ON THE EDGE OF EMPIRE: GENDER, RACE, AND THE MAKING OF BRITISH COLUMBIA, 1849–1871

On the Edge of Empire is a well-written, carefully researched, and persuasively argued book that delineates the centrality of race and gender in the making of colonial and national identities, and in the rewriting of Canadian history as colonial history. Utilizing feminist and postcolonial filters, Adele Perry designs a case study of British Columbia. She draws on current work that aims to close the distance between 'home' and 'away' in order to make her case about the commonalities and differences between circumstances in British Columbia and those of the 'Anglo-American' culture that was increasingly dominant in North America, parts of the British Isles, and other white settler colonies.

On the Edge of Empire examines how a loosely connected group of reformers worked to transform an environment that lent itself to two social phenomena: white male homosocial culture and conjugal relationships between First Nations women and settler men. The reformers worked to replace British Columbia's homosocial culture with the practices of respectable, middle-class European masculinity. Others encouraged mixed-race couples to conform to European standards of marrrige and discouraged white-Aboriginal unions through moral suasion or the more radical tactic of racially segregated space. Another reform impetus laboured through immigration and land policy to both build and shape the settler population.

A more successful reform effort involved four assisted female immigration efforts, yet the experience of white women in British Columbia only made more pronounced the gap between colonial discourse and colonial experience. In its failure to live up to British expectations, remaining a racially plural resource colony with a unique culture, British Columbia revealed much about the politics of gender, race, and the making of colonial society on this edge of empire.

(Studies in Gender and History)

ADELE PERRY is an assistant professor of history at St Paul's College, University of Manitoba.

STUDIES IN GENDER AND HISTORY

General editors: Franca Iacovetta and Karen Dubinsky

On the Edge of Empire

Gender, Race, and the
Making of British Columbia,
1849–1871

ADELE PERRY

UTP 100 1901-2001

UNIVERSITY OF TORONTO PRESS
Toronto Buffalo London

© University of Toronto Press Incorporated 2001
Toronto Buffalo London
Printed in Canada

Reprinted 2002

ISBN 0-8020-4797-1 (cloth)
ISBN 0-8020-8336-6 (paper)

∞

Printed on acid-free paper

Canadian Cataloguing in Publication Data

Perry, Adele
    On the edge of empire : gender, race, and the making of British
    Columbia, 1849–1871

    (Studies in gender and history series)
    Includes bibliographical references and index.
    ISBN 0-8020-4797-1 (bound)   ISBN 0-8020-8336-6 (pbk.)

    1. British Columbia – History – 1849–1871.*   2. British Columbia –
    Social conditions – To 1871.   3. British Columbia – Colonization.
    I. Title.   II. Series.

    FC3822.P47 2001   971.1′02   C00-931748-1
    F1088.P47 2001

University of Toronto Press acknowledges the financial assistance to its
publishing program of the Canada Council for the Arts and the Ontario
Arts Council.

This book has been published with the help of a grant from the Humanities
and Social Sciences Federation of Canada, using funds provided by the
Social Sciences and Humanities Research Council of Canada.

University of Toronto Press acknowledges the financial support for its
publishing activities of the Government of Canada through the Book
Publishing Industry Development Program (BPIDP).

Contents

Acknowledgments

I have been writing this part in my head for a long time. It goes something like this. This manuscript began as a doctoral dissertation. It was completed at York University under the expert and thoughtful guidance of Craig Heron, Bettina Bradbury, and Kathryn McPherson. Susan Houston, Nick Rogers, and Ramsay Cook also generously shared their advice and knowledge. Sylvia Van Kirk's wise comments helped to turn the dissertation into a book. As a postdoctoral fellow at the University of British Columbia, I benefited from the sage counsel and scholarly support of Jean Barman and Veronica Strong-Boag. My new colleagues in the Department of History at the University of Manitoba have welcomed me and my research to this other edge of empire.

I shopped parts of this manuscript around fairly widely, and benefited from critical comments from the Toronto Labour Studies Group, the University of Toronto Women's History Discussion Group, the University of Toronto Gay and Lesbian History Discussion Group, the Early Canada Research Group, the York University Women's History Group, the Farley Series on Gender History, and audiences at the Canadian Historical Association in St John's and the International Congress of Historical Sciences in Montreal. In different ways, Lisa Chilton, John Gay, Mona Gleason, Cole Harris, Victoria Heftler, Martha Kanya-Forstner, Richard Mackie, Fiona Miller, James Moran, Steve Penfold, Carolyn Podruchny, Gillian Poulter, Myra Rutherdale, Becki Ross, Ruth Sandwell, Nandita Sharma, and Sharon Wall provided helpful commentary, feedback, and support. Emily Andrew, Jill McConkey, and Gerry Hallowell of the University of Toronto Press and series editors Karen Dubinsky and Franca Iacovetta each helped hone this volume and shepherd it through the publishing process. Eric Leinberger made the maps.

Archivists and librarians in Victoria, Vancouver, Ottawa, Toronto, and London supported this project ably. Martha Kanya-Forstner, Colin Mooers, Penny Perry, Lara Perry, and Marie Campbell put me up and put up with me on my various research trips. In an era of declining state support for scholarship, I was lucky to receive generous assistance through a doctoral fellowship from the Social Sciences and Humanities Research Council of Canada, a Queen Elizabeth II Ontario Scholarship, and a Social Sciences and Humanities Research Council of Canada Post-Doctoral Fellowship.

There is personal in the academic just as there is in the political. My father, Clay Perry, first showed me that there was a connection between social justice and social history. My mother, Penny Perry, taught me that there was much to value and evaluate in British Columbia. Both supported me and this project above and beyond the obligations of parental duty. Peter Ives certainly knows more about colonial British Columbia than he ever wished. Our daughter Nell Ives Perry was born as I finished this book, and she has brought unspeakable joy into my life and helped to keep it in perspective as only a baby can. Throughout it all, Kate McPherson has taught me much about the writing of social history, about Western Canada, about feminism, about teaching and, ultimately, about friendship. So this book is for her.

ON THE EDGE OF EMPIRE:
GENDER, RACE, AND THE MAKING OF
BRITISH COLUMBIA, 1849–1871

Introduction:
Analysing Gender and Race
on the Edge of Empire

Mid-nineteenth-century British Columbia hung precariously at the edge of Britain's literal and symbolic empire. A three- to six-month sea voyage separated the colony from its imperial headquarters, and a substantial portion of North America stood between British Columbia and its closest colonial cousins, Red River and the Canadas. The society that developed in this far-flung shore also hovered dangerously at the precipice of Victorian social norms and ideals. Racially plural, rough, and turbulent, British Columbia bore little resemblance to the orderly, respectable, white settler colony that imperial observers hoped it would become.

Gender and race loomed large in observers' assessments of why British Columbia remained on empire's edge. In this book I probe the connections between gender, race, and the making of colonial society during British Columbia's years as a separate colony. Between 1849 and 1871 British Columbia's gender and racial character challenged normative standards of nineteenth-century, Anglo-American social life. First Nations people outnumbered whites dramatically, and within the small white community, males outnumbered females even more sharply. White male homosocial culture and mixed-race heterosexual relationships were common and persistent reminders that British Columbia fell short of Victorian standards.

In response to the alleged problem of British Columbia's gender and racial character, reformers mounted a significant if disjointed regulatory program that aimed to create an orderly, white settler colony anchored in respectable gender and racial behaviours and identities. Journalists, politicians, and missionaries, as well as other reformers attempted a series of social transformations, labouring to make rough backwoods men into temperate and responsible patriarchs, to render white-Aboriginal relationships compatible with European marriages, and to turn a small and disorderly white population into a large and prosperous colonial community. If moral reform could not work these transformations, then surely white women, that well-worn imperial panacea, could. With a sizeable migration of white women, reformers argued, British Columbia would finally fulfil its destiny as a stable, respectable, white society. In these ways, gender and race were a sharp edge of colonial politics, programs, and policies in mid-nineteenth-century British Columbia.

But these colonial visions were ultimately pipe dreams. Despite the grandiose ambitions of reformers, British Columbia remained on empire's edge, a racially plural, sparsely populated resource colony in the period 1849 to 1871. Indeed, it did not support a white population equal in size to its Aboriginal one until late in the nineteenth century. British Columbia's colonial project was a fragile one that was constantly challenged both by First Nations resistance and by white unwillingness to conform to prevailing constructions of appropriate behaviour and identity. In its failure to live up to imperial expectations, British Columbia revealed much about the politics of gender, race, and the making of colonial society.

Reckoning with the history of gender and race in mid-nineteenth-century British Columbia has led me far away from the shores of the north Pacific. I draw, selectively and sometimes episodically, on four theoretical schools. First, this study is rooted in a large body of feminist theory that explores gender as the social organization of manliness and womanliness. When we put this idea to work historically, we find that gender is doubly significant as a social factor and as a category of scholarly analysis. Second, I borrow from Marxism the contention that historical change is material in character and that class relations are central to social relations in the capitalist era in general and to imperial relations in particular. The contention that the daily experience of ordinary peoples needs to be understood and explicated in order to meaningfully explain social change follows from this. Third, while leery of the notion that we are now 'post' colonialism, I draw from post-colonial literature the fundamental insight that imperialism and race are crucial to social experience and thought on both sides of the imperial divide. Fourth, I utilize post-structuralist insights around the necessarily discursive character of all sources and, more importantly, the historically constructed character of social relations. This leads me to the contention that both race and gender are not inevitable and fixed categories, but rather historically constructed ones that are not created through biology as much as they are normalized through biological discourses.[1]

These rarefied considerations have practical ramifications for how this study is conceived and executed. In keeping with a social constructionist perspective, I try to respect the flexibility and historicity of racial categories and territorial designations. A burdgeoning litera- ture suggests that whiteness is an especially slippery yet significant racial category. To be defined as white, scholars like David Roediger have persuasively argued, is to have a race like any other.[2] Interrogat- ing whiteness as a race challenges the assumption that whiteness is normal and brownness, blackness, and redness the problematic 'others' in need of explication. It also accurately reflects the prevailing racial categorization of nineteenth-century British Columbia. As Paul Tennant points out, settler British Columbians called themselves white and drafted laws that reflected the identity and power this conferred.[3] It is for these historical and theoretical reasons that this book refers to 'white' peoples and aims to interrogate the meaning and politics of whiteness.

Given imperialism's long and heavy history of categorizing indig- enous peoples, it is tougher to develop a politically and intellectually satisfactory way of describing British Columbia's First Nations. Despite contemporary longings for the days when nomenclature was self-evi- dent, nineteenth-century whites could not agree on how to describe indigenous peoples. They used a suspicious array of words to describe them, including Siwash, Native, Indian, and savage, not to mention a vast range of specific national names. People of mixed heritage were dubbed half-castes, half-breeds, half-bloods, half-whites, or bloods. The many terms used to connote local peoples affirms the point that racial categories are fictive and changing rather than real and stable. But to argue that race was constructed is not to suggest that it lacked social import: to acknowledge that houses are built is not to suggest that they are somehow unreal. That race was made and constantly remade in mid-nineteenth-century British Columbia reflects rather than mitigates its import.

Race was simultaneously flexible and critical. This study tries to reflect its ambiguous character and historicity by, whenever possible, using the specific national names generally favoured by contemporary First Nations. If this national name differs significantly from the nine- teenth-century version, the latter follows in parentheses. When such specificity is neither possible nor intended, I utilize the two terms – First Nations and Aboriginal – generally adopted by late twentieth-century indigenous people and assume that these terms apply to people of full or mixed-heritage unless otherwise indicated. In nineteenth-century British Columbia, some people were thought to be of mixed race. I concur with Ruth Frankenberg that the term 'mixed race' has an air of biological determinism and suggests that there is a pure, whole, or real state of race that some folks depart from. But I also share her inability to develop an alternative and use the terms 'mixed race' and 'mixed blood' to refer to both individuals identified as Aboriginal and European descent and to personal relationships between white and First Nations individuals.[4]

Nations, colonies, and other ways of organizing space and polity are, like races, mutable human inventions. To simplify the many perambulations of the colonial state on North America's north Pacific coast, I usually refer to 'British Columbia.' If a distinction is relevant, I follow contemporary local practice by referring to 'Vancouver Island' or 'the Island' and to 'British Columbia' or 'the Mainland.' The book also uses the term 'colonial British Columbia' as a shorthand for the years between the establishment of Vancouver Island as a British colony in 1849 and the colony's entry into Confederation in 1871. This does not imply that the relationship of colonialism existed only within the tidy parameters of these dates, but simply indicates a specific moment in state formation.

Rather than treat British Columbia as a wholly unique entity, this study emphasizes how it fits within a broader context of European colonialism.[5] British Columbia shared much with other British colonies like Australia and New Zealand that were economically and socially tied to resource extraction and politically committed to settlement. It had more common ground with the colonial societies of India and Africa than scholars have generally acknowledged. British Columbia's status as a white society may seem obvious in the late twentieth century, but it was not so in the nineteenth century. This supposed obviousness is also more an artefact of the success of imperialism than a sign of its absence. But to reckon with British Columbian history as colonial history goes against the grain of much popular and scholarly tradition. As Cole Harris has recently pointed out, white British Columbians are reluctant to recognize home-grown colonialism and instead 'associate colonialism with other places and other lives.'[6] Canadian historians as a whole are even less enthusiastic. In the 1930s, historian George Stanley did analyse colonization, albeit in whiggish and altogether laudatory terms – the unrelenting march of Western civilization, Stanley assures his readers, necessarily vanquished the 'primitive' Métis rebellions of 1869 and 1885.[7] Possibly in reaction to such celebratory accounts and certainly in response to a general postwar discomfort with colonialism, historians have largely abandoned discussions of imperialism in favour of analyses of settlement. Inasmuch as this term suggests that nobody was there, it subtly depoliticizes the process whereby white people came to dominate First Nations territory.

To acknowledge the salience of international patterns of imperialism is not to deny the local, the particular, and the idiosyncratic. Perhaps the greatest accomplishment of recent colonial historiography has been the shift away from totalizing analyses of imperialism as a coherent monolith.[8] British Columbia was not Batavia, and neither was it Bermuda. Like other recent scholars of particular colonialisms, I find the notion of the 'colonial project' an effective way of navigating the analytic pulls of the local and the imperial. Nicholas Thomas defines a colonial project as 'a socially transformative endeavour that is localized, politicized, and partial, yet also engendered by larger historical developments and ways of narrating them.'[9] Seeing British Columbia as a colonial project illuminates the always important and often contested relationship between London and Victoria, between local histories and imperial patterns. These stories and conflicts are further illuminated by the techniques of social history. The messy practice of actual colonial space profoundly challenged imperial dreams and ideals: it was in the backwoods that the programs of pundits were transformed into hybrid local expressions. To examine colonialism from the vantage point of the periphery highlights the disjuncture between imperial ideals and practice, and reminds us that colonialism was a popular social experience as well as a political arrangement and literary discourse. This is a point that can be lost when imperialism is examined, as it has so often been of late, exclusively through the lenses of literature and politics.

Gender is key in charting the particular trajectories of local colonial projects, including British Columbia's. In arguing for the significance of gender for both the colonized and the colonizing, I draw generally on feminist scholarship pressing for the mutually constitutive character of gender and race. This utility of this maxim has been amply demonstrated by historians of gender and imperialism such as Antoinette Burton, Catherine Hall, Anne McClintock, Mrinalini Sinha, and Ann

Laura Stoler. Each of these scholars, in different ways and in different contexts, has demonstrated that the processes of colonization cannot be understood without attention to gender, and that gender, similarly, cannot be adequately comprehended outside of the politics of race and colonization.[10] In British Columbia, white and First Nations did not meet as ungendered, undifferentiated racial subjects, but as men and women, and to fail to recognize this is to fundamentally misunderstand the processes of cultural contact and colonial development. Similarly, to analyse gender as an independent and autonomous force is to misunderstand its character. 'A conception of the interlocking and mutually constitutive character of social categories,' Ruth Pierson points out, 'explodes the notion that gender rotates simply around a single axis of polar opposites' by demonstrating how gender is classed, raced, and sexualized.[11]

The growing canon of Canadian gender history helps to hone this analysis. Recent scholarship has worked especially to refute the notion that gender is a fancy word for women and instead conceptualize gender as a dynamic structure that gives shape to the identities and experiences of both men and women. Masculinity, like femininity, is a historical phenomenon deserving analysis.[12] Despite the anxious claims made in a peculiar and inappropriately polarized debate around the merits of *gender* versus *women's* history,[13] this work shares, at root, a common *feminist* commitment to critically analysing gender inequity and difference.[14]

Recognizing gender as important should not lead us to conceptualize it as autonomous. Rather than examine gender in relative isolation, this study investigates how gendered experiences, identities, and structures were produced and reproduced in intimate partnership with other social divisions. It aims, to borrow the language of recent feminist scholarship, to examine social identities and cleavages as intersectional rather than separate or serial. While paying some heed to the importance of class and sexuality, I especially emphasize the importance of race to the social experience of gender in nineteenth-century British Columbia. In doing so, I am responding to anti-racist critiques made most powerfully by women of colour who have demanded, in Hazel V. Carby's words, that 'white feminist researchers should try to uncover the gender-specific mechanisms of racism among white women.'[15] I hope that this effort will particularly contribute to Canadian historiography which, while possessing a rich literature on the relationship between gender and class,[16] is only beginning to develop its analysis of gender and race.[17] By treating race as what Joan Scott might call 'a useful category of analysis' for white as well as non-white peoples, I also try to demonstrate the intellectual utility of race not simply for studies of people of colour, but for Canadian history as a whole. In emphasizing the histories of white and Aboriginal, I do not mean to minimize the significance of non-white settler groups, but merely to probe the fault line that cut most strongly through British Columbia at this particular moment in history.

I am not alone in asserting the utility of theory to historical analysis and the centrality of race to British Columbian history. A small spate of recent assessments have conclusively demolished the perception of nineteenth-century British Columbia as a bucolic and harmonious frontier society. Post-structuralist and post-colonial analyses have proven particularly influential in this reinterpretation, with historians such as Tina Loo and Elizabeth Vibert, geographers such as Cole Harris and Kay Anderson, and literary scholars such as Christopher Bracken utilizing critical theory to trace the contours of conflict, struggle, and contestation in British Columbia's past.[18] Yet with the important exception of Vibert, none of these authors use gender as a central category of analysis. Rich periodical literatures on women in nineteenth-century British Columbia[19] and First Nations women and colonization,[20] however, suggest both the necessity and possibility of a new, critical gender history of British Columbia. Such a scholarship can challenge both gender-blind historiography and the existing hagiography celebrating white women's roles as pioneers.[21]

However far this study travels, it remains very much an analysis of one particular edge of empire. In the eventful years between 1849 and 1871, British Columbia went from a diverse, First Nations territory to a fur-trade colony, to a gold-rush society grafted on a fur-trade settlement, to a resource-oriented colony with an emergent settler society. People have lived and developed complex cultures on northern North America's Pacific coast at least since 12,000 BC. But British Columbia was born in the first half of the nineteenth century, the awkward and disappointing child of the fur trade and British imperial expansion. Explorers pushing the limits of European geographical reach visited the Pacific coast from 1778 onwards, travelling a path that would be followed by British, American, and Russian traders.[22] Their approach was matched by the arrival of the land-based fur trade in the first decades of the nineteenth century. Before 1849 no European power asserted a conclusive territorial claim, but Harris is correct to argue that the fur trade established a 'protocolonial' presence in the interests of profit.[23]

Based on the politics of fear and, after 1821, the strength of Hudson's Bay Company (HBC) monopoly, this protocolonial presence asserted itself in a territory that was both densely populated and culturally complex. While earlier estimates put the First Nations population at contact at roughly 100,000, scholars now estimate the population as hovering between 300,000 and 400,000.[24] Speaking over thirty-four distinct languages and possessing distinctive political, and economic structures, Aboriginal society in British Columbia defies broad generalizations.[25] The most salient division was probably between the large, highly structured, hierarchical, and rank-oriented cultures of the coast, and the smaller, egalitarian societies of the interior. Yet even this rudimentary distinction masks significant cultural, economic, political and historical differences.[26] While historians debate the impact of early contact and trade, it is safe to state that the fur trade reorganized First Nations trade patterns, cultural practices, and political alignments, and brought new diseases and intensified existing ones.

Formal colonial authority established on Vancouver Island in 1849 transformed a protocolonial presence to an overtly colonial one. But British Columbia remained firmly at empire's edge. As Jack Little notes, Britain colonized Vancouver Island because, in spite of declining interest in North America, it wanted a political foothold on the northern Pacific. Britain's desire for political presence was reconciled with fears of financial commitment when the old colonial system of the Caribbean was evoked and the HBC was granted proprietary rights to the island. Between 1849 and 1863 the colony slowly acquired all the constitutional trappings of settler colonies, namely, a governor and bicameral legislature.[27] While comprehensive white settlement of the island remained a vague goal, what Richard Mackie dubs 'a viable colony' did develop along local lines.[28]

The discovery of gold on the mainland's Fraser River profoundly shifted the trajectory of British Columbia's colonial project. Thousands of miners, chiefly American, arrived in the sparsely colonized and loosely organized colony in the spring of 1858. 'Never perhaps was there so large an immigration in so short a space of time into so small a place,'[29] opined one journalist. A transient, shifting gold-rush economy was thus awkwardly affixed to the existing fur-trade society. Politically, this simultaneously raised the possibility that British Columbia might be home to a white society and suggested that it might be neither

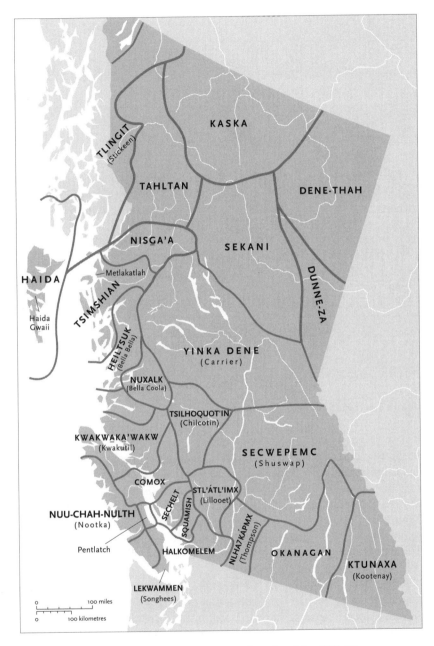

Map 1: Aboriginal presence in colonial British Columbia, 1849–71.

Colonial authority and Aboriginal persistence: the HBC's Fort Victoria in 1854.

British nor law-abiding. In response, the Colonial Office established a separate colony on the mainland and declared Vancouver Island Governor James Douglas governor of the new colony. It was not until 1863 that British Columbia would be granted a Legislative Council with a limited 'popular' element and a separate governor. In 1866 Vancouver Island was effectively absorbed by the mainland, the united colony retaining the name British Columbia but the island capital of Victoria. The colony joined Canada as a province in July 1871 and brought the colonial period to a close.[30]

These perambulations of the colonial state were motivated by the hope that an agricultural, white settler society akin to the Canadas or Australia would emerge in British Columbia. This chequered social and political history suggests how, despite these hopes, British Columbia remained on the edge of empire. Established during a low point of

TABLE I.1
White British Columbia by gender, 1855–1870

Year	White males	Males as % of white population	White females	Females as % of white population	Total white population
1855	509	65.8	265	34.2	774
1861	1456	88.3	192	11.7	1648
1862	1991	86.0	326	13.9	2317
1863	6978	95.1	360	4.9	7338
1864	1419	80.0	354	20.0	1773
1865	5708	91.3	547	8.7	6255
1866	2629	85.6	443	14.4	3072
1867	5410	77.5	1569	22.5	6979
1868	4806	74.8	1618	25.2	6424
1869	5811	70.3	2456	29.7	8267
1870	5782	67.4	2794	32.6	8576

*Note the impact of shifting political boundaries: 1855 figures include only those people inhabiting Vancouver Island, while 1861 through 1866 include only those living on the Mainland, while 1867 through 1870 include both the Mainland and the Island.
Source: W. Kaye Lamb, ed., 'The Census of Vancouver Island, 1855,' *British Columbia Historical Quarterly* 4:1 (1940) 51–8; Great Britain, Colonial Office, 'Blue Books of Statistics, British Columbia, 1861–1870,' British Columbia Archives, CO 64/1, Reel 626A.

imperial expansion, the colony received limited financial, military, or political support from Britain. While it slowly acquired the administrative accoutrements of a British settler colony, settler colonies are fundamentally premised on the existence of a large and relatively stable settler population. Drawing and retaining such a white society to British Columbia proved a slow and profoundly difficult process.

The continued demographic dominance of First Nations people stands as the sharpest evidence of the local colonial project's fragility. In 1855 Douglas estimated Vancouver Island's white population at 774.[31] Numbers of non-Aboriginal people peaked during the Fraser River gold rush and again during the Cariboo gold rush of 1862–4 (see Table I.1). Yet it remained concentrated in a handful of colonial enclaves, most notably Victoria, New Westminster, Nanaimo, and in shifting interior towns on the Fraser River, throughout the Cariboo and along fur-trade routes. It never came close to rivalling the First Nations population. As late as 1871 observers estimated that the Aboriginal population on the mainland alone was roughly 45,000, while the 'settled' population of *both* the mainland and island was only 19,225.[32] Shifts in white–First

Nations population ratios were caused not as much by natural growth or white immigration as they were by Aboriginal deaths. Disease, especially during the massive small-pox epidemic of 1862, took its toll: there were twice as many Aboriginal people on the eve of the Fraser River gold rush as there were in 1870.[33] Even aided by such population decline, the colonization of British Columbia occurred slowly. As Jean Barman argues, it was only in the fin de siècle that the 'fragile settler society on the frontier of the western world became a self-confident political and social entity.'[34]

The smallness of the setter population was matched by its diversity. Most colonists came from the United States and Britain, and smaller proportions hailed from Canada, Australia, and continental Europe. But colonization was never an all-white endeavour: Kanakas or Hawaiians settled in the wake of the fur trade, African-Americans clustered in Victoria and Saltspring Island, and the Chinese gravitated towards colonial centres or interior mining towns: in 1865 one observer put Quesnel's population at one hundred white men and one hundred Chinese.[35] This racial and ethnic heterogeneity was a characteristic that British Columbia shared with other settler societies.[36] Struggles to assert the whiteness were articulated not only in response to the Aboriginal population, but in relation to non-white and more especially non-British settlers.

Whatever their background, settlers worked in an unstable, resource-oriented economy centred around, but never entirely dominated by, the gold economy. The fur trade continued, and underground coal mining was initiated at Nanaimo and Fort Rupert. Commercial agriculture, attempted since early days of the HBC's Pacific trade, was stimulated by the demands of the trade in gold. Lumbering and fisheries employed a small workforce, but large-scale exploitation would not occur until the advent of new technology.[37] As the boom of the gold rushes faded, the economy diversified. In 1865, 72 per cent of the paid labour force was concentrated in the mining industry, while by 1870, 61 per cent of the waged labour force was in other occupations, about half of them in agriculture.[38]

British Columbia's emergent class structure reflected the significance of imperial ties, the importance of resource industries, and the continued influence of the fur trade. Three groups competed for the role of colonial elite. A tightly interwoven fur-trade cabal, with deep and often familial ties to Aboriginal society, maintained their significant political power throughout the colonial period. Led by men such as Douglas,

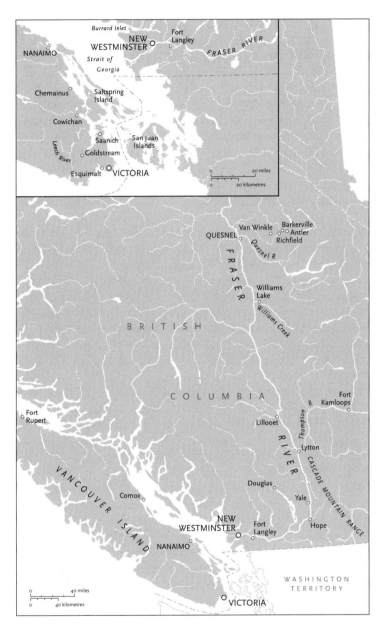

Map 2: Principal colonial settlements in British Columbia, 1849–71.

Roderick Finlayson, W.H. Tolmie, and John Work, this faction of the bourgeoisie were also major landowners, especially around Victoria.[39] Their right to rule was constantly contested by a self-styled 'reform' group energetically if informally represented by journalist–politician Amor de Cosmos and his Victoria newspaper, the *British Colonist*. Frequently with Canadian, Maritime, or American roots, this aspiring elite had ties to the gold and merchant economy and a firm belief in the colony's potential as an agricultural, white settler society.[40] Anglican Bishop George Hills led a third elite. Connected to British missionary agencies and with meaningful support from naval circles, they sometimes sided with the fur trade or reform party, and sometimes they used their considerable ideological muscle to challenge the legitimacy of both.

As traders, reformers, and clerics struggled for the upper echelon of colonial society, ordinary white men and women created the outlines of a working and middle class. A nascent, highly mobile, male, working-class culture was created as sailors, loggers, labourers, tradespeople, and especially gold miners combined independent commodity production with wage labour. In interior towns and urban enclaves – especially in the off-season – young, white, working men were a loud and sometimes disturbing presence. Their rough culture provided a convenient 'other' for the emergent middle class to construct itself in opposition to. Made up largely of shopkeepers, petty government officials, merchants, schoolteachers, and other 'middling' folk, this small middle class was centred in Victoria and, to a lesser extent, New Westminster. Through reform work, they were beginning to constitute themselves as a separate and identifiable class, although one that regularly spilled over into both working-class and elite society.

Settler society had a distinct gendered character as well as a racial and class one. British Columbia's settler society was overwhelmingly and persistently male. The resource industries that nurtured the colonial presence in British Columbia were gendered male here as elsewhere in the nineteenth-century Western world. Fur trading, gold mining, and the other trades that fed colonial British Columbia fundamentally depended on the back-breaking labour of men, especially young working-class ones, and it was young men that constituted the overwhelming bulk of migrants to this edge of empire. Colonial policies, while nominally devoted to securing a more gender-balanced settler population, did not counter the social patterns forged by economy and society. Contemporaries remarked regularly on the paucity of white women on both the mainland and the island, an impression that is reaffirmed by the available statistics. According to James Douglas's 1855 census, Vancouver Island was home to 150 white females over the age of fifteen compared with 338 males of the same age.[41] The female proportion of the mainland's settler population was considerably smaller. Women hovered at somewhere between 5 and 15 per cent of the white population on the mainland between 1861 and 1865. Following the decline of the gold economy after the Cariboo rush and the incorporation of Vancouver Island into British Columbia, the percentage of women in the white population eventually rose, but only to the 1855 levels of about 30 per cent (see Table I.1).

Most of the white female population was concentrated in Victoria and, to a lesser extent, New Westminster. An 1870 census recorded 1,645 white males and 1,197 white females in Victoria or roughly three women for every four men. In New Westminster there were 891 white males to 401 white females, or four women for every nine men.[42] In the colony's upper country, white women were truly a tiny minority. In the Cariboo in 1864, one observer estimated the white population at five hundred men and thirty-four women, or one woman to fifteen men.[43] There were four white women to twenty-seven white men in Lytton in 1861, while eight years later a colonial counter found 460 white males and 89 white females there.[44] That things were not substantially different in agricultural Vancouver Island is suggested by an 1864 census that found eight white women and forty-nine white men in the Comox Valley.[45]

The society that developed in colonial British Columbia was one that substantially departed from Victorian social norms and ideals. It was hard to reconcile an overwhelmingly male, racially diverse settler society living among a much larger First Nations population with mid-nineteenth-century dreams of sober, hard-working men, virtuous women, and respectable families. This social disruption was measured in numbers, but felt in everyday social interaction. Some white women complained of loneliness and social dislocation, while others remarked on the apparent maleness of social life. Conceptualizing it as a regional as well as colonial issue, one poet envisioned all men living in mining districts, leaving their female counterparts ironically to dominate town society:

'We're all off in the Spring to Cariboo,'
Celestial and Siwash, Gentile and Jew;

Of the pants-wearing sex in Col' and Van.'
There'll stay but one representative man;
Representing us men, and our Lady the Queen,
In his delegate charge of our dear Crinoline.

Whilst fathers and sons are up in the mines,
'Raising the wind' in church up to their chins,
The female folk 'as one man' will rise
To assume our late responsibilities;
Mammas and 'the girls' pack the little papooses,
And work our home claims, whilst we're working our sluices.

A Harbour-mistress will collect the dues;
A Post-mistress our letters send, and news.
A Cosmic love shall teach Victoria's types
To lash the world with Editorial stripes.
And members – petticoated – merely add bohea
To the' usual business of the House of M.P.P. ...

Convicts by female jailors will be made
To work in Crochet, Berlin-wools and Braid;
Found skilled already in the plainer parts
Of 'whipping,' 'felling,' 'running,' and like arts.
Unwhiskered 'Tigers,' smelling fire will prick their ears,
And girls' schools, rank and file, turn out as Volunteers ...[46]

This bit of hyperbole captures the sense of topsy-turvy Anglo-Americans felt when they encountered a society where gender and race were organized in different and often challenging ways.

White male homosocial culture and mixed-race heterosexual relationships were the sharpest symbols of what happened to gender and race on this edge of empire. This book analyses these two social phenomenon in chapters 1 and 2 respectively. I then turn to reformers' efforts to reorganize the gender and racial character of colonial British Columbia. In chapter 3 the book examines efforts to reform white men, while chapter 4 turns to the episodic attempts to reconfigure mixed-race relationships, and chapter 5 examines bids to build and shape British Columbia's white population. I then explore how reformers repeatedly returned to a well-worn imperial panacea, white women, to solve British Columbia's colonial ills. Chapter 6 explores how white women were constructed as effective imperial agents and examines efforts to directly import them to the colony. Chapter 7 submits that white women's experience suggests the profound limits of colonial discourse. In conclusion, I turn to the thorny question of the history of race in British Columbia and tease out some implications of our years spent on the edge of empire. Analysing gender and race in colonial British Columbia challenges us to think about our history in new ways and to consider how that history is put to work to explain our present and imagine our future.

This is the very stuff of colonization on one edge of empire. Settler colonies like British Columbia are organized around the double need to dispossess indigenous societies and build a settler population in their stead. In both scholarly literatures and popular discussions, these goals are generally presented as distinct ones: colonization and immigration are presented as wholly separate topics with little in common. Their seemingly discrete character is a fiction of a confident colonizing project where settler dominance is assumed to be normal and inevitable. It is a powerful fiction that masks the fact that dispossession and resettlement were and are deeply and irreparably intertwined, and indeed they derive their social power from that connection. Gender is where the abiding bonds between dispossession and colonization become most clear. Notions and practices of manhood and womanhood were central to the twinned businesses of marginalizing Aboriginal people and designing and building a white society. To probe the role of gender in British Columbia's colonial project is thus not to quibble with a minor historical matter. It is to reckon with the very process that put British Columbia on the edge of someone's empire.

Chapter 1

'Poor Creatures Are We without Our Wives': White Men and Homosocial Culture

In May 1862 a young Englishman named Charles Hayward sat in the Victoria home he shared with two male companions. 'We manage very well in our little Cabin,' he wrote. One man lit fires and prepared meals. The other two spent their days labouring in a building shop. But Hayward, who would later become mayor of Victoria, was uncomfortable doing his own marketing on Saturday nights, and more troubled still to be without his beloved female partner, Sally. 'Poor creatures are we without our wives,' he told his diary.[1] The combination of loneliness, competence, and mutuality that characterizes Hayward's experience says much about white men's relationship to race, gender, and the making of colonial society. In settler British Columbia, in the years between 1849 and 1871, customary gender relations were disrupted by the overwhelming demographic dominance of men. One result of this disruption was that white men developed a rough homosocial culture that existed side-by-side and occasionally overlapped with the mixed-race community. It did not challenge male power, but it did provide an alternative practice of racial and gendered identity.

The mid-nineteenth century witnessed the refashioning of dominant ideologies and practices of both masculinity and race throughout the English-speaking world. Middle-class masculinity especially was recast in the mould of the self-controlled, temperate, disciplined, and domestic patriarch. While this process was in many respects particular to the middle class, its implications were substantially broader. For the working classes, Wally Seccombe has persuasively argued, this ideal found expression in the male breadwinner norm, which mandated that men ought to earn sufficient wages to enable women and young children to live in uninterrupted domesticity.[2] Simultaneously, notions of racial difference hardened under the influence of imperial expansion and 'scientific' theories of race and racial hierarchy. Interracial sex was increasingly constructed as necessarily dangerous, and a vision of valiant imperial manhood circulated throughout popular culture.[3] The cumulative result was the creation of a dominant white masculine ideal in which European men were complete only when living in heterosexual, same-race, hierarchical unions.

The racially plural milieu and overwhelmingly male character of British Columbia's settler society rendered these ideals at best difficult to achieve. Alternatively, they encouraged and nourished a vibrant culture formed among and by white men. This homosocial culture was not entirely unique and had approximate equivalents in other culturally diverse societies with resource-extractive economies and heavily male populations like Australia, California, or Northern Ontario. Yet it was at heart a local phenomenon, with deep roots in the Fraser River gold rush of 1858 and the Cariboo gold rush of 1862–4. Some of its components reworked dominant gender norms and practices, while others reconfirmed them. Whether challenging or conforming to dominant norms, this homosocial culture was forged out of the everyday social relationships located in male households, friendships, and sexuality, and practices like labour, drinking, gambling, violence, and ideologies of racial solidarity and exclusion.

Reworking Masculinity: Male Households, Friendships, and Same-Sexuality

Male households were a key component of homosocial culture throughout colonial British Columbia. To create homes without white women was to challenge increasingly hegemonic concepts of gender and domesticity. In what Mary Poovey has called the 'binary logic' of nineteenth-century gender systems, women were assigned the domestic and moral spheres, while men weathered the capitalist economy and liberal polity. This division was explicitly racialized: the 'home' and the public-private split on which it was premised were constructed as both symbolic and constituent of Anglo-Saxon culture. If, as Poovey argues, women's need for waged work exposed the fallacies of this binary logic, so too did the domestic spaces white men created in white women's absence.[4]

It was the social and economic conditions of colonial British Columbia that so unsettled the tenets of dominant metropolitan discourse.

TABLE 1.1
Male households, Victoria, 1871

	Number	% of male households	% of all households
Total households	1025	n/a	100
Total male households	377	100	36.8
White single male households	186	49.3	18.1
White male group households	76	20.2	7.4
Chinese male group households	41	10.9	4.0
Chinese single male households	39	10.3	3.8
Black single male households	18	4.8	1.8
Mixed-race male group households	11	2.9	1.1
Black male group households	6	1.6	0.6

Source: Vancouver Island, 'Charge Book,' British Columbia Archives, GR 0428.
Numbers are rounded off, and two households could not be classified.

Popular literature routinely promoted male households as an appropriate adaptation to the insurgencies of immigrant life. John Emmerson, a middle-aged British miner, suggested that groups of six, including one experienced miner, were ideal for Cariboo-bound immigrants. Others advised farmers to do the same.[5] Authors made clear that the goals of group immigration were not simply economic since group living ensured among other things that the sick would be 'carefully tended.'[6]

Whatever the advice, white men joined together to create households both in and outside the cities. Probably because of the colony's imminent entry into Confederation, an Esquimalt police constable took a door-to-door census of Victoria in the spring of 1871. Recorded in dull pencil at the back of a notebook, this relatively untapped source found that over one-third of Victoria's homes contained no resident females whatsoever, even though Victoria's white female population was proportionately much larger than elsewhere. It also suggests important variations in male households (see Table 1.1.). Most housed a solitary white man, while a significant minority were group households made up of two or more white men. Chinese and Black men displayed not entirely dissimilar residential patterns, while First Nations men were less likely to live alone. Men did not necessarily live in same-race groups: there were at least eleven mixed-race male group households.[7]

The form as well as membership of male households varied. Most miners' homes in 1858 Victoria were reported to be 'simple tents,'[8] and canvas remained a common building material throughout the colonial period. In 1861 a magistrate found a few log cabins in the mining town of Antler, but reported that 'the rest of the miners were living in holes dug out of the snow.'[9] Other male households more closely conformed to conventional Anglo-American domestic space. Captain Phillip Hankin, between careers in the navy and colonial service, spent a month with five men 'in a very comfortable log cabin' in Barkerville. 'The house consisted of one fairly sized room, about 15 feet long, by 12 feet wide, with 5 bunks round like a large ship's cabin, and opposite the entrance door was a fire place with large logs on the ground, which were burning brightly, and a kettle hanging from a hook over the fire,' he wrote.[10]

While some male households were fairly stable, the membership of others was fluid. As Jock Phillips notes in his study of masculinity in frontier New Zealand, 'mateship was a relationship of circumstance.'[11] The readiness of miners to share their homes with veritable strangers became proverbial. 'The gold miner is rather an enigmatical character, pecuniarily speaking he is generous to a fault, his purse and cabin are alike open to friend and stranger, countryman and cosmopolite,' wrote one commentator.[12] Such backwoods hospital led tired and hungry overland traveller R.H. Alexander to rethink his assumptions about dependence and mutuality. 'The people are very kind,' the Canadian wrote. 'It is not begging – you just tell them you are broke and hungry and of course you get a meal.'[13]

Bonds easily forged could be bonds easily broken. Miners followed the excitement from rush to rush, moving from California to the Cariboo to Australia to the Fraser and Thompson rivers. Naval officer Edmund Hope Verney thought that mobility infected the entire colony. 'The Cariboo diggers are rushing down to Salmon river: the Stickeen diggers are tearing away to Cariboo, and the Salmon-river diggers are mad to get up to the Stickeen: numbers of the diggers are coming down the country and settling to work at Victoria, and numbers of Victoria work-men are going up the country to turn diggers: so we are all like the boiling water in a kettle, and no end of bubbles.'[14] Youth both rein-forced and reflected this fluidity. Thirty-nine-year-old Canadian Jessie Wright was exceptionally old for a gold miner. In 1866, he told his fifty-one-year-old brother that he was too old for the Cariboo and its life of 'the pick and shovel, with hard fare and harder knocks.' 'I am known here by the cognoun of Old Man,' he wrote, 'what would be your position[?]'[15]

Easy hospitality and mutuality never extended to all. As critics of the

A male household in the backwoods. Leech River, 1865.

homosocial culture, missionaries were often forced to 'batch it' without mates. In 1859 Methodist missionary Ebenezer Robson lived uneasily and alone in what he called a 'strange home' in Hope. Yet he soon learned to take pride in the labour required to keep it, equating bachelor domestic competence with attaining a university degree. 'Bought some housekeeping articles and have made up my mind to keep bachelor's hall,' Robson told his diary. 'So if they do not allow me to graduate at Victoria College and take the degree of BA, I will have the honor of being B something in British Columbia.'[16] Wealthy naturalist John Keast Lord not only lived alone but advised others how to do so in painstaking detail.[17]

Singly or collectively, living without women necessitated reconfiguring the process whereby domestic duties were assigned and performed. A few relied heavily on wayside houses and saloons and a few employed servants, but most found ways of domestic survival that did not rely heavily on the market. Some men cared only for themselves, others assigned an unemployed member domestic responsibility, while still others devised schemes whereby work could be performed collectively. These arrangements departed from traditions of institutional group lodging for working men found in Hudson's Bay Company (HBC) 'bachelor halls' and military barracks which were maintained by employers, subject to employer discipline, and reliant on paid staff for domestic services.

Recreating the domestic required white men to come to grips with skills and labours that were often radically unfamiliar to them. Cooking was particularly trying, especially in the upper country where provisions were scarce, limited, and expensive. Besides hard physical labour with little return, wrote disillusioned gold miner Charles Major, 'you go home to your shanty at night, tired and wet, and have to cook your beans before you can eat them.'[18] Some men never adjusted. One Comox farmer's meat, fish, and potatoes were poor, but 'his bread was the crowning atrocity.'[19] Other men adjusted and took pride in their culinary knowledge and accomplishments, treating small victories with a bravado that betrayed their inexperience. 'Last evening we had the pleasure of hearing some very intellectual discourses by some of the residents of this thinly populated district of Goldstream,' wrote one in 1865, including 'an animated discussion on bush cookery, and a number of valuable hints were thrown out.'[20] 'I was cook,' wrote future Indian Agent Henry Guillod, 'which I confess took up nearly the whole of my time.' He produced a competent but overly dry apple pudding, but was particularly proud of his talent at 'throwing a fritter or "slap jack" in firstrate style.' He promised to show his mother how to cook backwoods specialties on his return.[21] Such gendered renegotiations around the cook-fire led one female commentator to speculate that, in British Columbia's backwoods at least, the best cooks were frequently men.[22]

Without white women to clean and maintain households, men became inventive. The Norwegian who shared his Saltspring Island home with Blair and his brother Bill for the winter of 1863–4 'thought himself Very Clean but never used a Dish Scloth but his Briti[sh] flag.'[23] Emmerson's party washed their clothes in rivers and dried them by hanging them off their backs.[24] Housekeeping supplies were valued articles, sometimes carried from place to place across the backwoods. When a road-making crew found Duncan Munro's starved body between Williams Creek and Antler, they found no provisions or papers, but they did notice that the 'deceased had plenty of thread, pins and needles.'[25]

Like cooking, housework could be time-consuming. Chores dominated Richfield's Anglican missionary R.C. Lundin Brown's day, filling it with 'the lighting of the fire, fetching water from the spring, preparing breakfast, not to speak of sweeping the floor with an improvised broom, and sundry other little jobs.'[26] He was not alone. Missionaries argued that domestic responsibilities interfered with men's ability to perform their religious ones. Weekday services were impossible in Antler as 'directly the men were off work they had their suppers to prepare, and found themselves fit only to turn in and sleep after the meal was over.'[27] The Sabbath in Lytton was not a day of faith, but instead 'the grand account-settling, clothes-washing and mending, marketing and drinking day.'[28] Miners themselves inverted such critiques by appropriating the language of Christianity to describe the necessity of performing domestic tasks on Sunday. 'The Fourth Commandment' of the widely reprinted 'Miners' Ten Commandments' went 'Six days thou mayest dig or pick all that the body can stand under; but the other day is Sunday, when thou shalt wash all thy dirty shirts, darn all thy stockings, tap all thy boots, mend all thy clothing, chop thy whole week's firewood, make and bake thy bread and boil thy pork and beans.'[29]

Hardships aside, some represented their encounters with male households positively or even romantically. Lord called living in the bush an 'art' and could think of no other way of achieving 'a more perfect independence.'[30] R.H. Pidcock, a British minister's son who became a

Men cooking during the Fraser River gold rush. From *The New El Dorado: or British Columbia*, 1858.

Comox farmer, fondly remembered living rough with his mate in 1862. 'I and Fred took to it at once and notwithstanding all we had been through never felt so happy and well as when we had nothing but our bed of branches and our blankets to lay on.'[31]

The tough reality of household maintenance convinced others that domestic patriarchy was a better bargain than they had previously estimated. 'Coming in from work, hungry and tired – firewood to provide and prepare – the fire to make on – supper to cook – the things to wash up – the floor to sweep – shirts, towels, stockings, &c., to wash and mend, and all the paraphernalia connected with housekeeping to attend to, there was not much comfort belonging to it,' wrote Emmerson about the Victoria house he shared with another man. 'I had by this time made a grand discovery,' he declared. 'It was simply this: "I had found out the real value of a good wife and home comforts."'[32] Hayward had a similar epiphany. 'Have been reading to the boys an account of Belashazzors feast and it teaches The influence of women. We realize their value now.'[33]

Others lamented the loss of female company and the bonds of kin, reflecting a dominant culture that increasingly associated the emotive and the caring with the presence of white women and the domestic space of family. James Thompson wrote many sad letters to his wife Mary in Canada West, regretting his decision to ever leave her and their children for the dubious charms of Williams Creek. 'I sometimes wonder how I ever came to leave a kind and affectionate wife and all that the heart of man could desire of a family to sojourn in this land,' he regretted.[34] While Emerson waxed romantic about his male comrades, he was frequently suicidal and haunted by dreams of his wife and seven children, whom he missed terribly.[35] Hayward also deeply regretted his decision to leave his wife Sally in Britain and mourned her absence constantly, especially on Sundays.[36] Like the California miners studied by Andrew J. Rotter, these men found homosocial culture empty and isolating.[37]

Households were not the sole arena of white male homosocial culture. British Columbia created a broader male culture that fostered same-sex social, emotional, and sometimes sexual bonds. Nicknames symbolized the ties of men to each other and their membership in a distinct social world. In his private journal, Anglican Bishop George Hills noted that 'The appellation of all miners is "boy." Their chief is "Cap." All are called Dick, Tom, or Harry. Men are not known by their real names.'[38] Such language denoted affinity and occupational solidarity, but sometimes spoke of deeper ties. Illness and death made these bonds explicit. The sick and ailing of the Cariboo, thought the local press, were often 'tended with all the care and kindness they would have received in the bosom of their own families.'[39] A missionary noted the care an ailing miner received from his mates, describing the large attendance at his funeral as 'a good instance of the great sympathy and cordiality that exists even among these rough men.'[40]

The dissolution of male friendships could cause considerable torment. The parting scene was painful when Emmerson's group separated at Williams Lake. His mate William Mark wrote that 'we had shared the troubles and dangers together, for ten thousand miles, and here we part, in a strange, wild country, perhaps never to see each other again!'[41] Robert Stevenson, a miner who spent his old age in Kamloops writing virulent defences of his companion, 'Cariboo' Cameron, left a business diary containing affectionate, formulaic poetry and addresses of male companions. One read: 'Forget me not I only ask / This simple boon of thee / And let it be a Simple task / To sometimes think of me.'[42] One miner reputedly committed suicide after the death of his partner.[43]

White men could be many things to each other. Together, they constructed new versions of traditionally heterosocial activities. Some parties, like a Comox one, cancelled the dancing 'owing to the absence of crinoline.'[44] Others were more inventive in the face of gender's disruption. At a dance in Yale in 1858, 'The few ladies present had no lack of partners, while most of the men were forced to dance with each other.'[45] Travel writer R. Byron Johnson recalled meeting an old miner, Jake, who told of a winter ball on Williams Creek. When Johnson asked about ladies, Jake replied that they had none except for an African American washerwoman, a French madam, and the blacksmith's wife. 'But we danced some, I tell yu! It were stag dancin' of course, fur a hundred an' fifty men was too many fur three females, but it all came off gay.'[46] A largely male milieu was also no barrier to the performance of Anglo-American theatre. Journalist Edgar Fawcett remembered being cajoled into female roles in Victoria's Amateur Dramatic Club since 'female talent was scarce.'[47] One visitor speculated that actors must have shaved permanently for such roles.[48]

This homosocial culture was not necessarily a poor imitation of allegedly real, natural, or legitimate gender organization. While white men's desire for white women was often assumed, the lives of many of backwoods British Columbian men – lived in lifelong bachelorhood, with no apparent quest for formal marriage – suggests that same-race, heterosexual desires were not universal. One miner wrote that 'generally gold diggers are not marrying men. They work, spend their money in drink, and work again.'[49] Naval officer Richard Charles Mayne argued that gold miners' 'hard, wild life' ultimately 'unfit them for domestic existence.'[50] Historian of American masculinity Anthony Rotundo agrees on the importance of same-sex bonds, but argues that men's romantic friendships were a product of a distinct phase of the life cycle – youth. This explanation seems insufficient for explaining male bonds in colonial British Columbia. Steven Maynard suggests that the backwoods provided an environment where men could have their primary social and emotional bonds with other men. In much the same way that historians have persuasively argued that all-female institutions like settlement houses and female colleges offered a social space where early twentieth-century women could live a female-centred life, so the backwoods of British Columbia allowed men to create and maintain a social life revolving around same-sex ties and practices.[51]

Some members of this homosocial culture seem simply disinterested in conventional gender and familial organization, while others were actively fleeing from it. Mid-nineteenth-century British Columbia provided a useful haven for men on the lam from the unwanted encumbrances of wives and families. One local politician commented that three letters went up to the Cariboo for every one that went down.[52] Some of those unanswered letters were pleading ones in search of errant kin or their support. Ann Scott, living at the Alms House of Blackwell's Island, New York, wrote to local clergy about her husband who was reputedly living in Victoria. She particularly wanted to know if he had another family, and told the cleric: 'You will understand my feelings, and agree with me, that it is best for me to know the truth, one way or other.'[53] Inquiries from wives and families overseas were frequent enough to prompt the Colonial Office to ask Victoria to clarify their responsibility on the matter.[54] As Scott feared, some men did flee their families only to form new ones. An act requiring the registration of births, marriages, and deaths was supported on the grounds that it would assist in the prosecution of bigamy cases.[55] New York divorce lawyers saw a market in this mobile world and advertised their services in the Cariboo press.[56]

Not all members of this homosocial culture showed interest in recreating conventional family relationships. In poem and prose, some white men celebrated their distance from the world of white women and the nineteenth-century discursive corollaries of religion and 'the social.'

Manhood was transformed by the backwoods. 'To the Diggings and from the
Diggings,' from 'To Cariboo and Back: An Emigrant's Journey to the Gold
Fields of British Columbia' in *Leisure Hour*, 29 April 1863.

They represented their world as rough and masculine and made clear that these were admirable attributes. 'The man in the mines and the same man at home, with the influence of a loving mother, a wife, or virtuous sisters around him – bear no analogy to each other,' wrote one miner.[57] Sometimes the line between celebrating the maleness of the backwoods and misogyny blurred. Women at home, one wrote, would hardly recognize men at the mines since so rough and ready were the former fine gentlemen. 'There is no denying it, gold is all powerful and is the true mistress of destiny.'[58]

No clear line definitively and irreparably divided the homosocial from the homosexual. Historians of sexuality argue that before the widespread dissemination of a homosexual *identity* in the late nineteenth-century, homoerotic behaviour and desire was usually conceived as an 'act' rather than a persona, and subject to various levels of social regulation.[59] One letter writer announced that 'murderers, sodomites, and burglars have few sympathizers in Victoria,'[60] but the social history of the regulation of male homoerotic behaviour reveals a more complex history. D.W. Higgins's stories suggest how colonial British Columbia's homosocial culture could challenge conventional sexuality as well as gender. One grapples with the male narrator's ambivalence about his attraction to a young man named Henry Collins. 'I could not understand my feelings. Why should I be attracted towards him more than to any other young man? ... Were the mysterious forces of Nature making themselves heard and felt?'[61] Higgins – a journalist and future speaker of the British Columbia provincial legislature – resolves the potential subversion of homosexuality by having Collins turn out to be a passing woman. But real life did not always end so tidily. Between 1849 and 1871 at least four men were charged with sodomy or buggery in three separate trials.[62]

Read for broadly social rather than narrowly legal evidence, the case of John Butts especially indicates the relative importance of homosexual behaviour and demonstrates how its regulation was shaped by the context of colonial British Columbia. Butts was simultaneously central and marginal to Victoria society in the 1850s and 1860s, a famous outcast who performed tricksterlike functions in local society. Of English extraction and Australian birth, Butts moved to Victoria in 1858 after a sojourn in San Francisco. He was initially employed as the town crier and bell ringer. But, when the magistrate was out of earshot, Butts reportedly changed his proclamation to '"God Save (a pause of a few seconds) John Butt."' For this act of disloyalty he was deposed as town crier, and became a garbage collector until officially barred from the trade for charging customers for hauling the same rubbish back and forth across town.[63] Butts then became the most celebrated habitué of Victoria's police court, chain gang, and jail. In the early 1860s he was arrested for, among other things, stealing photographic equipment and a keg of porter, selling a stolen goose, 'rowdyish and disorderly conduct,' and for being a rogue and a vagabond. He also continued to work as something of a freelance town crier and a street cleaner, occasionally hiring a First Nations assistant.[64] Yet it was Butts's petty crime that earned him significant gaol time and titles like 'the hero of a hundred committals,' and, more often, 'the notorious John Butts.'[65]

Butts received censure not only from Victoria's police court but from the townfolk of Victoria. He was ridiculed in public, as when he was used as an exhibit by a travelling phrenology lecturer, caricatured in the local press, or shouted down when he asked to be appointed town crier.[66] That Butts was also considered an appropriate object of violence was confirmed when he charged a war hero named J.M. Simpson for beating him. Simpson's lawyer argued that it was 'shameful that a man of Butts' character should be allowed to slander gentlemen in this town.' Despite testimony that Simpson gratuitously beat Butts, the court commented that, given his poor character, Butts 'richly deserved the dressing he got.'[67]

This daily routine of mockery and casual violence served as a backdrop for the prosecution of Butts's same-sex activity. In January 1860 he was charged for 'an abominable offence on the person of a little English boy, employed at the Union Hotel.'[68] The state marshalled an impressive amount of evidence about Butts's sexual relationships with the illiterate William Williams, described in the local press as 'a rather good looking youth of about sixteen years of age.'[69] That Williams himself was initially held in gaol on charges of 'buggery' suggests that he was initially seen as a participant rather than a victim. Yet he was released after a couple of weeks and eventually served as the Crown's star witness,[70] testifying that he met Butts at a hotel, and that the older man offered him work and a place to stay. 'I went there, and went to bed with him, he had connection with me, and ever since I have been in great pain,' said Williams.[71] Other residents of Butts's household confirmed Williams's story, and in doing so, inadvertently revealed an intimate, crowded, and exclusively male world.[72]

This was not the first time Butts had propositioned young working-class boys who depended on older men for employment or shelter. A butcher recalled overhearing Butts make advances to a lad known as Ginger.[73] Ginger, or Francis Jackson, testified that Butts had approached him on three separate occasions, offering the homeless boy a job and a bed in exchange for sex. 'He told me he wished he had me in bed with him, and he put his hands on his privates and said if he had me in bed with him he would give me that,' Jackson testified. He spurned Butts by likening homosexual and interracial heterosexual sex. 'I told him if he wanted to fuck anything to get a squaw and he could do as much as he wanted.'[74] For Jackson, the 'squaw' or dangerous Aboriginal woman was presumed to be sexually available to all white men and an illicit enough object of desire to serve as a workable analogy to homosexual sex. These fraught connections between sexual identity, respectability, and race were also raised when the butcher chastised Butts not for suggesting sex to another man, but for doing so within earshot of what he called 'a lady'[75] – undoubtably a white woman. For him, Butts's language or behaviour were not inherently indecent, but merely not suitable for white women's ears.

It is not surprising that Butts's trial was a controversial one. The state mounted a serious case against which the poor and isolated Butts was unable to defend himself effectively. When tried by the attorney general in February 1860, Butts faced the court alone, without legal representation or even witnesses. Butts tried to turn these disadvantages to his favour with a elegantly pitiful self-representation, asking the court for mercy and explaining that 'the men I expected as witnesses have gone up the river and I am left without any.'[76] At nine o'clock in the evening after the trial, the jury announced that they could not agree on a verdict; the judge responded by locking them up until the following morning. After requesting 'instructions,' the jury declared that it was 'impossible for them to agree.' The judge dismissed them and impanelled a new jury.

The new jury, if nothing else, was efficient. They met for a mere five minutes before acquitting.[77] Butts, for one, had always maintained his innocence, testifying: 'All I have got to say is that this case is got up to extort money from me'[78] – an unlikely explanation given his obvious and indeed infamous poverty. But Butts's dealings with the local police were far from over. He was kept in jail for a spell after his acquittal and thereafter his petty theft continued apace, as did his to penchant for casual violence.[79] In July 1866 the court put an end to Butts's long career by charging him 'with being a rogue and a vagabond, and the associate of thieves.' In a peculiar and informal local variation on transportation, he was ordered to leave the colony, and, when he failed to do so, jailed for three months. He was released two months later when he signed articles to sail for either China or Australia.[80] The *Cariboo Sentinel* celebrated his final outlawry: 'Adieu! poor houseless, homeless vagrant. Your offenses against society have been many, and your punishment often severe.'[81]

The Butts case raises important connections between homosocial culture and homosexual behaviours. Witness testimony divulges a tightly woven homosocial milieu anchored in young white men's shared domestic and social ties. In Butts's crowded house, women only existed as infrequently invoked symbols of either propriety or danger. Homosexual acts seem to have been a relatively regular part of this homosocial milieu. Butts was known to proposition other men, and this behaviour does not seem to have been considered inherently problematic as much as it was inappropriate in certain circumstances – such as when white women were within earshot. Young men's testimonies reveal that they were easily fluent with language specifically describing homosexual sex.

That colonial British Columbia was a society that tolerated a certain amount of male same-sexuality is reaffirmed by other cases, as is the tendency of certain men to be singled out for their same-sex practices. In British Columbia as elsewhere, there was a special connection between seamen and same-sex practice. In 1866 Matti Rasid, a Greek sailor belonging to the HBC's *Princess Royal*, was found guilty of sodomy in a case that initially indicted Rasid and another sailor for a series of sexual acts committed with four boys over at least a three-week period and inadvertently revealed a working-class shipboard culture where sex between men was not uncommon.[82] In 1870 or 1873 a popular sailor named John Kingswell was found guilty of having attempted sodomy with another sailor at the Ship's Sun, an Esquimalt pub.[83]

No surviving records from the years between 1849 and 1871 indicate that any men were prosecuted for male homosexual sex in up-country British Columbia, including the overwhelmingly male mining towns. In large part, this reflects the limited reaches of the colonial state in British Columbia which, as Tina Loo has shown, was never able to establish conclusive legal authority over the backwoods.[84] Yet it also mirrors a particular pattern of sexual regulation that developed in colonial contexts. Historian Ronald Hyam explains male same-sexual practice in colonial settings as a situational response that was 'almost entirely opportunistic or the product of circumstance, and without prejudice to relationships with women.'[85] Others challenge this simplistic heterosexism. In *Colonial Desire: Hybridity in Theory, Culture and Race*, postcolonial theorist Robert Young suggests that fears of miscegenation could eclipse fears of homosexuality in imperial contexts. Same-sex sex, he writes, 'posed no threat because it produced no children; its advantage was that it remained silent, covert, and unmarked.'[86] Colonies could foster an environment of passive tolerance towards same-sex erotic practice because, however threatening, it did not create the boundless brown bodies whose very existence challenged racialized boundaries of rule. Such comparative tolerance would also have been fostered by the existence of a colonial community where men's social and emotional attachments to each other were nourished and reinforced by a wider homosocial culture.

Reconfirming Gender: Labour, Drink, Gambling, Violence, and White Identity

Some of the most compelling symbols of the homosocial culture of British Columbia's backwoods were those that reworked or challenged conventional gender organization. But much of the daily practice of this culture was not dissimilar from that of working-class men throughout the Anglo-American world. British Columbia's homosocial culture was rooted in labour, especially the hard work generated by gold rushes. Like many rural, nineteenth-century British North Americans, gold miners were independent commodity producers who drifted in and out of wage labour as need and opportunity dictated. To suggest miners were anything other than self-actualizing, wealth-seeking individuals goes against much that is dear in the white gold mining lore so ably analysed by Julie Cruikshank.[87] The notion that gold mining effortlessly drew together men of disparate class backgrounds appealed to nineteenth-century British Columbians as well. 'Socially we are a combination of all ranks from the proud aristocrat to the mean despicable city vagabond,' contended Cariboo resident and constant letter writer Tal. O Eifion. 'The great barriers of rank which exist in most countries has [*sic*] entirely broken down among us.'[88]

To some extent, the image of gold mining as an egalitarian industry where luck was the only authority was rooted in the peculiarities of placer mining. Yet this image mystified more than it mirrored. Gold mining was enmeshed in an industrializing economy and developing liberal state, and wage labour was more important than promotional

The Cariboo's Minnehaha Claim was a large gold-mining enterprise, ca 1867.

literature and romantic recollection suggested. Most non-white miners were wage labourers.[89] In the Kootenay mines in 1864 there were roughly fifty sluice companies with between five and twenty-five employees apiece.[90] 'It is estimated that the number of miners who make over wages is one in five hundred; and the number that do well in the mines is one in a thousand,' wrote Major, who never earned more than his 'grub.'[91]

The reputation of gold mining as a rough, disreputable trade reinforced its connection with wage labour. It was explicitly physical labour in an era where the division between manual and non-manual labour increasingly bespoke class division. Working individually or in small, sometimes collective groups, miners disrupted normative patterns of authority and deference. The non-industrial, seasonal rhythms of placer mining also ran up against the patterns of steadiness, reliability, and discipline that industrial employers were working to inculcate. Perhaps most fundamentally, gold mining suggested that wealth could be produced through luck, fortune, or chance, an affront to a society that increasingly connected financial success with moral virtue and disciplined labour. Such factors combined to give gold mining a reputation as a disorderly trade that infected all who came into contact with it. 'There is something disreputable about gold hunting,' pondered Hayward.[92]

The disrespectable image of gold mining could be a powerful lure for white men disillusioned with industrial capitalism and the visions of masculinity it offered. Embittered by the false promises of capitalism, they sought an environment where hard work would secure them manly self-sufficiency and respect. American cultural historian Gail Bederman suggests that the latter half of the nineteenth-century witnessed increasing disillusionment with the visions of self-controlled, temperate, disciplined, and domestic masculinity that gained hegemony earlier in the century.[93] In response, white men refashioned definitions of manliness and civilization and also sought environments where a reinvigorated vision of white manhood could flourish. Nineteenth-century gold rushes, much hyped and oft-promoted, especially promised white men a new vision of manhood unencumbered by the burdens of industrializing society. Some thought they found it. George Grant, secretary of Sir Stanford Fleming's party, declared a Thompson River prospector a genuine 'specimen of Anglo-Saxon self-reliant individualism.'[94]

Drink, like rough work, was indelibly marked on British Columbia's

The archetypal gold-miner in 1864, working alone and with simple tools.

homosocial culture. It was something of a colonial pastime. In 1853 Douglas called drunkenness 'the crying and prevalent sin of this Colony,' and not much changed in the following years.[95] Drink, rather than the church or the domestic, seemed to sit at the centre of colonial society. HBC servant Robert Melrose, whose 1853 diary enumerated the days he and his friends were one-quarter, one-half, or fully drunk, argued that drink was symptomatic of Vancouver Island's colonial condition. 'Here we are settled on this Island, just lying as Nature finished it, among a band of untutored Indians, here we have no Church to go to, no tailor to make our cloths, not a shoemaker to sole a shoe for us; but thither that accursed Grog has found its way, and a temple of Bacchus erected.' The 'god of wine,' he concluded, was truly 'revered in the north-west of America.'[96]

Drinking was the special preserve of the colony's settlers and men. Aboriginal people were legally denied the right to imbibe by statute in 1854 and thereafter the 'Indian liquor trade' was policed by gunboat.[97] The justice of denying First Nations people legal drink was occasionally debated, but the white community seems to have usually enjoyed its monopoly on lawful liquor.[98] Access to liquor was a significant enough citizenship right that non-white settlers fought to defend it, as when Victoria's Black community challenged white barkeepers for denying them drink at least twice in 1862.[99] Like citizenship, drinking was gendered as well as raced. 'It is considered a heinous offence against public morals that a lady should be anything but a teetotaller,' opined Johnson.[100]

Among white men, sailors and gold miners were especially famed for their enthusiasm for drink. So much did sailors love their liquor, the *Victoria Press* commented, that 'it is likely they would be equally as contented and happy in jail as on board ship if they could get their daily allowance of grog.'[101] Drink was the main focus of sociability in mining towns where there were few enough other options. That saloons and wayside houses were often the sole public meeting places in the up-country is suggested by how frequently missionaries held services in them.[102] Regulated by the necessity of ritual 'treating,' drinking in these places was an intensely social activity. Aristocratic travellers Viscount Milton and W.B. Cheadle described the protocol at wayside houses, those combination saloon, restaurant, and hotel that were dotted along the colony's back roads. After the men unloaded their packs, a drink was proposed by 'some one of the party less "hard up" than his friends, and the rest of the company present are generally invited to

Drinking in the backwoods. Ward's store at Leech River, ca 1865.

join in.'[103] Men who refused ritual drinks, like German mathematician Carl Friesach, were treated with disdain.[104]

Drinking took place all year and in all locales, but the winter and the town held a special place in British Columbia's political economy of partying. Miners and other seasonal workers who moved back in forth between city and woods converged on Victoria for the slack season. 'Miners spent money lavishly – chiefly in public houses and dance houses and extravagance in general,' remembered John Helmcken.[105] Dance houses primarily provided places where white men and First Nations women could socialize, but also, according to their defenders, were a necessary space for miners' seasonal binges. Admitting that his kind were 'a little gayer than ordinary,' one miner argued that long periods of deprivation gave miners a natural 'desire to spree a little.'[106]

Opponents of dance houses challenged the idea that they were needed and comfortable spaces for working-class sociability. Instead, they presented them as hotbeds of mixed-race immorality superintended by shrewd and devious profiteers. Dance houses, attested Methodist missionary Ephraim Evans, really catered to 'tangle leg manufacturers, illicit traders in small wares with the Indians, receivers of goods from parties whose possecorry [sic] rights are not too strictly scrutinized, light-fingered gentry who are not scrupulous as to the means of acquisition; and kindred characters, are not to be confounded with an honest and industrial population.'[107] Yet others defended drink as a potent and appropriate symbol of the homosocial culture of the backwoods. 'The Bard of the Lowhee' wrote a 'A Reminiscence of Cariboo Life,' which began, 'Oh, I love to snore/On a bar-room floor/And sleep a drunk away!' adding pearls like 'I love the barley bree!' and 'I love the jolly spree!'[108]

Whether it occurred in a saloon, wayside house, or dance house, drinking often went hand in hand with gambling, another activity associated with British Columbia's homosocial culture. In British Columbia gambling was constructed as equivalent or endemic to mining, a product of its privileging of chance and easy gain above hard work, ambition, and obedience.[109] Gaming was sometimes superintended by the shrewd and prominent professionals that troubled mining towns, vying for power and influence with local colonial officials, yet it was generally a casual affair intermeshed with other forms of sociability. Men played for drink more often than money, and gaming often went hand in hand with music, drinking, and bare-fisted prizefighting.[110] Like drinking, gambling could both link white men together as well as

A Way Side House.—Arrival of Miners.

A Way Side House at Midnight.

An evening at a wayside house. From *Cheadle's Journal of Trip across Canada, 1862–1863*.

divide them. As Gunther Peck points out in his study of the Comstock Lode, gambling and other risk-taking activities 'strengthened rather than weakened miners' commitment to a working-class moral economy that celebrated maleness, mutuality, whiteness, and the power of chance.'[111]

Violence was another keynote of this homosocial culture. An October 1866 prizefight between George Wilson, 'the Cariboo Champion,' and George Baker, 'the Canadian Pet,' prompted the local press to comment that 'Cariboo has never witnessed the assemblage of so many people since the white man came to work this "illihe" [land].'[112] Violence was not isolated to the spectacular and ritual. As in the Oregon context analysed by David Peterson del Mar, the settlement process gave white men an 'intimate knowledge' of violence and normalized the use of force to control others.[113] While Justice Matthew Begbie worked hard to construct the British Columbian frontier as uniquely peaceful,[114] it was hard to ignore the barroom and back-alley brawls. 'As you may imagine where there is so much young blood & no female population,' wrote British surveyor and diarist Charles Wilson about Victoria in 1858, 'there are sometimes fierce scenes enacted & the bowie knife & revolver which every man wears are in constant requisition.'[115]

Violence regulated relations within the white male community and reinforced its authority over both women and non-white peoples. The threat of violence could solidify male community: one author advised group emigration as a means to 'resist aggression.'[116] But solidarity could also encourage the use of force when mates came to each others' defence. The *Cariboo Sentinel* remarked: 'Every man has his friends, and it is not unlikely that some of these fights may end in a general row between the friends of the combatants, and where the strong and the weak fight in a mining camp serious consequences are sure to follow.'[117] Women and Aboriginal peoples were also targets of white men's violence. Such violence was often but not only sexual and conjugal. 'The white men kick the Indians about like dogs,' commented one observer.[118]

This suggests how white male homosocial culture was rooted not simply in identification as men, but in its members' tendency to identify as *white* men. The oft-remarked ethnic and racial plurality of backwoods British Columbia could challenge homogeneity and hierarchy. But it should not blind us to the centrality of whiteness to homosocial culture. The racial plurality of some gold-mining milieus could intensify rather than modify the significance of whiteness, as white men

Male community – in this case heavily armed community – could challenge as well as reinforce racial barriers. Ah Bau and two companions, 1858.

worked to assert their racial solvency in a context where it was cast into doubt. Immigrants carried racial ideologies premised on the distinctiveness of the Anglo-Saxon race and its dual superiority to and responsibility for all others with them from their home societies to British Columbia. There, notions of white supremacy were reinforced and reformulated against both the ethnic diversity of the settler population and the large Aboriginal population.

White men read First Nations people through the always clouded and often conflicted lenses of mid-nineteenth-century racial discourse. Some reported finding them less threatening and more admirable than anticipated.[119] Others expressed feelings of disgust, hostility, and revulsion regarding Aboriginal people's simple existence. Guillod told his family in England that 'a journey out here soon destroys all romantic illusions with regard to the Indians; instead of anything noble they are dirty, immoral, and fond of tawdry finery.'[120] Other white men pledged that they would assist in the gradual creation of a white society in this territory; some singled out gold miners as uniquely fitted as harbingers of civilization, as 'destined to raise up great and powerful nations of the Anglo-Saxon race in countries hitherto considered inhospitable and unfit for colonization and settlement for civilized man.'[121] Missionaries and moral reformers would disagree with such sentiments, arguing that miners' sexual and social excesses unfitted them for the true task of racial domination. But if others disputed their membership in the brotherhood of Anglo-Saxon men, white men in British Columbia rarely shared these doubts.

Prescribed gender organization was profoundly disrupted in colonial British Columbia. Among the results of this disruption is the complex homosocial culture forged among white men in the colony, which coexisted and sometimes overlapped with the mixed-race community. In the backwoods and urban enclaves, white men reconstructed domestic space without white women, creating their own structures of household life. They formed social, emotional, and sometimes sexual relationships with each other. In reconstructing these bonds, white men in British Columbia embraced same-sex relations at the same time heterosocial modes of sociability and domesticity were becoming hegemonic in middle-class Anglo-American culture and shaping expectations of working-class life. Similarly, white men drank, gambled, and fought, elevating these acts to social prominence and value at the very moment that metropolitan, middle-class visions of self-controlled, self-contained, and temperate manhood were constructed as both normative and necessary. When these pastimes held on in the working-class taverns and streets of metropolitan communities, British Columbians claimed them as prominent cultural practices and values.

Through daily practice and self-representation, this culture constructed a particular if fragmented vision of what it meant to be white and male. Whether it was reworking or reconfirming dominant practices of masculinity, this vision of white manhood did not reject, but rather reinforced, the power accorded white men in a colonial and patriarchal society. A shared white identity was celebrated, and men's authority over both women and First Nations people was reinforced through myriad daily practices. As much as the particular alignment of race and gender in colonial British Columbia gave birth to a homosocial white male culture, it also fostered intimate relationships between settler men and First Nations women.

Chapter 2

'The Prevailing Vice': Mixed-Race Relationships

In 1870 Anglican missionary R.C. Lundin Brown urged the English public to support his evangelical efforts in Lillooet, British Columbia. In a little wooden church among the mountains, he annually preached a sermon, usually in the week of Lent, against what he dubbed 'the prevailing vice, concubinage with native women.' Brown went on to speak of 'troops of young Indian girls' who annually migrated to Lillooet to live with white men in 'tumble-down cabins.' Such relationships, more than damaging Aboriginal women, imperiled the morality of their white partners. None, pondered Brown, 'could live intimately with persons of low tone and habits without sinking to their level.'[1] Brown's tirade was born out of his deep discomfort with the wide-spread practice of mixed-race relationships in British Columbia between 1849 and 1871. Sex lay at the heart of both British Columbia's colonial project and critiques of it. On this edge of empire, gender was organized in different and challenging ways, and heterosexual unions forged between settler men and Aboriginal women were among the sharpest reminders of this.

In colonial British Columbia, cultural contact was literally gendered insofar as the political economy of the colonial project tended to bring settler men into contact with Aboriginal women. Prevailing patterns of European migration and a resource extractive economy meant that men made up an overwhelming percentage of the white population, while simultaneously the imperatives of the local labour market and sexual economy meant that women were overrepresented in urban First Nations communities. An 1868 census, for instance, recorded almost twice as many Aboriginal women as Aboriginal men in Victoria.[2] That social and discursive space literary scholar Mary Louise Pratt calls the 'contact zone'[3] was, in British Columbia, explicitly gendered, bringing together men and women rather than ungendered racial subjects.

Cultural contact was also highly sexualized. The topic of mixed-race relationships in colonial British Columbia, however, is as slippery and charged as it is important. The limited resources available to nineteenth-century historians relying primarily on written sources necessarily impose restrictions on the extent to which any scholar, particularly a non-Aboriginal one like me, can deduce (let alone 'speak for') First Nations experiences. Even white perspectives on mixed-race relationships can be difficult to read. Few authors commenting on mixed-race relationships were themselves members of white-Aboriginal unions, and those that were rarely admit it. Discussions of mixed-race relationships come chiefly from missionaries and journalists, authors whose adherence to specific literary norms often leads to sensational portrayals of colonial life. Missionaries were especially empowered by their social position to comment on aspects of others' lives that most nineteenth-century people felt honour-bound to ignore, at least in print. Their discursive access to the sexual and domestic lives of others renders missionary records unusually revealing sources for social history, but also deeply colours both their form and content.

The laden character of available source material renders it impossible to construct a tidy division between the experience and representation of mixed-race relationships, a complexity this analysis tries to respect. Yet this source material does indicate that, for many, these unions amounted to even more evidence in colonial British Columbia that gender and race were lived in different and perhaps dangerous ways. Premised on the construction of First Nations women as sexually dangerous, this discourse represented mixed-race relationships and their children as inimical to the establishment of a respectable white settler colony in British Columbia.

Constructions of First Nations Women

Beliefs about the dangerous character of First Nations women were the bedrock upon which constructions of mixed-race relationships were built. Ranya Green suggests that Europeans saw North American women through a powerful dualistic lens: the 'squaw' was lustful and threatening to white men, while 'Pocahontas' was pure and helpful, a cultural mediator, who, like her namesake, protected white interests. A related discourse represented the squaw as overworked and abused, the firm-

White men like photographer J.C. Eastcott were fascinated with what they saw as First Nations women's bodily character. A Lekwammen (Songhees) group in 1867–8.

est evidence of Aboriginal savagism.[4] In mid-nineteenth century British Columbia, as in the prairie context recently studied by Sarah Carter in *Capturing Women: The Manipulation of Cultural Imagery in Canada's Prairie West*, the image of the squaw predominated.[5] Aboriginal women were constructed as lascivious, shameless, unmaternal, prostitutes, ugly, and incapable of high sentiment or manners – the dark, mirror image to the idealized nineteenth-century visions of white women.

First Nations women were represented as overtly sexual, physical, and base. White men were simultaneously attracted and alarmed by what they saw as Aboriginal women's sexual availability, signified most powerfully by their dress. James Bell, a draper visiting Victoria, found that 'among the Females there is a *painful* and *provoking* scarcity of petticoats.'[6] Others were unsettled by different politics of physical space. One found Northern women's curiosity about men's bodies 'frightfully disgusting' for 'a man of healthful proclivities.'[7] Thomas Bushby, a young middle-class British emigrant, saw the same physicality but interpreted it positively. He was deeply enamoured by his future wife, Governor James Douglas's mixed-blood teenage daughter, Agnes, especially with what he saw as her darkness and her willingness to engage in rough, physical play. He wrote that 'they say she looks with no savage eye on me – & true she is a stunning girl. black eye & hair & larky like the devil.'[8]

The grotesque helped hone the image of Aboriginal women. White observers were fascinated with Aboriginal cosmetics, adornment, and body culture, foisting uncomfortable attention on the practice of head-flattening and facial jewellery.[9] The construction of First Nations women as base and bodily was given meaning and shape by a usually unspoken but always present comparison with white women. 'Lines to a Klootchman [Aboriginal woman],' a poem reprinted from the American *Puget Sound Herald*, rendered this comparison explicit:

Sweet nymph! although of dirtier hue thou art
    Than other ladies brought from eastern climes,
To Thee I yield the tribute of my love,
    To Thee I dedicate these humble rhymes;
And if too faint I string my trembling lyre,
Great Pocahontas! thou my verse inspire ...

Thy well-squeezed head was flat as flounders are,
    Thy hair with dog-fish oil resplendent shone,

Thy feet were bare, and slightly inward turn'd
  Thy slender waist and swelling limbs did bind;
A mild but fishy odor round thee clung,
As though dried salmon thou hadst been among ...

But though thou smellest strong of salmon dry,
  Though innocent of soap thy hands appear,
Although thy toes turn inwards with a curl,
  And though thy skull is smash'd from front to rear;
Though nameless animals thy hair infest,
Still do I love thee of all maidens best.

Then give me a blanket and a mat,
  Dried claims and fish my only food shall be,
My only house a half-upturn'd canoe,
  Whiskey my drink, and love alone for thee;
Thus fair-haired dames for me will vainly shine
In all the charms of hoops and crinoline![10]

Fishy, infested, flattened, and barefoot, this klootchman is a grotesque foil for Western ideals of womanhood. As Terry Goldie suggests, images of 'anti-erotic' Aboriginal women paradoxically imply 'a fear of their attractions.'[11]

White men's perception of First Nations women as sexually available was justified by the contention that Aboriginal cultures, especially North-Coast ones, did not promote chastity. While interior nations valued female chastity, reported naturalist John Keast Lord, 'among the fish-eaters of the north-west coast it has no meaning, or if it has it appears to be utterly disregarded.'[12] Anglican missionary John Good considered Tlingit (Stickeen) and Haida women 'licentious beyond conception' and Tsimshian only a slight improvement.[13] Such comments hint at how in British Columbia images of the generic 'Indian woman' were tempered by culturally specific representations, especially those rooted in the ongoing reality of Haida, Tsimshian, Nisga'a, and Tlingit military and political power and presence.

The construction of First Nations women as licentious relied on the assumption that they lacked social censure and also self-regulation and its most powerful foot-soldier, shame. When an Aboriginal women drank from the remnants of a broken liquor bottle, white passersby in Victoria shouted 'halo shame,'[14] or 'no shame' in Chinook jargon, the

Settlers were fixated on head flattening among First Nations women. From *Four Years in British Columbia and Vancouver Island*, 1862.

joual of the West Coast. In 1865, when an Aboriginal woman named Lucy was charged for being drunk and disorderly in Victoria's police court, the *British Colonist* reported that the magistrate asked 'if she was not ashamed of herself.' The politics of their conversation were not lost on Lucy, who replied, '"Nowitka, nica patlamb, halo shame nika" [Indeed, I was drunk, but I am not ashamed].'[15]

First Nations society was thought to compromise maternal affection as well as self-governance. Yet commentators faced logistical difficulties in balancing notions of the 'naturalness' of gender with the specificities of race. A drawing of an 'Indian Woman and Child' uneasily balances images of dark and slatternly womanhood with motherly protection. Some went beyond the uneasy balance to construct motherly love as a powerful force that spanned racial boundaries, as when Aboriginal mothers in Victoria were said to have a 'true motherly affection for their young.'[16] Others considered race a significant enough force to compromise such affection. Methodist missionary Thomas Crosby wrote that 'heathenism crushed out a mother's love.'[17] A British travel writer emphasized First Nations women's willingness to abort, calling 'extinguishing life in the womb' a common habit.[18]

Discourses of prostitution were especially handy tools for defining respectable and unrespectable femininity in British Columbia as in Red River.[19] A convenient shorthand for signifying the immorality of First Nations womanhood was the suggestion that Aboriginal women were, by definition, prostitutes. The magistrate of Lillooet referred to 'the wholesale prostitution of the young women and even small children.'[20] Communities located around the city of Victoria received the lion's share of this scorn, reflecting the belief that Aboriginal people were necessarily degraded by cultural contact. In 1870 colonial official Joseph Trutch wrote that 'prostitution is another acknowledged evil prevailing to an almost unlimited extent among the Indian women in the neighbourhood of Victoria.'[21] Cultural rhetoric justified the intimate connection between Aboriginal women and prostitution. The sex trade was associated with First Nations gift-giving ceremonies, seasonal migration, social organization, and gender norms. Navy surgeon Edward Bogg wrote that 'the open practice of habitual Prostitution is not considered as a disgrace, but as a highly legitimate and very lucrative calling, nor does the Indian warrior consider it as in any way derogatory to his manhood to subsist on the earnings of his Squaws at this shameful trade.'[22]

As much as they were said to embrace what Europeans saw as

A mixed message: images of caring maternity existed alongside notions of First Nations women's depravity. From *Four Years in British Columbia and Vancouver Island*, 1862.

disrespectable sexuality, First Nations women were thought unable to appreciate the finer points of Western love. A missionary describing life on Haida Gawaii argued that 'the beautiful attachment and heroic constancy of affection ending only in death, amongst civilised or Christian nations, is to them unknown.'[23] A popular poem contrasted the romantic words and lofty promises of a white man with the ignoble response of his Aboriginal intended. While he promises her eternal affection and high sentiment, she replies with an offer, in Chinook, to sell him clams:

> Come maiden of the wilderness,
>   And linger by my side;
> We'll fly away across the sea,
>   If you will be my bride ...
>
> The maiden raised her lovely head
>   With eyes meek as a lamb's,
> She gazed into his manly face,
>   And softly whispered, – C-K – Clams.[24]

Where 'Lines to a Klootchman' contrasts white female delicacy with Aboriginal vulgarity, this poem contrasts European romance with First Nations coarseness.

First Nations women were critiqued for 'native' hygiene, dress, and habits and also mocked for adopting the conventions of white femininity. In Victoria the local press derided 'Mary, Sunox, Carol, Kate, Emelie, and Mush, squaws belonging to the northern tribes,' for wearing hoop skirts at court.[25] Remembering a Quesnel dance, naval and colonial official Phillip Hankin found women's refusal to dance with men to whom they had not been introduced truly ironic. 'I recollect,' he wrote, 'asking one of the Kitty's in Chinook to dance with me and she drew herself up in a very dignified manner, and said "Halo introduce" [no introduction] which signified I had not been introduced to Her! and I couldn't help laughing which made her very angry.'[26] Incorporating the manners and clothing of European femininity did not guarantee Aboriginal women the respect accorded to ladies.

The logical extension of the representation of First Nations women as the mirror image to white women was the exclusion of Aboriginal women from the category of 'woman' altogether. In British Columbia the category 'woman' was given racial contours in both casual and

Embracing the latest Victorian fashions rarely convinced white observers that First Nations women were respectable. Lekwammen (Songhees) people in 1867–8.

formal acts. Local officials responded to queries about their gaol facilities by commenting that 'no woman had been imprisoned' and that 'drunken squaws have ... been locked up until sobered.'[27] Hankin's reminiscences mention dancing with First Nations women and not being 'fit to sit down at table with Ladies' in one passage.[28] Just as the jail's 'squaws' were not women, Hankin's ladies could not be of the First Nations.

This image of Aboriginal women was a homespun, localized construct, as cultural historian Carrol Smith-Rosenberg suggests, based on the settlers' need 'to refute the positive representations of indigenous Americans found within British imperial discourse.'[29] The construction of First Nations women in colonial discourse bore little relationship to actual women's lives. Yet the image was an enduring one that continues to shape First Nations women's experience. Janice Acoose/Misko-Kìsikàwihkwè (Red Sky Woman) powerfully demonstrates how the image of the 'easy squaw' legitimates violence against Aboriginal women, like the brutal 1971 rape and murder of Helen Betty Osborne in small-town Manitoba.[30] In colonial British Columbia, the construction of First Nations women as the dark and dangerous opposite of white women was given addition meaning by a related discourse on white-Aboriginal relationships. Colonial discourse built upon its representation of First Nations women as dangerous by constructing mixed-race relationships as an active threat to white men's fragile moral and racial selves.

Constructions of Mixed-Race Relationships

Secular and religious observers alike were compelled to notice the existence of heterosexual relationships between settler men and First Nations women throughout British Columbia. They especially associated them with the colony's fur-trade community that both Sylvia Van Kirk and Jennifer Brown have documented.[31] Even if mixed-relationships were losing their widespread acceptance among the higher echelons of the fur trade, wage earners remained deeply enmeshed in conjugal relationships with Aboriginal women. In 1861 an experienced Orkney servant reported that 'the custom of living with Indian women was universal in the Hudson's Bay Company (HBC) service.'[32]

Yet mixed-race relationships were not confined to the fur trade. Disillusioned miner John Emmerson wrote that only one unmarried man in the interior mining town of Douglas had failed to take an Aboriginal partner.[33] White male homosocial culture and mixed-race sociability overlapped: mining towns like Douglas were not as much without women as they were without white women. George Grant, secretary of Sandford Flemming's surveying party, noted that around Kamloops, 'most of the settlers live with squaws, or Klootchman as they are called on the Pacific.'[34] Methodist missionary Ebenezer Robson, visiting Salt Spring Island's north settlement, despaired that of nine men '5 are living with Indian women in a state of adultery.'[35]

Mixed-race relationships were a part of city as well as bush, country, and mining life. The census of Victoria enumerated a total of 581 family households by race in the spring of 1871. In excluding the Lekwammen (Songhees) settlement and deeming people of mixed heritage like James Douglas's family and a plethora of lesser-known individuals as white, the census taker employed a definition of whiteness that was unusually expansive by nineteenth-century British Columbian standards. Yet it still found that sixty households or over 10 per cent of all family households contained an adult First Nations female and white man, thirty-one of which had resident children. These families were clustered in the poorer districts lying at the city's outskirts: almost one-quarter lived on Store Street alone and over 80 per cent were located on Store, Johnson, Cormorant, Pioneer, and Broughton and Kane streets.[36]

Mixed-race relationships frequently departed from the conventions of European marriage. Missionaries described encountering couples who had lived together for years without the benefit of white ceremony. It was usually the event of marriage, rather than the relationship itself, that occasioned notice. Crosby remembered that five mixed-race couples with children were married in one missionary visit to Chilliwack.[37] Some mixed-race couples challenged missionary sensibilities by explaining that their relationships were unchurched by choice. Anglican Bishop George Hills wrote about one Fort Rupert couple who had lived together for thirteen years. The white man 'objected to marriage because if she knew he was legally bound to her she would probably fall back into her old habits & perhaps cohabit with Indian men & expect him to be home to keep notwithstanding, he said this had happened in several cases when men had married.' Yet when Hills asked this man if 'he intended life long fidelity,' he replied, 'Yes.'[38] Another missionary wrote that white men blamed 'their Klootchmen' for refusing legal marriage.[39]

Other mixed-race couples conformed to the conventions and ceremonies of European marriage. In doing so, they revealed something about the character of their relationships. Sifting through the incomplete information included in the marriage registers of five Anglican churches – St Paul's of Nanaimo, St John's of Victoria, St Mary's the Virgin of Sapperton, St John the Divine of Yale, and Christ Church of Hope – it is possible to identify sixteen mixed-race marriages out of 126. These marriages are marked by significant age differences between the men and women, differences that probably exacerbated racial and gendered difference. Of the twelve couples for whom ages were given, the men were on average 31.25 years old, while the women were an average of 21.6 years of age. These were hardly extreme examples. Qwa-Wail-Yah or Madeline Williams, a Halkomelem woman from the Musqueum village, remembered becoming the second wife of 'Gassy' Jack Dieghton when she was only twelve.[40] These marriage records also confirm that mixed-race relationships were not confined to the fur trade. Except for the three men who married daughters of the fur-trade elite, all the

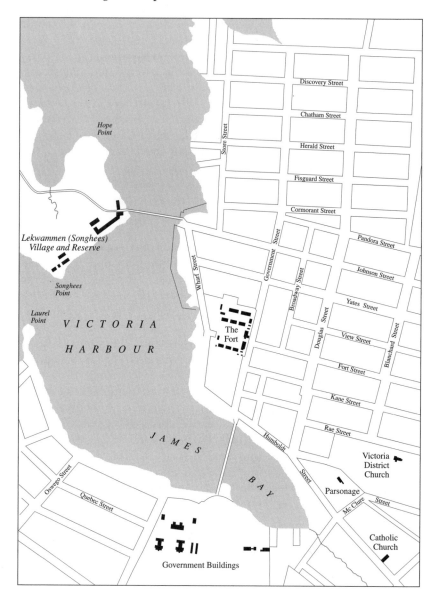

Map 3: Victoria, 1862

grooms had working-class occupations characteristic of a coastal, resource economy: they were sailors, miners, and building, industrial
and retail workers. All the women hailed from British Columbia, and
most were members of Coast Salish nations whose territories abutted
white settlements like the Lekwammen (Songhees), Halkomelem, and
Sechelt.[41]

Aboriginal custom probably served more often than did the Christian ceremony. In 1866 Bishop Hills described a union of a white man
and a Tsimshian woman: 'Married that is not of course with Xian
rites or in legal union but as Indians marry, & as I suppose would
satisfy the essentials of marriage, as for instance in Scotland.'[42] In the
1930s an influential Halkomelem elder from Musqueam, August Jack
Khahtsahlano, described nineteenth-century marriage ceremonies to
Vancouver archivist Major J.S. Matthews:

> Major Matthews: – I was talking to Mrs Walker ... and she told me that her
> father married an Indian girl at Musqueam, and that it was done with
> much ceremony; that Old Kiapilano took 'Portuguese Joe' by the arm, and
> another chief took the Indian girl by her arm, and put them together, and
> said they were going to be man and wife, and then gave them a lot of
> blankets, and then put all the blankets in a big canoe, and sat Joe and his
> wife on top, and they set out for Gastown. What do you think of it?
>
> August: – That's the way all Indians Marry. S'pose I've got a son, and he
> wants to marry. I go to you and say, 'My son want to marry your girl.' And
> he says, 'Alright, come on Tuesday,' or someday like that. And, they tell all
> their friends and each one of them come with his blanket; and the boy
> come with his blanket; and that's the way the Indian get married.[43]

Khatsalano describes a ceremony where the only evidence of Europe
lies in the trade blanket given and, sometimes, the European bride-
grooms.

Where Khatsalano saw 'the way all Indians Marry,' many Europeans
saw casual and temporary relationships. Naval officer Richard Mayne
wrote, 'Whenever a white man takes up his residence among them,
they will always supply him with a wife; and if he quits the place and
leaves her there, she is not the least disgraced in the eyes of her tribe.'[44]
Despite Mayne's equation of short relationships and Aboriginal tradition, fleeting unions were also a part of European culture. For some
white men, casual connections with Aboriginal women were part of the
travel experience. Canadian R.H. Alexander's journal of his 1862 over-

land trip from Canada to British Columbia includes mundane mention of his interaction with Aboriginal women. Passing through Fort Garry, he wrote that 'we went through the bush after some Indian girls and had some great fun.'[45]

Notions of the transiency of mixed-race relationships probably legitimated the ease with which some white men abandoned their Aboriginal partners. In 1861 a white man in Nanaimo fought with, and subsequently replaced, his First Nations wife. In response, the first wife hung herself. This led one letter writer to note that 'surely Indian life is held cheap here.'[46] Burrard Inlet sawmill owner S.P. Moody abandoned his Aboriginal family when his white wife joined him from Victoria, as did Okanagan rancher John Hall Allison.[47] Even if cherished by their partners, Aboriginal women could be rejected by their white in-laws. Qwa-Wail-Yah was denied the money intended for her and her son by her partner's family, and Khatsahlano's sister Louisa was evicted from her home after her husband's death. 'But that's the way they do with Indian woman who marries whiteman,' Khatsahlano argued, 'when their husbands die, they kick the woman out – because she's "just a squaw."'[48]

These experiences confirmed white observers' fears that mixed-race relationships were necessarily degraded ones. That Aboriginal women were 'used as slaves, and turned off at will' and that white men 'pursued a system of debauchery and vice, in their keeping Indian women, and exchanging or abandoning them at their pleasure' became key points in melodramatic and paternalistic missionary discourse.[49] The excesses of this rhetoric should not blind us to the presence of coercion and violence in intimate relations between white men and Aboriginal women. The regional historiography is replete with happy stories among which the long marriage of James Douglas and Amelia Connolly is probably the most famous. These stories are a necessary corrective insofar as they challenge that nineteenth-century discourse that predicted doom for all relationships forged across racial lines. Yet we also need to be wary of how stories of love and affection across racial lines can obscure both coercive details and the larger brutality of colonialism. Pratt argues that the 'transracial love plots' of imperial discourse are 'imaginings in which European supremacy is guaranteed by affective and social bonding.'[50]

Violence in mixed-race relationships belied such transracial love plots. The *British Colonist* reported that 'fights between squaws and squaw men' were a daily occurrence.[51] A Nanaimo missionary reported that

British Columbia's much-lauded and much-criticized mixed-race bourgeoisie. Sir James Douglas, ca 1860s, and Lady Amelia Connolly Douglas, 1862.

one white settler beat his First Nations partner constantly and was reputed to have caused his childrens' deaths. 'His poor woman is constantly in a state of fear,' he wrote, 'he has beaten her so severely three times in the last nine weeks, each time the poor thing has taken to the woods only returning when driven to it by starvation she is now suffering from her last ill-treatment having had her head severely cut by a broken bottle.'[52] While this abuse was similar to that meted out in same-race relationships, the connections between conquering land and conquering women, explored by Anne McClintock in *Imperial Leather: Race, Gender and Sexuality in the Colonial Contest*, reinforced the bonds between heterosexual violence and the colonial project.[53] Judge W.H. Franklyn, referring to the many First Nations women 'persuaded to live with the white men,' argued that such relationships caused 'an ill feeling against the whites.'[54] Scientist Robert Brown thought that 'the causes of nearly every quarrel between whites and Indians on this coast may be summed up in three lines,' the first of which was 'White men taking liberties with their women.'[55]

Resorting to court was not necessarily an expedient solution to such 'ill feelings.' Hills counselled two Aboriginal women who complained of white men's sexual assault 'to appeal to the English magistrate' since 'he would be their friend, and not allow such conduct.'[56] Yet women following Hills's advice could find themselves battling the assumption that all Aboriginal women were sexually available to white men. In October of 1862 Mary Vauliere and Margaret Garbourie, described as 'both Indian women legally married,' charged two Saanich settlers with rape. The preliminary inquiry focused on establishing whether the women had grounds to claim coercive sex:

> The first witness, Mary Vauliere, when questioned as to her knowledge of the obligations of an oath, replied, through her interpreter, that she believed in the truths of Christianity; she had been baptized by a priest who had given her first name; and she knew that if she did right she would go to heaven; if wrong, that she would go to hell. The two complainants were heard, and they seemed to stand cross-examination very well. They both asserted that they were faithful and sober wives, but confessed to having imbibed a few glasses of liquor before the occurrence which led to the trial. The only white witness, George Fey, testified to both women being drunk and to their being well known as prostitutes. Mr John Coles was called to prove that the women were both addicted to loose habits and drunkenness.

After hearing testimony, the magistrate decided 'that though a prostitute was equally entitled to protection,' the evidence was insufficient and dismissed the case.[57] Christianity, a tough courtroom demeanour, legal marriage, and corroboration were not enough to convince this court that Aboriginal women were not the sexually available 'squaws' of colonial discourse.

First Nations communities were not passive in the face of violence. Some responded with the retaliatory violence that was said to motivate events like the Tŝilhquot'in (Chilcotin) Uprising or, as it was more often known, Bute Inlet Massacre.[58] Women sought and sometimes received the protection of the local courts. Arguing that 'the cowardly habit indulged in by certain men of beating squaws, was becoming as common as it was disgraceful,' Police Court Judge Augustus Pemberton superintended something of a crackdown against white batterers of Aboriginal women in Victoria in the spring of 1862.[59] But occasional intervention did not answer First Nations communities' sense that the abuse of women was symbolic and symptomatic of larger inequities and oppressions. The depth of Khahtsahlano's anger led Matthews to note that 'August deeply resents such treatment of Indian wives of whitemen.'[60]

Settlers associated the exchange of cash or goods as well as violence with white-Aboriginal unions. A poem by 'Mosquito,' published in the *Cariboo Sentinel*, recounts a white man cajoling a First Nations woman into living with him. Calling her 'love,' he offers her liquor, a wallpapered cabin, a bed, a stove, messages from friends, and 'klosh wawwaw' (good talk) in exchange for cohabitation:

Oh Mary, dear Mary! come home with me now,
The sleigh from Mosquito has come;
You promised to live in my little board house,
As soon as the pap'ring was done –
The fire brightly burns in the sheet iron stove,
And the bed is made up by the wall;
But it's lonesome, you know, these long winter nights,
With no one to love me at all,
Oh, Mary, dear Mary! come home with me now,
Old George with his 'kewton' is here;
You can, if you like, have your drink of old Tom,
But I'd rather you'd drink lager beer –
I've come all the way thro' the cold drifting snow,

And brought you a message from Yaco;
And these were the very last words that she said:
'Klosh waw-waw delate mika chaco.' [Good talk, really, you should come]
Oh, Mary, dear Mary! come home with me now,
The time by the watch, love, is three –
The night it grows colder, and George with the sleigh,
Down the road, now, is waiting for me,
She stopped by a stump on her way up the hill,
And whisper'd for me not to follow,
But pressing my hand ere I left her, she said,
'Delate nika chaco tomollow' [Really, I will come tomorrow].[61]

While such exchanges were hardly dissimilar from those analysed by Karen Dubinsky in her study of heterosexual conflict in Ontario,[62] settlers in British Columbia read the evidence in overtly racial terms, often equating it with slavery. 'It was not an uncommon thing for these poor blind heathen parents and relatives to sell their little daughters to the white men for the basest of purposes,' wrote Crosby.[63] Amateur ethnographer and businessman Gilbert Sproat saw white men's trade in women as a variation of Aboriginal slavery.[64] Such comments may describe indigenous practices, but they may also confuse them. The exchange of cash or goods could be a version of bride price, a symbol of women's value, not men's disdain. As anthropologist Wilson Duff points out, 'Marriages arranged to form alliances between social groups, and accompanied by exchange of gifts, looked to the whites like a violation of the right of individuals to choose their own mates, and like the "sale" of brides.'[65]

An extension of the conflation of gift exchange with slavery was the likening of mixed-race relationships to prostitution. This was part of a larger tendency of nineteenth-century, middle-class moralists to deem all non-marital sex as prostitution. Despite the presence of settler prostitutes, it was generally assumed the Aboriginal women alone plied the sex trade in colonial British Columbia. The road to Esquimalt and the area outside of Victoria's theatre were especially famed for sexual commerce.[66] Hankin reported that there were 'about 200 Indian prostitutes living in Cormorant, Fisgard, and Store Streets in a state of filth, and dirt beyond all description.'[67] Dance houses, dubbed by one journalist 'no better than brothels,'[68] were also thought to facilitate sexual trade across racial lines.

Does settler society's evident concern for exchange and coercion add up to a critique of the inequities of heterosexuality in general and mixed-race relationships in particular? Some whites were aware and critical of the extent to which violence against Aboriginal women was both common and condoned. An editorial in the *Nanaimo Gazette* noted the lack of legal protection afforded to First Nations women. 'Shall the Indian woman remain open to coarse and obscene insult from every ruffian, without the slightest appeal to justice?'[69] They recognized that this was about race as well as gender. While First Nations men were dealt tough sentences for sexual crime, white men's attacks on Aboriginal women were accepted or even lauded. 'The offence, if it must be called such,' they wrote, 'when committed by a white man is called a lark, a spree, a good joke, a bit of fun.'[70]

Yet whatever critique of white-Aboriginal relationships was offered in mainstream colonial discourse was blunted by paternalism and essentialist, pejorative visions of racial mixing. Observers were surprised when mixed-race relationships departed from preconceived notions of degradation. A Cariboo correspondent told the Victoria press that the Aboriginal women who attended a 1868 party 'conducted themselves during the whole performance in such a becoming and ladylike manner as to stand the hardest test of security from any Puritan whatever' and were 'very gently handled throughout by the rough-bearded part of the assembly.'[71] Preconceptions were more often confirmed by tales of Aboriginal female disgrace and white male treachery. Borrowing on images of the 'noble savage' and its female representative, Pocahontas, colonial discourse could present First Nations women as moral, dutiful, and beautiful in her native realm yet soiled by contact with white society. One poem told of a pristine Stl'àtl'imx (Lillooet) woman besmirched by sexual contact with a white man:

The smoke of her wigwam curling rose
Where the sparkling Lillooet swiftly flows,
To join the impetuous Fraser nigh;
And the blood-red salmon hung to dry
By the lodge where the artless untutored maid
Sprung up like a flower in her native glade ...

But the white man came and his proffered gold
Purchased her ornaments untold,
And the maiden so coy in her native guise
Now courts the rude gaze of admiring eyes,

And her cheeks despoiled of their blushing red
Now wear the vermilion's hue instead.

Her limbs, which scant robes erst confine,
Are now encased in stiff crinoline;
And her brow which with flowers bedecked we knew
And stoops to a band of less graceful blue.
Supporting a cradle bestrung with bells
Which the maiden's misfortune plainly tells.[72]

The 'maiden' here can only be recognized as a victim if she is first envisioned as 'coy in her native guise.' In this poem, there is little room for the recognition of Aboriginal women's agency, nor for an analysis of men's violence that transcends stereotypes of racial mixing, or for a serious grappling with the connections between imperialism and sexual brutality. Genuine critiques of violence, coercion, or abuse in mixed-race relationships were buried under the heavy weight of condescension, romantic racism, and essentialist images of cultural purity and racial identity.

British Columbian critics were generally more concerned for their nascent and struggling white society than for Aboriginal women. Marriage was constructed as the ultimate bulwark maintaining appropriate racial segregation; breaching it imperiled not only individuals, but society as a whole. 'There is not perhaps any dislike to the negro or the Indian population, except in view of their intermarrying with whites or attaining the full privileges of Citizens,' wrote Judge Matthew Begbie.[73] The equation between sexual contact and equality were also articulated in discussions about relationships between different settler groups, especially Black and white. If white liberals really thought Africans were equal, one wrote, they should 'intermarry with the blacks, take them to your houses, your tables, your parlours, your *beds*, but do not whine about "social equality" with negroes until you do something to show that you are in earnest.'[74] Local Black leader Mifflin Winstar Gibbs exposed the hypocrisy of such sentiments. 'It comes with a bad grace for Americans to talk of the horrors of amalgamation,' he wrote, 'when every plantation of the South is more or less a seraglio, and numbers of the most prominent men in the State of California have manifested little heed to color in their choice of companions in an amorous intrigue or a nocturnal debauch.'[75]

While sex and domesticity across all racial lines was considered a threat, in British Columbia white-Aboriginal relationships were constructed as especially dangerous for white men, whose appropriate behaviour and identity would guarantee an orderly settler colony. White men who wedded First Nations women were said, first, to be on a fast road to moral turpitude. Such connections could even imperil public officials. In the late 1840s critics evoked the HBC's seeming acceptance of mixed marriages to challenge their ability to serve as proprietorial rulers of the new colony of Vancouver Island. While company defenders argued that officers were 'exerting themselves to check vice, and encourage morality and religion,'[76] the connection between the HBC and white-Aboriginal relationships persisted as a key rhetorical plank in anti-company discourse. Governor Douglas's mixed-blood family was used as a causal explanation for what critics saw as his poor government and the fur-trade elite's inherent corruption.[77] But fur traders were not the only public officials thought to be imperiled by their mixed-race attachments. One letter attacked magistrates who formed relationships with First Nations women. 'Sorrowful has it been to mark many of the victims of this deadly gangrene,' it went, 'who once were men of mark for amiability and respectability – now how fallen!'[78]

Other men were also said to be imperiled by mixed-race attachments. Pemberton worried that local youth were 'demoralized' by First Nations women who led them to steal.[79] One impassioned letter writer wrote to the *British Columbian* that white men who lived with First Nations women were almost inevitably stripped of their manhood:

Almost without an exception those men who have sunk so low as to live with native women are degraded below the dignity of manhood. For instance, look at that creature, long-haired, badly dressed, dirty faced, redolent of salmon, who may be seen lounging at the door of almost every log cabin in the country, and tell me can that be a man? Enter any up-country dancing house; can that half-inebriated sot, who whispers obscene love speeches into the ear of yonder unfortunate squaw bedizened in all the finery which his bad taste and wasted money can supply, be a man? Can this fellow offering three horses and ten sacks of flour to yonder old pander, who haggles as to the price of his own flesh and blood, be a man? Or can that ruffian whom I see cruelly beating – whaling I believe is the term – the poor slave whom he has bought with his money, corrupted by his own foul nature and language, and diseased by his vices, be a man? Surely not, or we have indeed cause to be ashamed of our species.[80]

White men who married First Nations women were thus seen as dangerously flirting with relinquishing their place among the responsible gender and, more profoundly, the civilized race. They were, in other words, in danger of being deracinated. Observers identified fur traders as having already suffered this process. One travel writer thought that many 'shunned the haunts of civilisation, even after plunging beyond its pale, and so marrying native women, whom they became as attached to as they could have been to women of their own English, French, Canadian, or American race.'[81]

These fears and judgments were based on the assumption that white men who lived with First Nations women became more savage, rather than did their partners more civilized. Some personal narratives did tell of white men 'elevating' their First Nations partners to intelligence and cleanliness.[82] But most envisioned an opposite process. Civilization was thus constructed as a fragile state that might easily be undone by the more powerful force of savagery. Vancouver Island's first 'independent' settler, Walter Colquhoun Grant, wrote that 'though several White men have intermarried with the women of the various tribes, the result has always been that the white man has lowered himself to the standard of the wife, instead of the savage becoming at all elevated herself by the connexion.'[83] Good commented on a Tlingit (Stickeen) woman dying far from home in Nlha7kápmx (Thompson) territory. Her extensive contact with white men, he thought, had been wholly unelevating. 'Yet, though she has lived in the closest intimacy with these men for years, she has never gathered from their conversation or habits one single worthy notion of God, or duty towards Him,' he wrote, adding, 'How much worse than heathen lives such men live!'[84]

These men lost both their general racial status and the particular hallmarks of the Anglo-Saxon race. Their commitment to agriculture, a uniquely civilized pursuit, diminished. The British Columbian farmer was a failure, thought one journalist, because he 'has become half-savage with his Indian woman.'[85] 'It is your ignorant, slothful, unpolished subject,' argued the *Cariboo Sentinel*, 'who digs about a few acres, hunts and goes fishing, and then after having done just sufficient to satisfy the typical wolf at the door, sits down in front of his log shanty and smokes his dodder with his aboriginal companion of the softer sex.'[86] Colonial backwardness, class, and rurality were encapsulated in mixed-race relationships. The *Mainland Guardian* argued that 'men living away in the interior, isolated from the centres of population, are fain to console themselves with companions, that too often, render them regardless of the future, and rob them of all energy and ambition.'[87] Mixed-race unions, agreed scientist Brown in 1864, were both symbol and substance of British Columbia's poor economic development. That settlers in Cowichan, Chemanius, and Saltspring Island, often former gold miners, lacked the necessary ambition for economic progress was signified not only by their poverty and lack of refinement, but by their Aboriginal partners. He wrote that their 'only ambition (it is no use mincing matters by refined Language) seems to be "a log shanty, a pig, a potato patch, Klootchman (Indian woman) and a clam bed!"'[88]

White men who engaged in mixed-race relationships ceased to be white and became nearly and sometimes entirely Aboriginal. A white man who married among the Halkomelem-speaking Keatsy people of the Lower Fraser was assumed to have effectively become Keatsy. He 'shares with them in pot and lot,' wrote the *British Columbian*, and 'is, in fact, as one of them.'[89] John Helmcken argued that deracination was an inevitability. In his memoirs, he wrote, 'Living among natural people one gets naturalized and imbibes a good many of their natural conceptions ... In fact become Indianized!'[90]

More than an individual process, deracination was a palpable threat to the entire white society. Racial mixing, obviously, compromised specific colonial policies that depended on the self-evident character of racial identity and separation. When white married Aboriginal they threatened the reserve system by disrupting the process of racial identification and land allocation; they challenged the suppression of the liquor trade when Aboriginal wives drank their husbands' legal booze.[91] Aboriginal people's presence in white settlements compromised their status as imperial bastions. The Lekwammen (Songhees) reserve hovering on Victoria's outskirts was deemed 'a disgrace to the Government, a scandal to religion and an offence to our boasted civilization.'[92] It was especially embarrassing that this blight survived in 'the capital of an English colony.'[93]

More profoundly, white men who cleaved themselves too closely to Aboriginal women violated white notions of racial distance and superiority. When mixed marriages took place, 'you make any *true* relation between the aboriginal people and the settlers an impossibility,' said Samuel Wilberforce, the Bishop of Oxford, at a London meeting of the Columbia Mission.[94] Rather than suggest the possibility of equality, white people ought to affirm their racial difference and supremacy.

The persistence of First Nations peoples in colonial settlements continually disturbed white observers. Lekwammen (Songhees) housing in Victoria, 1867–8.

Instead of cohabiting with First Nations women, thought one letter writer, white men ought to 'assert our own superiority by ceasing to associate with them on equal terms, and let them feel themselves to be what they really are – less than civilized and far worse than savage.'[95] Missionaries were shamed when whites 'let down their side' and failed to behave with the superiority colonial discourse accorded them. 'Alas! instead of teaching Christianity to them, they make them more de-graded than they were before,' moaned Anglican Brown.[96]

In these discussions, mixed-race relationships function as a symbol of imperialism gone awry. They speak of an explicitly white working-class vision of colonialism based on rough, racially plural sociability, one that differed sharply from models of imperialism rooted in racial distance and difference. The *British Columbian* argued that 'their daughters have been lured on by the white man's wiles to lives of shameless vice and perpetual misery, and even their lawful wives enticed away from them to become the obedient paramours of the proud invaders of their soil.'[97] A poet used the figure of the brightly dressed dance-house worker as a sign of the success of one form of cultural contact over another. If missions had not compelled her, the businessmen who prof-ited from the dance house had:

What a sad and sober moral,
  Are we thus compelled to draw,
From the missionary's teaching –
  From the Christian's moral law.
Years and years of good men's efforts
  Seen thus exercised in vain,
Fiddle and the toe fantastic
  Is the way we're to reclaim
All the Indian tribes around us,
  From their wild and savage life,
And we'll teach them all the fashions,
  All the vices that are rife.
And to Donald F. and Cary,
  And to noble Cochrane J.
And to those who have an interest
  In the Market Company,
We will sing the loudest praise,
  For their calm and Christian efforts
Teaching squaws the Christian's ways.[98]

Here, Aboriginal women's work at dance houses demonstrates the triumph of rough, popular white culture over the missionary's vision of a Christian, racially separate civilizing project. Such ideas do not critique colonialism itself as much as they defend one vision of colonialism over another.

This discourse did not, of course, reflect social practice. The lives of mixed-race couples, like Aboriginal women, persisted and persistently defied those seeking to caricature, classify, or denigrate them. A handful of critics built on this resistance by explicitly and purposefully defending both the respectability First Nations women and mixed-race relationships. Bogg argued that not only were Nanaimo's Aboriginal women decent wives and housekeepers, but that their domestic talents outstripped those of their white counterparts. 'It is worthy of remark that those miners who have *English* wives generally have their houses in a dirty, slatternly condition, while, on the other hand, those among the miners who have *married* Hydah or Tsimshian women have their houses kept [in] patterns of cleanliness, neatness, and comfort,'[99] he wrote. A Nanaimo resident admitted 'that there are a great many white men living with Indian women,' but denied the charge that their lives were ones of 'debauchery and vice.' Their moral character, indeed, was equivalent to that of their attackers.[100]

Yet these discursive disruptions were infrequent challenges to the construction of mixed-race relationships as deeply dangerous. Unless functioning as symbols of pristine culture, Aboriginal women were rarely the primary objects of concern. Rather, writers feared that mixed-race relationships imperiled white men's morality, manliness, and ultimately their claim to racial distinction and superiority. Since an orderly, large, and industrious population was key to the creation of a respectable white settler society, the tendency of mixed-race relationships to deracinate white men compromised British Columbia's colonial project. So too did the simple existence of mixed-race people. These people were constructed as inherently inferior, physically and morally weak, and a threat to the colony's political stability.

Constructions of Mixed-Blood Peoples

If sexual, domestic, and emotional relations between First Nations women and white men disturbed Victorian gender and race systems, the offspring of these unions also deeply troubled the imaginations of white British Columbians. In this sense, their fears were explicitly heterosexual ones, premised not so much on a fear of sex, but on a fear of reproduction. This tendency was reinforced by the fact that the mid-nineteenth-century was a watershed in the development of 'scientific' racist thought, particularly as it related to reproduction.[101] While metropolitan in origin, these developments were not lost on this edge of empire. The invention of the word miscegenation in 1864 was duly noted by the Victoria press.[102] Hills owned a book that classified racial types and advised him on how to categorize any humans one might encounter.[103] The onset of a sustained and major white settlement in British Columbia thus occurred simultaneously with the increasing dissemination of theories of 'scientific' racism. The intensification of white settlement in British Columbia was surely enabled and encouraged by changes in racial thinking, but they did not cause it. The rise of racism and settlement were not so much causally connected as they were inextricably and largely accidentally bound by chronology.

This combination meant that race and reproduction were not solely intellectual issues for colonial British Columbians. As Homi Bhabha suggests, the hybrid, mixed-blood subject was both deeply symbolic of and troubling to colonial enterprises.[104] Certainly for many white observers, the simple existence of mixed-race people was confusing and often disturbing. Mayne wrote, 'You frequently see children quite white, and looking in every respect like English children, at an Indian village, and a very distressing sight it is.'[105] Charles Gardiner expressed a similar unease with the mixed-race community he encountered at a Fort Langley. 'There were the English, Scotch, French and Kanackas present,' he commented 'and all so thoroughly mixed with the native Indian blood, that it would take a well-versed Zoologist to decide what class of people they were, and what relation they had to each other.'[106] Such discomfort suggests how racial mixing challenged ideals of racial separation. The absence of clear markers separating 'the pure Indian to the comparative civilization of the race of partly white and partly red blood, and thence upwards to the pure white' thwarted attempts to develop race-based legislation.[107]

Many white observers were more than confused. Influenced by prevailing theories of race and reproduction, they constructed mixed-blood people as a unique and particular kind. A minority thought this specificity positive. Navy surgeon Bogg made a detailed argument about the physical fitness, reproductive prowess, and political reliability of British Columbia's 'half-breed' population: 'The offspring of intermarriage between the white and aboriginal races are generally of

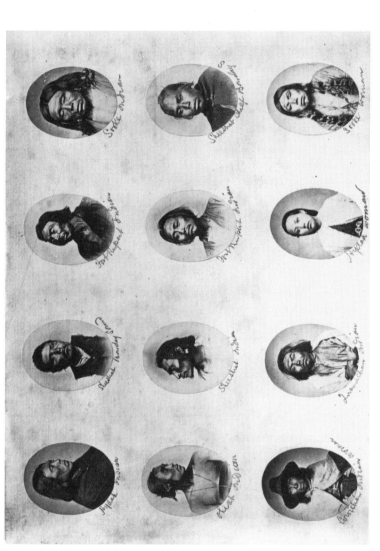

The mid-nineteenth-century mania for racial categorization comes to British Columbia. Frederick Dally's 'Types of British Columbia Indians,' ca 1860s.

medium height, well-formed, and muscular, having a very light olive complexion, and high cheek-bones, while, to the intelligence of the Father, they add the quickness of observation and restless activity of the Savage. They are prolific, and are calculated to become a fine and intelligent race of people. Their antipathy to the Aborigines is very violent and intense, and should any serious difficulty arise with the natives, the Half-Breeds will afford valuable assistance in quelling the disturbance.'[108] Canadian politician Malcolm Cameron agreed. After visiting British Columbia, he told Montreal's Young Men's Christian Association that 'it is a mixed race which produces a great people, a powerful nation.'[109] But most settlers utilized notions of mixed-race specificity to an opposite end.

They evoked ideas of mixed-race degradation not in scientific jargon, but in everyday, common-sense language. Often, commentators repeated the trope that mixed-race people combined the worst of both races. To 'Indian abandonment to vice and utter want of self-control,' thought Mayne, there 'appears to be added that boldness and daring in evil which he inherits from his white parent.'[110]

Such ideas rested on the assumption that sex across racial boundaries was necessarily pathological. One commonly observed pathology was 'half-breed's' supposed physical weakness and inability to reproduce. In the treatise 'Physiological Characteristics of Halfbreeds,' naval surgeon P. Cormie wrote that mixed-blood people were 'very deficient in vitality and inheriting none of the good qualities of either race.' More particularly, he thought them 'weak and prone to tubercular diseases and polyps [with] very little powers of procreation.'[111] Sex between people of different racial groups was also said to lead to venereal disease. Ironically calling Britain a '*Syphilised*' nation, Cormie identified venereal disease as one of the 'pathological phenomena which have been observed in the case of two Races coming into Contact in the Same Country.'[112]

The inferiority of mixed-blood people was thought to manifest itself in political and social terms as well, threatening British Columbia's colonial development. Congregationalist minister Matthew Macfie elevated the widely held fear of hybridity's political ramification to new levels of rhetorical excess. He traced the existence of twenty-three kinds of racial '*crosses*,' which, he feared, imperiled British Columbia's colonial future.[113] Macfie's later book on racial theory particularly addressed the impact of east Asian immigration on Western society. Despite his shift in focus, his feelings about mixed-blood peoples had not changed.

'The result of union between American Indians with all sections of the Aryan race,' Macfie wrote, 'is uniformly unsatisfactory, for in the *cross* that incapacity for improvement, which is the marked peculiarity of the Indian, is retained.'[114]

Other observers shared the fear that British Columbia's social institutions were unable to cope with a large mixed-blood population. Hills worried about how to educate these people, whose impulses for disorder were apparently so strong.[115] Fear of the potential political power of mixed-blood peoples intensified after the Red River Resistance of 1869.[116] In 1871 the Chief Commissioner of Lands and Works, B.W Pearse, argued that only an intense state-driven reform program could compensate for mixed-blood people's ill-fated origins. Even with the establishment of a system of common schooling, he wrote, the colony's 'race of half-castes' would 'prove a curse to the Country in the next generation,' since 'the important part of the education necessary to make a good citizen will still be wanting in these young half castes, who can never have the tender care and virtuous teaching of a Christian mother, and who, being so neglected, will be too apt to copy the vices without emulating the virtues of the white man.'[117]

These related discourses about First Nations women, white-Aboriginal relationships, and mixed-race children never determined the course of peoples' lives. Yet they did set some significant parameters. Whatever their character, mixed-race relationships were lived against a discursive backdrop which, especially after the early 1860s, constructed them as dangerous both to individuals and to colonial development. At root, these ideas were premised on the representation of First Nations women as the dark, dangerous opposite to idealized images of white women. If white men cleaved themselves to their racial inferiors, they would be rendered immoral, unmanly, and, above all, deracinated; if children were born to the union, they would painfully bear the marks of their shoddy beginnings. When Brown preached his annual sermon about 'the prevailing vice' in Lillooet's little church, he was speaking to widely held concerns. Reformers responded to white-Aboriginal relationships and rough homosocial culture with a series of efforts designed to inculcate the gendered and racial identities and practices cherished by metropolitan Anglo-American culture.

Chapter 3

Bringing Order to the Backwoods: Regulating British Columbia's Homosocial Culture

At the 1861 opening of Victoria's Young Men's Christian Association (YMCA), its promoters promised that it would reclaim the colony's errant, footloose young men. The YMCA, they pledged, would 'be a healthy check against dissipation which has made fearful sacrifices in countries like ours where a large portion of the young men were deprived of the society of home.'[1] In British Columbia the continued strength and visibility of Aboriginal people unsettled visions of white hegemony as did settlers' unwillingness to live up to the narrow roles accorded them by colonial discourse. Young white men severed from familial restraint loomed especially large in discussions of unruly settlers. The rough, homosocial culture of the backwoods offered a special challenge to colonial visions, a challenge reformers met with efforts to promote a model of bourgeois, metropolitan manhood. The disorderly fellows of the backwoods would have to change if this edge of empire was to be drawn closer to the centre.

The missionaries, politicians, journalists, and freelance do-gooders who launched this campaign to reform white men were not a unified movement with coherent aims and techniques, but a fragmented collection of social actors sometimes united by nothing more than a vaguely middling class position. But despite meaningful differences in motivations, techniques, and aims, all sought to regulate, reclaim, and otherwise reform the society they found in British Columbia and can, for that common purpose, be dubbed reformers. A particular object of their reforming efforts were white men, and their attempts to transform this group left an identifiable discourse on whiteness, masculinity, and reform. It is these organizations and the public discourse they created, rather than the individuals behind them, that deserve our historical attention. Through temperance campaigns, the creation of alternative sites of male sociability, and missions to white men, reformers sought to render male identity and behaviour compatible with the larger aims of the colonial project.

Temperance

Drink was an object of reform as well as a key component of rough homosocial culture. Colonial officials and employers like the Hudson's Bay Company had always discouraged drinking when it interfered with profit or rule, and the colony witnessed formal anti-drink campaigns from 1859 onwards. They were never a roaring success: Jan Noel is correct to argue that the temperance movement in colonial British Columbia made 'lacklustre progress.'[2] But their constant efforts demonstrate the range of ways reformers encouraged drink in the interests of reshaping colonial masculinity.

Some temperance groups aimed to recast male communities in the mould of sobriety and respectability. The Sons of Temperance formed all-male divisions in Victoria and Hope in 1859.[3] They were regarded as a watershed in the colony's transition to a stable, respectable settler colony that was indicative, according to the *British Colonist*, of the existence of a responsible male community who were nobly 'willing to deny themselves, by setting an example, of total abstinence, in order to reclaim, by moral suasion and fraternal kindness, their erring brethren.'[4] After the Sons of Temperance atrophied around 1860, their mantle was taken up by the Dashaways. The Dashaways were a local group with roots in San Francisco.[5] The *Weekly Victoria Gazette* thought this organization particularly suited to the hard-drinking, irreligious population of British Columbia, having 'adopted a system which renders them more likely to obtain members.' Instead of demanding a permanent temperance pledge, the Dashaways suggested a six- to twelve-month promise and also took pains to ban 'the subject of Sectarian Religion or Politics' from their meetings.[6] The Dashaways worked to establish alternative places of sociability to replace the morally perilous social spaces of the saloon and the dance house. In 1860 they opened a gym, hoping to encourage young men to spend their leisure hours in vigorous, moral, and manly physical recreation. Their public performances, the local press thought, deserved support because the 'progress of these athletic amusements is as great an evidence of enlightenment in a community.'[7]

CONSTITUTION

AND

BY-LAWS

OF THE

DASHAWAY ASSOCIATION

OF

VICTORIA, V. I.

PRINTED BY AMOR DE COSMOS,
AT THE COLONIST OFFICE, VICTORIA, V. I.

The Dashaways' public face, 1860 or 1861.

Other temperance campaigns worked with an explicitly Protestant idiom to rescue settler society from its penchant for drink. Anglican Bishop George Hills remained suspicious about the plebian, suspiciously secular tone of anti-drink groups, commenting in his private journal that they fostered 'lower standards than the true.[8] Other Anglicans were more enthusiastic. At an 1866 Nanaimo meeting, Alexander C. Garrett spun tales of liquor's 'disastrous effects attendant on its introduction within the domestic circle – chilling, blighting, and poisoning wherever allowed ingress, and never satisfied until peace and love industry and self-respect were laid prostrate before it.'[9] Methodists particularly embraced the temperance cause. Missionary Cornelius Bryant noted the anniversaries of his temperance pledge in his diary and deemed drink 'one of the chiefest and most potent agents in this work of the Devil.'[10] Methodist-supported temperance meetings in New Westminster and Victoria gathered crowds from across the denominational spectrum, although an 1863 meeting of Nanaimo's Methodist-influenced Total Abstinence Society rustled up a mere seven pledges.[11]

Protestant and heterosocial organizing overlapped in British Columbia's Independent Order of Good Templars, a relatively long-lived Methodist-inspired anti-drink organization. Where the Dashaways sought to reformulate male sociability in a same-sex environment, the Templars created heterosocial events to rival the boozy affairs that dominated nineteenth-century plebeian life. An 1864 Good Templars' dance in Victoria was noted for being 'largely attended by the fair sex.'[12] In a local colonial culture where masculinity, drink, and same-sex sociability were closely connected, the press took pains to present the Templars' heterosocial events as a different, but by no means less festive, form of masculinity. An 1870 Templars' ball was said to disprove all the negative associations with temperance. 'Those among us who imagine that austerity and solemnity are the natural results of teetotalism, will learn tonight that a man or woman may be mirthful and rationally jolly without the impelling influence of the contents of the flowing bowl.'[13] The heterosociability of the Templars was reinforced by the fact that a minority of officers were identifiably female.[14] Amelia Beckwith's 1864 poem celebrated the formation of a new Templars chapter by stressing both the manliness of male Templars and women's participation in the movement:

Ah yes! your cause is just and holy,
And you fight a noble fight –

But your weapons are not hurtful,
They are truth and love, and right;
And though strong men well may wield them,
Woman's hand can grasp them too,
And can send conviction's arrow
With a steady aim and true.[15]

Here, the temperate life is again presented as a vehicle for a superior, explicitly heterosocial, masculinity.

Whatever their gendered politics, these temperance campaigns were less than mesmerizing for the bachelors of the backwoods. Despite their relative success in Victoria, Nanaimo, and New Westminster, temperance groups barely penetrated the interior. Even in the towns of the southern coast, support for temperance was centred around the urban middle class and small factions of the skilled, improving working class. In 1860 the Dashaways' president, Jos. A. McCraw, was an auctioneer; its second vice-president, Richard Broderick, was proprietor of Kaindler's Wharf; Samuel Bingham, the secretary, worked at the harbour-master's office.[16] In Nanaimo, the president of the Total Abstinence Society in 1863 was none other than future coal baron, union buster and self-improver par excellence Robert Dusmuir.[17] As in the Ontario towns studied by Lynne Marks, temperance appears to have appealed primarily to improving, skilled men rather than their 'rough' counterparts.[18]

Alternative Sites of Masculinity

Whether through the secular homosociability of the Dashaways, the godly ways of Protestant groups, or the heterosociability of the Good Templars, temperance groups aimed to refashion male community and present it as the most manly option. Other reformers directly provided alternative sites of masculinity like the YMCA, Mechanics and Literary Institutes, and the Sailors' Home. In doing so, they aimed to provide surrogate families for white men that would encourage them to forsake the rough culture of mining camps, dance houses, and sailor pubs in favour of a masculinity consistent with a respectable, white settler colony.

The YMCA brought to the fore the values of domesticity, thrift, self-improvement, and Christianity that were shot through the temperance movement. At the opening of Victoria's reading room in 1859, speakers presented the YMCA as an antidote to the mobile, disrespectable masculinity fostered in a gold-mining colony where white women were few and families scarce. A Congregationalist minister argued that this organization was especially needed 'where the population was so unsettled; where there was so little public opinion to influence and direct young men; whilst there were so many things incident to the love of money in a gold country to induce youth to contract habits adverse to the progress of morals and religion.'[19] Despite its much lauded beginning, the YMCA in Victoria had died by 1861, apparently a victim of its own piety. The *Victoria Press* opined: 'Were we to confine any association to *young men* and *Christians* we very much fear the eligible members of the community would make an exceedingly small show.'[20] Its commitment to whiteness also perhaps damaged the YMCA: Black men complained that they were excluded from membership.[21] A second YMCA established in 1862 languished in relative obscurity until it merged with the Mechanics Institute in 1865.[22] Attempts to create a New Westminster branch in 1864 were even more fruitless, despite the assistance of the city council and the Anglican church.[23]

The goals of domesticity, discipline, and sobriety embraced by the YMCA were given new life when reformers in British Columbia turned to what were interchangeably called Mechanics or Literary Institutes. Mechanics Institutes existed throughout the Anglo-American world, offering a path to self-improvement paved with libraries, self-improvement classes, and debating societies. In colonial British Columbia, Mechanics Institutes garnered special ideological strength from the perception that they were a compromise between white men's distaste for religion and love of rough sociability and reformers' commitment to sobriety, steadiness, and respectability. In 1865 the *Vancouver Times* mocked the pretention of churchgoers who complained about 'compulsory idlers,' but failed to support practical reform efforts like the Mechanics Institutes: 'There is great satisfaction in deploring in loud terms the prevalence of ignorance and sin, in denouncing with much complacency the wicked habits of our neighbours, in bemoaning, with sorrowful countenances, their social delinquencies, but all this will not mend matters nor afford a substitute for the many temptations to idleness and vice with which our city admittedly abounds. It is far better to supersede these places of gross and unhallowed pleasures, by giving substantial aid to the establishment of an attractive intellectual resort for compulsory idlers, than to be merely wasting time by whining about the immorality of the Colony.'[24] Mechanics Institute thus served the local colonial project by mediating the ongoing conflict between putative social mores and popular culture.

Mechanics Institutes would provide useful or at least harmless social pastimes to counter the deleterious pleasures of the backwoods. A Mechanics Institute would ensure that men's leisure hours were spent in rational self-improvement rather than the 'morbid attractions of billiard tables, and saloons.'[25] Vancouver Island Governor Arthur Kennedy concurred that one of the Victoria institute's greatest objects was 'to withdraw men from the haunts of vice and dissipation, to spend their leisure hours in improving and moral recreation.'[26] Yet Mechanics Institutes were commercial as well as moral tools. Commentators argued that they could keep wintering miners from fleeing with their dollars and pounds to the greater cosmopolitan attractions of San Francisco. The local press thought that 'apart from the valuable results arising from a widespread diffusion of knowledge, and the creation of more elevated tastes amongst the people at large, to say nothing of the humanizing influence of literature' an institute would help make Victoria 'attractive as permanent winter quarters for our migratory mining population.'[27]

These motivations led to the creation of Mechanics and Literary Institutes throughout the colony. Yale boasted a reading room in 1864; Nanaimo's Literary Institute emerged from the ashes of the St Paul's Literary Institute in 1863, and the racially plural lumbering settlement of Burrard Inlet developed a Mechanics Institute in 1868.[28] Victoria's Mechanics Institute opened in the winter of 1864 with a library, a speakers series, elocution classes, a reading class, and a debating club.[29] In a genteel, smoke-free atmosphere, white men dwelled in the realm of self-education and improvement and also pondered how to best implement and represent colonialism, debating 'Have we the right to dispossess the savage of the soil?' and reciting poetry commemorating the Bute Inlet Massacre.[30]

Such charms were insufficient to seduce the rough colonial men away from the bar and dance house. By 1865 Nanaimo's Literary Institute was a local joke and cause for cheap poetry.[31] Victoria's did not fare much better. In a public speech, Kennedy said: 'It had struck him as very strange that a community that could not support one Mechanics' Institute or one free school could support 85 public houses.'[32] The Victoria Mechanics' Institute revived itself only to have its survival again threatened in 1871.[33] New Westminster's reading room opened in July 1865 after two years of agitation, and it seems to have collapsed three years later.[34]

Ironically, Mechanics and Literary Institutes thrived where rough homosocial culture did, in the Cariboo. In 1864 a meeting of the Cariboo

Barkerville's library was a bastion of metropolitan respectability in the back-woods, 1869.

Literary Institute drew 450 people, 250 of whom were miners.[35] Its success, to be sure, was not constant: its reading room was closed in the summer of 1868 and only rebuilt with government aid after the Barkerville fire later that year.[36] Yet the Cariboo Literary Institute was comparatively prosperous, and this prosperity seems rooted in its ability to blend reforming culture with the easy white male sociability of the backwoods. The institute published a literary newspaper featuring the unique talents of miner-poets James Anderson and John McLaren.[37] McLaren used this work as a building block for a fleeting career in local politics, standing as the 'miners' candidate' for the mining board in 1866,[38] while Anderson developed something of a literary career, eventually earning the title 'poet laureate of Cariboo.'[39] In his 'Sawney' poems, Anderson described Cariboo life to a fictitious Scottish reader who functioned as a moral, domestic foil for the ribald tales of backwoods male life. In one, Anderson wrote about the weakness of religious institutions and centrality of informal secular organizations for miners:

> There's neither kirk nor Sunday here,
> Altho' there's mony a' sinner,
> An' if we're steep'd in a' that's bad,
> Think ye there's muckle winner?
> There is a little meetin' house
> That's ca'd the Cambrian Ha,'
> Its memers few – but these I view
> As saut preservin' a' –
> But if we hiina got a kirk
> We hae anither biggin
> (Altho' it may na point sae clear
> The way abune the riggin)
> That gies amusement to the boys
> An' brings them a' thegither
> Ae nicht a week for twa short hours
> To laught wi' ane anither
> I dinna ken what name to gi'ed,
> A 'Play-house' ye despise,
> Would 'Amateur Dramatic Club'
> Look better in your eyes,
> You Sayneys are a moral folk,
> Altho' ye will get fou!
> 'Twad do ye a' a sight o' guid
> Twa years in Cariboo![40]

Anderson's work certainly struck a chord: when he left the Cariboo in 1871 his departure was publicly mourned.[41]

Mechanics Institutes' all aimed to transform white men's gendered and class identities. They worked to replicate the political and social functions of the nineteenth-century, middle-class home. Victoria's Mechanics Institute was hoped to 'provide rational amusement to those among us who do not enjoy a *home*.'[42] In the place of bad habits, Mechanics Institutes, like the domestic families they modelled themselves on, would inculcate ones befitting a respectable settler colony. 'There are hundreds in this community deprived of home comforts and advantages; and to such the Institute presents the ready and convenient means of spending the spare hours of evening in rational amusement or mental improvement,' the *British Colonist* wrote, and thus was 'instrumental in keeping many a young man from a course which would make him less valuable as a citizen and less happy as a man.'[43]

Reformers further reinforced the connections with the bourgeois family by constructing the Mechanics and Literary Institutes as bastions of heterosociability. The press publicized white women's contributions, commenting when the Cariboo Literary Institute met at Jeanette Morris's house.[44] Women's presence at lectures was encouraged at the Victoria Institute, and at one celebration 'the ladies' auspiciously occupied chairs in front of the platform while members sat behind them.[45] Individual members were encouraged to bring women with promises of free admission or the comment that 'no member's company will be properly appreciated unless he is accompanied by a lady friend.'[46] Women's involvement, of course, was more than symbolic. When Miss Wilson left Cariboo in 1865, the reading room collapsed. Given that she owned 130 of the library's books, this was hardly surprising.[47] But white women's mission was also ideological. Kennedy constructed the Victoria Mechanics Institute and white women's civilizing mission as analogous. He encouraged women 'to give their support to this movement, and he assured them that a few hours spent in the rooms of the Mechanic's Institute would render the young men still more fit for their society.'[48]

Mechanics Institutes sought to foster a specific version of class relations as well as gendered identity. Reformers hoped that these organizations would particularly reshape the poor moral habits of the working classes that threatened colonial progress. Its first president wanted the Victoria Mechanics Institute to improve 'the condition of those who may be perhaps a step down in the ranks of society.' Kennedy supported him, reminding an audience that 'all colonial prosperity and respectability must mainly depend upon the basis of the working classes.'[49] The extent to which these institutes represented employer values was rendered clearest in towns with a single or major employer. In Nanaimo, the Vancouver Coal Company donated the site for the Literary Institute Hall.[50] Historian Robert A.J. McDonald writes that the Burrard Inlet Mechanics Institute was consistently operated by the local bourgeois, especially those tied to the mill.[51] Mill owner S.P. Moody helped pay for the erection of the Mechanics Institute Hall and later liquidated the organization's debt, a generosity that earned him unanimous praise from members and a role in selecting books.[52]

Even when major employers did not directly fund or support the organizations, Mechanics Institutes reflected the values of, and ultimately catered to, the middle class. Although naval officer and evangelist Edmund Hope Verney wrote to his father that a meeting of the Victoria Mechanics Institute 'was attended chiefly by working men,' and was particularly pleased to note that his participation was suggested by 'a working sawyer,[53] actual working-class participation was minimal. By 1868 the leadership of the Victoria Mechanics Institute was dominated by professional men, often with ties to the colonial state. Dr John Ash, a physician, was president; E.G. Alston, the vice-president, was a barrister and supreme court registrar of deeds, while Thomas Allsop, the secretary, was a land agent.[54] In New Westminster, the Mechanics Institute was criticized for placing 'the institution upon too narrow and exclusive a basis.'[55] It was perhaps their connections with the state and local bourgeoisie that earned the Mechanics Institutes relatively generous government funding, despite their sometimes obvious mismanagement or unpopularity.[56]

Domesticity and discipline also informed a small band of reformers to launch an unsuccessful but revealing campaign to create a Sailors' Home. Sailors' homes, like temperance groups and Mechanics Institutes, were not local inventions sprung from the peculiar minds of British Columbia's do-gooders. They existed in port cities throughout the Anglo-American world, working to tame sailors, those mythic nineteenth-century working-class libertines. As Valerie Burton notes, the image of the sailor was a powerful and largely unitary one: 'Footloose, careless and fancy-free, he roams the world without constraints of home and family, half hero and half reprobate.'[57] Sailors' homes sought to transform these characters into model industrial workers, inculcating what Judith Fingard calls 'middle-class notions of the qualities desired in wage earners of the industrial age: punctuality, hard work, temperance, thrift, and obedience.'[58] They aimed to domesticate as well as discipline the sailor, providing him with a surrogate home that would draw him away from both mixed-race and rough homosocial pastimes.

The possibility of opening a Sailors' Home in Victoria was first raised in 1867 after men at the Esquimalt naval base died while working drunk. A Sailors' Home would help to address the problem of drunken seamen, its advocates promised, by providing an alternative site of improving recreation with 'the comforts of a public house without its contaminating influences.'[59] Like the YMCA and Mechanics Institute, a Sailors' Home would serve as a surrogate family for the sailor who so clearly lacked appropriate restraining influences. Seamen, 'cut off as they are from all home ties, are forced to frequent public houses where the vilest of liquor is served out to them, and to contract habits that contribute to the demoralization of the individual and the destruction of his health, and are in the highest degree detrimental to the welfare and discipline of the services,' wrote the *British Colonist*.[60] Sailor's Home gained additional justification from the promise that they would simultaneously protect the sailor from his exploiters and the community from sailors' rowdiness. 'As the case stands now,' pondered the press, 'Jack finds all doors closed against him except those of persons who, playing upon the poor fellow's weakness and simplicity, seek to relieve him of his hard earned pay.'[61] A Sailors' Home would also protect the community from the disreputable antics of sailors on leave, since it was 'not fair to the quiet living citizens to let loose swarms of giddy men to play their fantastic tricks before the eyes of all.'[62]

Such impassioned pleas did not succeed in creating a Sailors' Home in Victoria. Naval authorities apparently considered providing a home in early 1868, but subscription lists were being circulated in search of alternate support six months later.[63] Harbour master Jeremiah Nagle, the moving force behind the campaign, was frustrated by low attendance at meetings and insufficient patronage from the local elite.[64] By 1870 Nagle had apparently admitted defeat, and the campaign to establish a Sailors' Home disappeared altogether. Yet this brief campaign serves as another example of the attempt to transform the rough, homosocial culture forged by white men in colonial British Columbia, saving men from themselves and society from them.

Missions to White Men

Encouraging rough fellows to become disciplined, sober, and steady was a goal shared by Anglican and Methodist missions. Since their arrival in the early 1850s, Protestants and Roman Catholics promoted a variety of social goals consistent with a larger program of piety and white supremacy. After 1858 and 1859 both Anglicans and Methodists identified settler men, especially gold miners, as a special object of their ministrations. Missionaries hoped to ensure that white men severed from traditional social restraints would be provided with new but similarly effective ones. Reverend William Burton Crickmer visually represented these efforts when he sketched himself preaching, a lone voice for Christianity perched on an old barrel among the racially

Crickmer's mission to men.

plural, liquor-filled, and working-class community at Derby (later Fort Langley).

The most sustained efforts to reign in the rough fellows of the colony's backwoods was orchestrated by the Anglican Columbia Mission, an offshoot of the Bishopric of Columbia founded by wealthy British heiress Angela Burdett-Coutts in 1858. The Columbia Mission was initially more interested in reclaiming Britain's errant sons, in ensuring that the 'self' did not become the 'other,' than in converting the othered 'savage.' Doing so would both protect white men and limit the influence of embarrassing representatives of whiteness on the First Nations population. Novelist Charles Dickens described the Bishopric of Columbia as a needed corrective to the undue influence of white, working-class men on the local colonial project: if the '"untutored heathen" were to be reclaimed from *their* vices, it must be by a somewhat purer agency than the hideous influence of these lawless godless whites, only occupied in digging up the earth for gold.'[65] In 1862 the Bishop of Oxford, Samuel Wilberforce, spoke at a London meeting of the mission and promised that Anglican clergy would provide the social regulation that Dickens's 'lawless godless whites' in British Columbia lacked. Gold miners, proselytized Wilberforce, 'have but a short harvest of a few weeks in the gold fields, and then, all unused to the possessions of wealth, all unfitted for its spending, all unable to invest it with no calls of the family upon them, no natural and healthy outlets for their new infusion of this new gold, go down for the rest of the year to some city upon the border of that land, and find there the leeches of dissipation and corruption, of lust and of drunkenness, ready to relieve them of the plethora of that unusual fullness, and so are exposed to a new form and set of temptations, against which nothing but habits of morality and religion deeply ingrained into their own nature will defend poor weak human beings suddenly subjected to them.'[66] Like Mechanics Institutes and Sailors' Homes, the Columbia Mission was conceived as a surrogate family able to shelter white men from the 'leeches of dissipation and corruption, of lust and of drunkenness' that reigned supreme in colonial space.

Despite its avowed interest in rough mining culture, the Columbia Mission initially had very little contact with it. No clergy lasted a Cariboo winter before 1866–7 and even their summer ministrations were minimal.[67] This peculiar combination of alleged interest and actual inattention evoked a protracted critique from Caribooites. Disparaging the manliness of Protestant clergy too weak to withstand the rigours of an up-country winter, one writer commented that it was appalling to see 'the host of men lounging along the streets' of Barkerville while 'the feather-bed "soldiers of the Cross," in the lower country, are indulging in good living and easy work.'[68] Inveterate letter writer Tal. O'Eifion opined that the immorality of the Cariboo was inevitable, given that 'those who were at one time sent amongst us to be our spiritual advisers, have entirely deserted us.' It was not surprising, he thought, that morality withered under such blatant ecclesiastical disregard. 'As a matter of course,' wrote Eifion, 'when the shepherds are absent the sheep are bound to go astray.'[69]

Clergy responded to such critiques by arguing that the Cariboo was a hostile field with little appeal for the aspiring missionary. It offered rough living conditions and isolation and lacked the two constituencies missionaries inevitably found most appealing: pious whites and romantic, untutored heathens. Even the ever-sincere R.C. Lundin Brown considered the Cariboo's dearth of piety daunting.[70] After an up-country tour in 1865, Alexander C. Garret commented: 'This emphatically is not the place for inferior men.'[71] Many residents were simply disinterested, explained another representative of the church, while some Cariboo miners were 'always ready to attribute sordid and avaricious motives to the clergy.'[72] The impasse between the daunted Anglican missionaries and the ambivalent Cariboo public came to a point in the summer of 1868 when Hills agreed to send a clergyman if a local committee could pay over half his salary.[73] One local likened this offer to 'an advertisement to run an express between Cariboo and heaven, fare $1500: if we don't like or can't afford to pay this, we may go to hell.'[74] These critiques soon succeeded in convincing Hills to appoint James Raynard as resident missionary to the Cariboo.[75] With this appointment, the Columbia Mission began a concerted mission to create responsible, Christian manhood where rough, homosocial culture reigned largely uncontested.

Raynard's mission was both literal and symbolic. That he was accompanied by his wife and children and therefore a living representative of domestic masculinity was constructed as a mission effort unto itself. Hills thought Mrs Raynard's 'presence there would do incalculable good, not only in supporting her husband in a fight almost too great for any man, unaided by human sympathy, but also in affording an example of the order and beauty (even amidst manifold privations) of family life, in a place where virtuous women were, to say the least, excessively scarce.'[76] In published reports, the Columbia Mission argued that the white missionary family had worked the intended reformatory effect on the single, rough men that surrounded them. Although, they argued, 'at first the miners were disposed to shun this family, as too uncomfortable a rebuke to themselves ... they are beginning to admire and appreciate, and better still to imitate; for Mr Raynard reports three marriages – a thing unheard of before on William['s] Creek.'[77]

Along with serving as an epitome of domesticity and heterosociability, Raynard actively worked to reconfigure homosocial culture. He launched the Cariboo Church Institute, an organization that, like Mechanics Institutes, offered men rational amusements and education. In the win-

The Church that Raynard built: St Saviours in Barkerville, ca 1869.

ter of 1868–9 the Church Institute sponsored elementary education, biweekly Bible classes, 'an entertainment of singing and reading, or lectures on popular science, or history, or music' on alternate Thursday nights and a daily class especially for Chinese men.[78] By aiming for a festive but improving atmosphere, Raynard tried hard to make his ministrations compatible with the easy sociability of white homosocial culture: 'I encourage the young men to be cheerful, not to consider their parson as a death's head. Our room is often full, and "the boys" are kept from the dance-house till ten o'clock, and then go quietly to their cabins. I am working this band, hoping to build a club-room attached to the Church Institute, where they can meet, smoke their pipes, have a song, or a game at chess. As it is, these things, harmless in themselves, are made to them sources of temptation and mischief.'[79] Raynard thus attempted to render his exertions compatible with the informal male community that thrived in the Cariboo and, in doing so, disassociate male community from rough and smutty pastimes that so often accompanied it. His efforts were matched by that of his Methodist counterpart, Thomas Derrick. In 1869 and 1871 Derrick directly challenged the prevailing local model of masculinity in a popular lecture on 'Manliness.' At Williams Creek and Van Winkle, Derrick argued that it was manly to be virtuous, self-reliant, and studied. More significantly, it was manly to be familial and domestic. 'Man to be manly must have a home and love it,' claimed Derrick.[80]

After Raynard's and Derrick's burst of reforming enthusiasm, Protestant interest in the rough men of the backwoods waned. By the winter of 1871–2 Raynard had abandoned the hard fare of Cariboo for the comparative urbanity of Nanaimo.[81] Derrick survived only three years of the 'peculiar and difficult' field of the Cariboo.[82] Like temperance groups and alternative sites of masculinity, missions to white men in British Columbia found fostering an orderly, respectable manliness consistent with the broader aims of the colonial project a difficult and generally thankless task.

British Columbian white men's ambiguous response to missions suggests their complex relationship to reforming efforts. Critiques of white male homosocial culture in British Columbia were premised, like much of evangelical, middle-class thought on gender, on a profoundly pessimistic view of what it meant to be a man. Men could only be adequate citizens, it suggested, if they were carefully regulated either by the family or by institutions that could serve in its stead. As much as this discourse pivoted on the romantic, idealized view of womanhood so often remarked on in the literature on women's history, it rested on a deep distrust of manhood, especially working-class manhood. In British Columbia, critiques of homosocial culture were also premised on an ambiguous view of settler men's claim to whiteness. To groups like the Columbia Mission, gold miners were an appropriate object of civilizing efforts akin to those directed against First Nations people locally and indigenous populations throughout the world. This suggests how, for many observers, settler men's claim to membership on the white side of the imperial divide was far from secure.

Colonial discourse's ambiguous view of white masculinity in British Columbia was not, it seems, shared by the rough fellows of the backwoods. Nor, however, was their opposition to reformer' views and actions clear and consistent. For the most part, white men responded to missionaries, temperance advocates, and alternative sites of masculinity with indifference. Yet they also, as in mid-1860s Cariboo, complained bitterly and publicly when they thought Protestant clerics neglected them. At other times, they bristled at reformers' attention, particularly challenging metropolitan missionaries' right to adequately represent them to metropolitan audiences. In the early 1860s the *British Colonist* waged a campaign against the Columbia Mission, claiming that 'ludicrous things are retailed to the venerating multitudes in England.'[83] The writers took particular umbrage at their characterization of British Columbia as 'homeless.'[84] In challenging the right of missionaries to depict their community as a hotbed of immorality, they disputed the imperial production of knowledge to defend their status as white men. By objecting to critical references to the absence of conventional families, they challenged metropolitan notions of manhood and respectability.

In reasserting their gendered and racial identities in the face of opposition, this critique suggested both the power of British Columbia's rough, homosocial male culture and the regularity and persistence with which it was criticized and attacked. Missionaries, politicians, journalists, and other self-appointed moral guardians saw the homosocial world of the backwoods as an immoral one inimical to the creation of a prosperous, respectable white settler colony. While many called for the emigration of white women, others worked to create institutions that, in their absence, would serve an analogous social function. A temperance movement encouraged hard-drinking white men to become sober. Alternative sites of masculinity aimed to serve as surrogate families and communities for young single men. Missions to white men offered living examples of domestic, familial masculinity and disseminated this model among the mining population of the Cariboo. The short life of most of these projects suggests that the objects of reform resisted attempts to reshape them. The persistence of reformers in devising new efforts indicates their abiding interest in rendering life on this edge of empire more compatible with the social ideals of the centre.

Chapter 4

Marriage, Morals, and Segregation: Regulating Mixed-Race Relationships

In the spring of 1861, in the pages of the *British Colonists*, two Protestant missionaries debated the merits of marrying a First Nations woman and an English man. One argued that to deny them nuptial rights would further degrade Aboriginal womanhood and Christian manhood alike, while the other contended that it was the marriage sacrament that would be debased by wedding civilized and heathen.[1] They were not the only reformers who pondered how to best regulate mixed-race relationships, and nor were they the only reformers who parted company on the question of tactics. While some worked to assimilate white-Aboriginal relationships to European sexual and social norms, others identified mixed-race relationships as fundamentally unredeemable and aimed to discourage them or, more radically, racially segregate urban space. All shared the motivating conviction that relationships forged between white men and Aboriginal women were indicative of the failure of respectable gender and racial organization to develop on this edge of empire. Like the rowdy male culture of the backwoods, mixed-race relationships would have to change if British Columbia was to become a respectable, white settler colony.

To identify a reform movement and to divide it into three camps is admittedly schematic. This was more a loosely connected set of initiatives launched by an equally loosely connected collection of individuals than a programmatic campaign. Some individuals, moreover, endorsed at least two of these approaches at different times and in different contexts. Yet it is the cumulative contour of the discourse they created, rather than the shifting individual positions, that deserves our attention. It was this discourse that flowed in three rough streams, one seeking to reshape mixed-race relationships in the mould of Christian, legal marriage, one working to discourage white-Aboriginal unions, and a third labouring to racially segregate urban spaces.

Reshaping Mixed-Race Relationships

Reformers who worked to render mixed-race relationships compatible with European values of Christianity, monogamy, and legality turned, in part, to the law. As Tina Loo points out, 'The Europeans who inhabited the area that became British Columbia took an active and critical interest in the law, seeing it as central to their identity and to securing their future in Britain's far western possession.'[2] That getting married was expensive and inaccessible in British Columbia lent additional purpose to legal reform. After 1859 Vancouver Island couples could wed by banns or alternately pay a fee and make a declaration at Victoria's Government House to secure a licence that would empower a recognized clergyman to wed them upon payment of another fee.[3] However difficult marrying was on the Island, it was much harder on the Mainland. Before 1865 marriage licences could be obtained only on Vancouver Island. This enraged Mainland critics, who took it as an indication of broader administrative failure. 'Amongst the numerous anomalies of our present absentee system of Government is the absence of any authority for issuing marriage licenses in this Colony,' complained New Westminster's *British Columbian*. 'Any one desiring to take unto himself a wife must either procure a license from the neighbouring Colony, or submit to the tedious process of publishing the banns in Church.'[4] It was not only 'expensive and inconvenient, but rather humiliating to be obliged to go to another Colony for such a purpose,' they later added.[5]

Confusion compounded expense and inaccessibility. British Columbia's colonial legislatures had considerable difficulties developing a uniform system of legitimating, registering, and conducting marriage. It was, at various points, unclear if dissenting ministers could perform a marriage, whether weddings had to be held in church, what were allowable hours for marriages, and who would benefit from the licence fees.[6] R.C. Lundin Brown, Anglican missionary to Lillooet, lectured the government on their administrative deficiencies when it came to marriages. Problems, he explained, flowed from 'the ignorance of clergy & everybody as to the marriage law in the force in the Colony ... and to mismanagement in response of your officials, which causes & has caused many vexatious & tedious delays.'[7]

Critics of the colony's marriage system promised that reforming it would not only address inefficiency, but lead Aboriginal-white couples to the registry office. Efforts to develop a uniform and accessible form of civil marriage were probably motivated by the mid-nineteenth-century retreat of sexual nonconformity and the increasing hegemony of legal marriage in Britain so ably analysed by John Gillis.[8] Yet they also gained additional strength from the local perception that mixed-race relationships were a special threat to the colonial project. In 1862 Anglican Bishop George Hills wrote to British Columbia Attorney General Henry Crease arguing that the ideal law should maintain the Christian sacrament of marriage, while providing for 'the convenience of those who cannot be married by Xian rites through one of the parties being heathen, but also may desire to live in legal not in illegal cohabitation for the sake of the offspring and morality.'[9]

Legislation passed in 1865 and extended to Vancouver Island in 1867 reflected these specifically racial and broadly social goals. 'An Ordinance respecting Marriage in British Columbia' allowed dissenting clergy to wed, empowered secular, government-appointed 'registrars' to conduct civil weddings, loosened the restrictions on the place of marriage, and removed the necessity of parental consent for underage girls whose guardians were overseas.[10] While the bill initially specified a five-dollar registration fee, this was later deemed inimical to the goals of the legislation and eliminated. One legislator claimed that 'there should be no impediment whatever thrown in the way of marriages in the colony.'[11]

The 1865 marriage law was initially part of a broader attempt to subject British Columbia to rational processes of gathering and creating information. It was twinned with a law mandating the registration of births, marriages, and deaths, commonly referred to as the census law and deemed a key index of colonial progress. 'A country without statistics is like a clock without a dial plate,' opined the *Victoria Press*.[12] As Benedict Anderson has recently argued, after 1850 the census was key in shaping 'the way in which the colonial state imagined its dominion – the nature of the human beings it ruled, the geography of its domain, and the legitimacy of its ancestry.'[13]

Efforts to subject British Columbia to rational methods of information gathering were inevitably thwarted by the mixed-race character of the colony which, officials argued, rendered it too confusing to count and classify. The 1865 census law was dropped owing to what the attorney general called 'the difficulty of procuring assent to the principle of compulsory registration, in a new Colony containing a large Indian population.'[14] In 1869, after being pestered by the Colonial Office to pass a law ordering the registration of births, marriages, and deaths for years, Governor Frederick Seymour explained that this racially plural colony was unknowable to the imperial state: 'I really do not know how a general system of Registration could be worked satisfactorily here. The population is greatly scattered. The majority are Indians whom we could hardly expect to register any one of the great events of life. Many of the white men are living in a state of concubinage with Indian women far in the Interior. They would hardly come forward to register the birth of some half breed bastard.'[15] This answer apparently satisfied the Colonial Office, whose queries about the absence of registration laws in British Columbia subsequently ceased. The difficulty of classifying a transient and racially plural colonial society peopled by mixed-race couples and their 'half breed bastards' continued to dog British Columbia's legislative efforts throughout the colonial period, and a registration or census law was never successfully developed.

Perhaps the 1865 marriage law survived because it was empowered rather than thwarted by discourses of racial plurality. Responding to the Colonial Office's concern that the law would invalidate 'all marriages celebrated by Native Indians among themselves,'[16] Crease explained that it was uniquely suited to the colony's racial character. That it ignored Aboriginal people was inevitable, given their fundamentally incompatibility with marital regulation, while 'the large class of persons who have an admixture of native and white blood' were as able to partake in the law as suited their geographical and social position. The law's special efficacy lay in its ability to bring legal marriage to mixed-race couples. 'There are many cases at this moment in the Colony of white men living in remote districts with Indian women as wives to whom the facilities for marriage afforded by this Ordinance will be a great boon,' Crease wrote.[17] The Colonial Office eventually ascended to this law, commenting that while it flirted dangerously with rendering marriage too accessible, there was more risk 'in requiring too much in respect of the leniency of such places, that marriages will not be solemnized at all.'[18]

A similar struggle to reconcile mixed-race, backwoods social formation and the mechanics of European morality emerged during a 1872 effort to pass legislation providing for the families of dead settlers. Chief Justice Matthew Begbie explained the situation to distant officials in Ottawa:

There is in this Province a large class of very useful, hard-working, but not very highly educated or refined set of men, who form as it were the van of settlers. They generally pre-empt land far up the country, and employ themselves in stock-raising or other agricultural pursuits, sometimes in mining, in isolated localities, or packing ... but generally in having a log house, which they consider their home, and generally an Indian concubine, whom they consider and treat in all respects as the wife of a man in similar circumstances of life would be considered and treated by him in Great Britain.

There is very often issue of the concubinage. These men, being enterprising, frugal and industrious, and their concubines being, in many respects, help more 'sweet' to them than women of European descent or education would be, live in a rude comfort, and often amass property of considerable value – from a few hundred dollars to $10,000 and upwards. They are generally men separated from the heirs or next of kin by long intervals of time and space, and often ignorant and careless whether there be anybody in the whole world living to claim kinship with them at all. The concubines, it is to be observed, consider themselves to be, and are according to the native customs, lawful wives generally.

In order that these families be provided for and distant 'legitimate' relations be kept from their booty, the provincial legislature proposed a 'Bill for providing for Indian Concubines, and Destitute Half-breed Children of persons dying intestate and leaving property in the Province.' It allowed the court to make provision for the 'concubine' and minor children of a man dying intestate with property, provided he recently and publicly supported them and no 'legitimate wife' in the colony objected. Canada's governor general refused to approve the law which would, in effect, legitimize children of 'illegitimate' unions, but Begbie continued to draw attention to the gap between legal recognition and popular practice in British Columbia's backwoods, a gap which ultimately served to disadvantage local families.[19]

The law was not the only site of reform for those who sought to reshape mixed-race relationships to conform to normative standards of white matrimony. Others worked to achieve the same goal by relying on timeworn techniques of moral persuasion: they urged, harangued, and beseeched mixed-race couples to wed. Journalists and missionaries used the overlapping languages of manliness, race, and morality to convince lax white men to protect both lesser beings and the reputation of their race and colony. Congregationalist missionary Matthew Macfie wrote that he was 'deeply anxious for the removal of the injustice and dishonor a considerable portion of the immigrants are bringing upon the native population in this island and British Columbia.' He therefore implored 'all who are conducting themselves improperly toward *clootchmen*' to wed by civil ceremony. In doing so, they would not only improve themselves, but the entire colony and, perhaps most of all, the tarnished reputation of their once-noble race. 'It has become proverbially a disgrace to civilization that the countries which send forth Christian teachers to toil for the temporal and spiritual welfare of aboriginal races are also the chief source of hinderance to the success of moral and religious mission,' Macfie wrote.[20] If white men would marry their First Nations partners, agreed an editorialist in the *British Colonist*, they would make an important step towards achieving the respectability that so far had eluded them. 'Humanise yourselves, civilise your paramours, and legitimise your children without delay,' the press urged.[21]

Reformers bade white men to marry their First Nations partners in order to cement their own racial and gender status and to serve as colonizers within their own families in face-to-face meetings as well as through mass media. Hills tried to convince a long-time fur-trade worker that he should marry his First Nations partner. When he defended the unmarried state as 'happier' and compatible with his cultural environment, Hills responded 'that the sin was the same here as in Britain.' Failing in his arguments, Hills responded by deploying two other missionaries against the unrepentant cohabitater.[22] When Methodist missionary Ebenezer Robson posted banns for the marriage of 'John Maleom and an Indian woman by the name of Emma,' he commented that he hoped that 'others who are living as he has been would take his example & follow it.'[23]

Other missionaries appealed to Aboriginal womanhood rather than settler manhood. Missionary Brown recounted preaching against short mixed-race connections and in favour of Christian marriage in a Stl'àtl'imx (Lillooet) keewolly or underground house in 1861. 'If any white man wanted honestly to wed with an Indian girl,' he wrote, 'they should be married; "leplate" [priest] would make them join hands, and give them God's blessing; they should then be no longer two but one, and live together as man and wife for ever till they died.' Any other sort of relationship was unacceptable. 'As for those temporary and unhallowed connexions,' Brown continued, 'they were thoroughly bad. Indians must steer clear of them, or their canoes would be smashed among the rocks; and if any girl there was already entangled in such a connexion, so degrading, so offensive to the Great Spirit, so deadly, – she must not hesitate, but do at once what God required of her, – she must break it off.'[24] While missionaries appealed to white men's racial pride, Brown employed threats of metaphorical and literal ruin to convince Aboriginal women of the dangers of consensual mixed-race relationships and the merits of European marriage.

Other missionaries devised education programs to prepare First Nations women to marry white men. These involved religious instruction directed to equipping First Nations women with the requisite 'Christian knowledge' to contract the sacred rite of marriage. In 1864, J.C.B. Cave, Anglican catechist to Nanaimo and Comox, listed the 'preparation of Indian women, cohabitating with white men, for baptism and marriage and confirmation' as one of his six main duties.[25] The work of Cave and his colleagues in this effort was regarded as successful. Hills later observed the confirmation of four Tsimshian women who lived with white men, noting that Missionary John Good 'has taken much pains with them, and their present improvement is a great contrast to their former selves.'[26]

Missionaries sought to instil broadly social as well as religious truths in Aboriginal women. They especially worked to school First Nations women in the productive disciplines of European femininity. At their Cowichan convent, the Sisters of Saint Ann taught 'young female Indians and half-breeds' to card wool.[27] Anglican missionary Anna Penrice spent three afternoons a week at Victoria's reserve school teaching 'women and children to work.'[28] Hills judged missionary wives insufficiently expert to instruct white women, yet admirably suited to educate First Nations.[29] His own wife taught Aboriginal women to knit stockings in Victoria's Humbolt Street mission in the late 1860s.[30] By harnessing the efforts of missionary wives, these missions offered, as Myra Rutherdale points out, a living model of white, domestic womanhood,[31] one that was especially directed at partners of settler men.

By bringing marriage to the masses, urging the dissolute and unwed to take holy or legal bonds, and training First Nations women, legislators, missionaries, and journalists hoped to encourage mixed-race couples to recreate themselves anew. Some had their efforts greeted with hostility, while others met with a quieter failure. Reforming British Columbia's marriage law did not prevent the backwoods press from complaining in 1871 that 'the Executive has failed to provide for the

Anglican Missionary John Good posed with his gender-segregated Nlha7kápmx (Thompson) flock, ca 1860s.

Missionaries, missionary wives, and First Nations parishioners in Cowichan. From *Columbia Mission Annual Report 1869*, 17.

connubial wants of the people of Cariboo.'[32] Brown became famed not only for encouraging legal marriage from the pulpit and in keewolly, but also for generating popular opposition. In his diary, Hills wrote that 'Mr Brown has very properly preached against this frightful evil & has of course given offence.'[33] Such offence suggests the very real limits resistance placed on the efforts of reformers to render mixed-race relationships compatible with normative, white Christian marriages.

Discouraging Mixed-Race Relationships

Those who sought to reform mixed-race relationships built on traditional missionary notions of progress and tutelage. While white-Aboriginal unions were immoral, they could, with correct and timely guidance from appropriate sources, become holy, righteous, and Christian, or at least legal. Others displayed no such familial faith in the potential of the mixed-race relationships. These reformers worked to discourage recognition, especially religious, of relationships that they viewed as inherently illicit and corrupt. Victoria's 1861 controversy clarified the differences between these two streams. Macfie launched the debate with a letter to the *British Colonist* complaining that another clergyman refused to wed a white-Aboriginal couple, who he united in a civil ceremony in order to relieve the Englishman from 'the alternative of living in a state of open guilt.'[34] Macfie, in providing a civil marriage but denying a religious contract, worked, like the makers of the 1865 marriage law, to reshape mixed-race relationships by encouraging them to conform to basic European norms of morality. In contesting Macfie's actions and views, Anglican Alexander C. Garret, missionary to the Lekwammen (Songhees) settlement at Victoria, clarified the motives of those who worked to discourage white-Aboriginal relationships. He claimed that he had refused to marry the couple in question because the Aboriginal women had insufficient Christian knowledge, and 'was therefore entirely incapable of making *any religious* promise or contract of a Christian kind.' It was a violation of religious sanctity to wed heathen and Christian. The 'object of the original institution of marriage was that the woman "might be a help-meet" for the man,' he wrote, 'and that for a Christian to respect an ignorant and idolatrous Heathen, to prove such is most extremely irrational.'[35]

For Garret, a relationship between a white and an Aboriginal could not be anything other than immoral, ill-begotten, and illegitimate. Garret's position followed the directions of his Bishop, Hills. While he

sometimes encouraged particular mixed-race couples to wed and supported the reformation of British Columbia's civil marriage laws, Hills
did not consider white-Aboriginal couples suitable candidates for Christian marriage. In 1861 he responded to queries from clergy about the
policies around what he called 'Marriage between a professing Xian
and a Heathen woman.' Quoting copiously from biblical and legal
sources, Hills argued that these marriages could not be considered on
the grounds of scripture, antiquity, marriage service, and reason. Instead of marrying mixed-race couples, he advised missionaries to counsel men in permanent relationships to seek immediate civil marriage
and work towards the long-term conversion of their partner. Those in
casual relationships should shun their Aboriginal partners but make
financial provision for them and their children.[36] Two years later, Hills
had not changed his mind. He wrote in his private journal that mixed-
race relationships were inherently unequal and untrue, and 'hence the
Church can never sanction by her blessing the union.'[37]

Hills's decision that white-Aboriginal couples should not usually
be wed by Christian ceremony was based, primarily, on deep fears of
white male deracination. He worried, like many other settlers,
that white men's morality would inevitably be imperilled by connections with Aboriginal women. Defending his decision, Hills wrote: 'An
untaught, an uncouth, superstitious heathen cannot be a fit companion
for a Xian.' He thought there was 'great danger of being led further
away from God both as to faith & morals.' While marriage to white
woman elevated men, marriage to Aboriginal women merely reinforced their base character. 'A man who seeks a Heathen wife must
have only his grosser appetites in view,' he thought. For these reasons,
concluded Hills, mixed-race marriages were 'unreasonable and fraught
with danger.'[38]

Missionaries worked to discourage mixed-race relationships in a
variety of ways. William Duncan, the messianic leader of the model
mission village at Metlakatlah, did this primarily by isolating Tsimshian
women in order to prevent mixed-race relationships from occurring.
He asked that the colony pass a special divorce law enabling Aboriginal
women to legally shed their immoral white husbands.[39] More successfully, Duncan established a much observed residential girls' home in an
ongoing effort, as Hills put it, to counteract 'the corruption of the youth
of the female sex through the evil influence of the Heathen homes & the
association at times with depraved whites.'[40] While Duncan was the
only Protestant missionary who successfully created a home dedicated

to cloistering First Nations women and girls from the deleterious attentions of white men before Confederation, it was a dream others shared.
James Raynard, faced with the difficult dilemma of providing women
with a practical alternative to white partners, wrote that 'I am longing
for the day when I can ask them to break such unholy bonds, and offer
them maintenance in some industrial school.'[41]

Duncan's superintendence of the residential school ironically gained
him a dubious sexual reputation among settlers who intrinsically
doubted the morality of a single white man living among Aboriginal
girls and women. In an effort to combat rumours, the Church Missionary Society urged Duncan to immediately accept a 'sensible, matronly
married woman' as assistant, appointed a married missionary to join
him in his labours, and tried, without success, to bully him into taking a
white wife. They were especially worried that Duncan would marry
one of his Tsimshian converts and himself join the ranks of those he was
supposed to be converting. 'We hope that he is not intending to marry
one of them,' they commented, 'as such marriages in other missions
have usually been great hinderance to a Missionary's usefulness.'[42] For
these observers, Duncan's efforts to prevent mixed-race relationships
led him closer, rather than further away, from them: in sheltering First
Nations women from white men, Duncan placed himself in dangerous
intimacy with them.

While missionaries were on the forefront of efforts to discourage
mixed-race relationships, they were not entirely alone. A secular critic
of public officials with First Nations partners urged that these men
'purge themselves *at once* from the pollutions with which they are
charged.'[43] Discursive demands had little effect on high-placed men,
but employers could more effectively prevent white workmen from
forming conjugal relationships with local women. After firing Leech
River's constable for living with an Aboriginal woman in 1865, Victoria's police force amended its conditions of employment to make clear
that 'the practice of Constables in out-lying districts living with Indian
women will not be tolerated.'[44] Other employer crackdowns met with
more resistance. Francis Poole was outraged when an Aboriginal woman
appeared in his copper-mining camp on Haida Gawaii, 'saying that one
of my workmen had told her to come and take up her residence there.'
He wrote: 'I could not of course mistake the meaning of that. The
proceeding was inadmissable for every moral and sanitary reason.' His
eight men, already angered by the lack of maple sugar and grog in their

rations, promptly revolted. 'It was a mutiny for all intents and purposes,' wrote the furious Poole. Only being empowered to act as magistrate, he thought, would have equipped him to manage the men he called 'white savages' and 'misguided louts.'[45] His workmen demanded not only the usual fruits of preindustrial paternalism – sugar and booze – but also their right to take Aboriginal partners. Yet Poole recognized neither the claims of his miners nor the possible legitimacy of their connections with local women.

While those who worked to recast mixed-race relationships found a friend in the law, those who aimed to discourage them were disappointed in the apparent unwillingness of the law to meddle with mixed-race relationships. Calling for a law 'whereby we could get rid of this pest of our community, viz: – the cohabitation of white men with Indian women,' a Nanaimo contributor to the *Victoria Press* asked, 'When will our *Christian* Legislature give their due attention to this subject?'[46] Methodist missionary Thomas Crosby had little luck convincing magistrates that mixed-race relationships involved the sale of girls and thus were slavery, that institution so repugnant to British justice.[47] Others were equally unsuccessful in suggesting that existing laws be used to discourage mixed-race relationships. The *British Colonist* suggested that 'the white and black men who glory in keeping' First Nations women should be prosecuted under the Vagrancy Act.[48] Hills's demand for the appointment of an 'Indian Protector' to help combat the 'frequent instances of the abduction of wives & children of Indians by dissolute white men' was similarly unsuccessful.[49]

Such bitter disappointment suggests how reformers' efforts to discourage mixed-race relationships were thwarted both by disinterest and resistance. In typical frustration, Crosby wrote: 'We reasoned with their parents and heathen relatives, but our efforts were in vain. We went to the cabins of white men and expostulated with them, and were driven out with fiendish curses and told that it was none of our business.'[50] Some journalists and politicians rejected moral suasion or calls for legal intervention and turned to the harsher strategy of racially segregating urban space. Rather than work on an individual level, they aimed to create an ordered society which would, by definition, prevent social and sexual contact across racial divides. Here, racial difference and hierarchy would be mapped spatially, and colonial settlements would be freed from the ominous presence of mixed-race, rowdy enclaves and disturbing encampments and reserves.

Segregating Urban Space

Throughout the mid-nineteenth century, local police forces worked to both minimize and direct Aboriginal women's presence in white settlements. Victoria's police court routinely charged them with petty offences like drunk and disorderly conduct, and sometimes enacted a specific punishment reserved for Aboriginal women alone – shaving their heads – which aimed to shame by associating them with both European female sexual deviants and Haida and Tsimshian slaves, whose shaved heads marked them from free.[51] Higher courts sometimes charged them with prostitution-related offences. Given the broader equation between First Nations women and prostitution in colonial discourse, it could take little to 'prove' their participation in the sex trade. When, in 1860, the courts prosecuted a Kanaka man named Nahor for keeping a disorderly house, the chief evidence against him was that First Nations women lived in his house and that when men passed by, they would say 'chako' (come) and 'cla-how-a' (how are you?).[52]

Along with policing Aboriginal women in white settlements, reformers attacked institutions explicitly connected to rough, mixed-race sociability like the dance house. To reformers' eternal horror, dance houses were tolerated by civic officials who were more concerned with attracting the business of seasonal male workers during the yearly slack periods than with protecting anyone's morals. Complaining of what they dubbed 'the disgraceful orgies practised there by permission of the civic authorities,' reformers bristled at the suggestion that '*legalized licentiousness is a social necessity*.'[53] Their fury was directed not only at the disorderly character of these institutions, but at their facilitation of mixed-race sociability and sex. The *British Colonist* opined that 'a dance house is only a hell hole where the females are white; but it is many times worse where the females are squaws.'[54] In response, critics gathered petitions calling for their closure and urged Victoria's civic government to deny them licences and thus state legitimation.[55] Failing that, they suggested that the government force them to locate outside of the white settlement, so that respectable families might be sheltered from their noise, immorality, and excess.[56]

Alongside these various piecemeal efforts, the cities of colonial British Columbia also sought to banish First Nations people from their streets altogether. While these efforts began earlier, it was the massive smallpox epidemics of the early 1860s that provided the necessary rationale for transforming occasional efforts, campaigns, and rhetorical outbursts into a sustained attempt to racially segregate urban space in British Columbia. In making this argument, I do not mean to suggest that smallpox was a ruse for the covert machinations of a beleaguered imperial minority. Smallpox was a material reality whose impact on Aboriginal British Columbia was, as anthropologist Michael Harkin argues, apocalyptic.[57] In 1862–3 alone, at least 20,000 Aboriginal people were slain, and there was an overall population decline of around 62 per cent, while the Northwest Coast population is estimated to have been decimated by roughly 90 per cent.[58]

However severe, the material history of disease cannot alone account for the fervour or shape of settler British Columbia's reaction to smallpox in the mid-century. Colonial officials and the local press readily admitted that there was little cause to fear that the disease would seriously infect the white community.[59] Smallpox precipitated radical responses because it crystallized white fears of sexual and social contact with the Aboriginal community and fuelled and legitimated existing visions of racial segregation. Even when framed in the language of public health, mid-century campaigns to control the spread of smallpox in white settlements were directed at regulating the contact of First Nations people with whites. Such connections between gender, race, and disease are no surprise to historians of sexuality. As Frank Mort persuasively argues, medical knowledge has long played a role in defining central meanings and power relations around sex. From the cholera epidemics of the 1830s to the AIDS crisis of the 1980s, social discourse suggested, in Mort's words, that 'promiscuous and "deviant" sex leads to killer disease.'[60] Colonial contexts filtered these connections in overtly racial terms. As John and Jean Comaroff note about South Africa, the Black body became 'specifically associated with degradation, pollution, and disease' and 'racial intercourse' intimately linked 'with the origin of sickness.'[61] Across the imperial world, colonial administrators conflated disease with local bodies, and control over space became control over native social and sexual relations, especially if they involved or threatened imperial subjects and interests.

This is as true for British Columbia as elsewhere in the colonial world. Imperial visions of orderly, white communities buttressed by distant and quiescent First Nations populations routinely ran up against the rough-and-ready mixed-race social practice of the colony and precipitated, in turn, efforts to racially segregate urban space. A crusade to evict New Westminster's Aboriginal population was launched every few years. In 1861 the *British Columbian* claimed that their removal was

First Nations people made their presence felt among the very bastions of imperial authority in Victoria. Sarah Crease painted Lekwammen (Tsartlip or Songhees) people settled outside of the Governor's Garden in 1860.

required to prevent 'that abominable licentious intercourse' which was 'a burning disgrace to any people claiming to be civilized or christian.'[62] The spectre of smallpox led to the creation of a reserve outside of New Westminster in 1862, a space designed to house this threatening population and remove it 'from the immediate contact of the depraved potion of the white population.' Yet it did not quell townsfolk's fears of their Aboriginal neighbours.[63] In 1868, the forced removal of First Nations people being deemed impossible, New Westminster's city council burned First Nations homes and cleaned others.[64] Smaller colonial centres like Lillooet also occasionally evicted their Aboriginal population in the name of smallpox.[65] But it was in Victoria that the campaign to segregate the population reached its apogee. This is hardly surprising given that Victoria's heritage as a walled enclave and the practical and symbolic headquarters of mercantile and political empire. Nor is it surprising given the stubborn fact of First Nations persistence within the city of Victoria.

Racially segregating Victoria was initially proposed as a necessary response to the crime, disorder, prostitution, and excess of Northern Aboriginals rather than to disease. Beginning in 1855, local burgers annually complained about spring-time visits of North-Coast nations, asking that the colonial government evict them or provide the whites with sufficient arms to mollify them.[66] Men evoked the chivalric duty as husbands and fathers bound to protect white women and children from threatening, non-white peoples, and missionaries and politicians alike promoted Aboriginal relocation and containment as a benevolent means of saving the benighted savage.[67] By 1859 their pleas convinced Victoria's Grand Jury to recommend First Nations people be removed from the city limits, a point they repeated the following year.[68] Soon after, orders were passed demanding that Aboriginal people leave the city at night. Initially, only men were included in this directive. After 1860, however, the ruling was expanded to include Aboriginal women.[69] It subsequently became common for the press to assume that these orders were directed against First Nations women specifically, who were, at any rate, the bulk of the urban Aboriginal population. This ruling, while of an uncertain legal nature, was enforced by local police forces who arrested First Nations women for simply being on the streets.[70] White men's presence in First Nations settlements, as a corollary, was also policed, as when a young white man was arrested for being found asleep in Victoria's Haida settlement, a place, according to the local press, 'where no person with morals other than lax should be found.'[71]

Efforts to rid Victoria of First Nations people continued throughout 1861. In April the police issued orders 'to drive all Indians found in town after 6 o'clock p.m. across the bridge' that effectively separated settler-Victoria from the Lekwammen (Songhees) reserve. Aboriginal people found on the wrong side of the racial divide after 10 p.m. were to be searched and prevented from returning until morning unless they could produce documentation of a clear and subservient relationship to the colonial community, namely, 'passes from white persons by whom they are employed.'[72] By August the press was complaining that the existing ban was being ignored and Aboriginal people were seen in numbers after dark.[73] The police responded, in part, by burning down the houses occupied by Northern nations. Some journalists and Anglican missionaries named this act as overly cruel,[74] but others called for a re-intensification of segregation efforts. In December of 1861, Methodist missionary Ephraim Evans complained about the lapsed segregation policy, arguing that the presence of the First Nations women was especially damaging to the fragile morals of local white men. In doing so, he rendered the fraught connections between race, morality, and disease explicit: 'A short time ago the constabulary had orders to oblige all Indian women to leave the town for their encampments after dark. Now they are to be harbored in the dance houses until half the night is spent, and turned out to roam at large in their drunken excitement. The whole system of permitting them to frequent the town, or to live in its vicinity, is radically wrong, and should be abrogated before a harvest of evil shall be reaped fearful to contemplate. Beyond the demoralization of the settled population occasioned by their presence, what must be the effect on the health, and the discipline of troops, should this be made a military station?'[75] The connections between gender, race, and disease were thus firmly in place before the arrival of smallpox in the spring of 1862. For Evans, the presence of First Nations women imperiled the apparently feeble morals of white men, especially plebeian ones, and rendered British Columbia's colonial project dangerously tenuous.

When smallpox broke out in late April 1862, voices like Evans's multiplied, and the campaign to remove all First Nations people from Victoria picked up speed. The disease legitimated white people's disgust at the simple presence of Aboriginal people within colonial settlements. The British Colonist raged that 'they line our streets, fill the pit in our theatre, are found at nearly every open door during the day and evening in the town; and are even employed as servants in our dwellings, and in the culinary departments of our restaurants and hotels.'[76] The spectre of First Nations women cohabiting with settler men was a special affront that was carefully noted in commentary about the spread of smallpox.[77] These sentiments, when coupled with fear of contagion, were sufficient to motivate a sustained program of forced removal. Throughout April and May, the police cajoled the Haida, Tsimshian, and Tlingit (Stickeen) to leave Victoria, eventually resorting to burning their homes and compelling them to leave by gunboat. Racial segregation, apparently, was to be as complete as possible, and white people were banned from walking on the abandoned and razed Aboriginal settlement.[78] Even the Lekwammen (Songhees), whose local territorial claims had previously exempted them from removal orders, were moved to the San Juan Islands.[79] In the first week of May, the police issued what was dubbed a 'sweeping' order 'to compel all Northern Indians and squaws to evacuate the city limits.'[80] They were again escorted up the coast by gunboat, and Nanaimo's townfolk prevented their canoes from landing farther up-island.[81] Not surprisingly, these efforts to segregate urban British Columbia succeeded primarily in one thing: spreading smallpox up the entire Coast, a fact acknowledged in the local press.[82]

But disease was not always foremost on settlers' and officials' minds. That segregation efforts predated meaningful outbreaks of smallpox suggests the extent to which the expulsion was motivated by broad fears about gender, race, and colonial society rather than narrow ones about disease. Local press reportage confirms this contention. Victoria's journalists made clear that their first concern was morality, a state they thought could only be achieved through racial separation. The *Victoria Press* hoped that 'the wholesale ejection of man, woman and child, will effect ... a marked moral change in the state of the town.'[83] Smallpox, they further explained, was not a disease as much as it was a punishment for racial mixing, a sharp reminder of the evils of admixture and the costs of plurality:

> When we come to look at the effects of the mere contact of the Indians with the whites the result has been truly frightful. For disseminating vice profligate whites received in return the most horrible of diseases. The place became a moral as well as physical pest-house, and all this was not only tacitly allowed, but actually encouraged by the authorities; for we had squaw dance-houses – no better than brothels – licenced during last winter. Now for all this mass of corruption in our midst, what was our compensation? The sale of a few blankets and trinkets to the Indians – 'cheap' labor at the expenses of a white immigrant population – and a large illegal traffic in poisonous liquors. The morality and health of the town were bartered away for these results. The justice of Nature could not allow such things to pass with impunity, and accordingly we are visited with a malady that clearly proves how rotten is the 'paternal guardianship' under which the 'poor Indian' reposed![84]

Here, the language of destiny and science are evoked to articulate disease as the inevitable and natural result of white people foolishly allowing First Nations to sleep, trade, dance, and work among them. While the language is overtly secular, missionaries also played this card preaching to Aboriginal communities, as when one Anglican told a First Nations audience that smallpox worsened when the dance house opened.[85]

The notion that disease was the result of interracial sex was not minor or incidental: it was powerful enough to fuel gunboats. Yet it was not always powerful enough to entirely mute white sympathy or guilt. Observing the forced removal of Northern peoples, settlers displayed the psychic dissonance and fracture one might expect of a community that had just evicted its neighbours to probable death. Some took philanthropic heart from stories of missionaries and physicians vaccinating Aboriginal people or contributed their own labour to relief efforts.[86] Others, like Garret, named the 1861 expulsion as unjust, likening it to the eviction of Irish tenants and in doing so, challenged the logic that normalized such experiences for non-white peoples.[87] Police Magistrate Augustus F. Pemberton defended his actions against these charges by arguing that Victoria had long evicted its Aboriginal populations, by explaining the benevolence of his actions, and by blaming 'mischievous boys' for setting the settlement alight. Pemberton called on metropolitan precedents to further exonerate his segregation efforts. Not only did British vagrancy laws mandate the punishment of those 'living in tents without any visible means of support and not being able to give a good account of themselves,' but it was the practice of London's police 'to remove the Gypsies when they become troublesome.'[88]

Yet Pemberton was rarely forced to defend his attempts to racially segregate Victoria. Settler quiescence was in part guaranteed by the increasingly influential ideology of the 'dying race.' The supposed inevitability of the demise of First Nations' individuals, and collectively, both explained and legitimated the actual death of real people from smallpox. Yet other white people felt compelled to make more exaggerated efforts to ignore the worst excesses of the colonialism that their community was premised on. One article denied the existence of racial conflict in the expulsion campaign by arguing that First Nations accepted and indeed concurred enthusiastically with the benevolent intentions of the smallpox campaign. The *Victoria Press* took care to point out that Aboriginal people cheerfully saw their expulsion as an opportunity for sightseeing. 'It is due to the Indians to remark,' they wrote, that they 'thoroughly understand the intention and spirit of these orders, and fully appreciate the humanity and wisdom of the regulation. They will take up their temporary abode upon some of the many beautiful Islands that lie between this and the Plumper Pass.'[89] Later, they argued that the Tsimshian burnt their homes 'without any compulsion.'[90] Such facile attempts to justify white behaviour suggest that however pervasive, ideologies of the 'dying race' were not always able to entirely abrogate settler guilt.

Ideals of racial hierarchy and separation were challenged more often

A hybrid place: Lekwammen (Songhees) shed-houses and canoes persisted in disrupting space in Victoria. From Admiral Hastings's album, 1866–9.

by social practice and popular resistance than by formal written discourse. Even when fuelled by the powerful politics of disease, visions
of racial segregation were unable to supplant the easy, mixed-raced
sociability of the British Columbia backwoods. Colonies, as a spate of
recent critical social histories of imperial spaces have so eloquently
attested, were hybrid, homespun places that constantly resisted efforts
to render them compatible with ideals of racial hierarchy and separation.[91] The efforts to order Victoria on racial lines in 1862 are a case in
point. Within a week of the May order being passed, the salience of
mixed-race consensual family formation and the resistance of First
Nations women forced administrative overhaul. While it was clearly
the refusal of Aboriginal women to leave the city and the support of
their white partners that was behind the action, the *British Colonist* felt
compelled to explain it in language of white male citizenship rights:

> The order from the Police Superintendent requiring all Indian men and
> women to leave the town and vicinity instantly ... reaches many citizens
> who have cohabited with native women for years, and by whom they
> have had children, without having the union legalised by marriage. This
> class of citizens are in a quandary. Their women have been warned off,
> and the men, as a matter of course, cannot accompany them, nor can they
> permit their offspring to do so, and thereby expose them to the small-pox
> and kindred diseases, to say nothing of the state of moral corruption and
> turpitude into which they would surely fall under the skilful education of
> their red-skinned friends of their maternal relatives. The women, with
> true motherly affection for their young, naturally refuse to be separated
> from them, and threaten, if sent away, to sulk in the adjacent forests and
> steal the children at their first convenient opportunity.[92]

Whatever the exact point of resistance, it resulted in the segregation
ruling being transformed into a pass law: First Nations partners or
servants of white men were allowed to stay in the city, so long as their
men obtained a permit from the police. This pass-law was apparently
popular, and many applications were received at the police office from
'those having Indian servants and wives.'[93] The *British Colonist* was
furious that consensual relationships and First Nations women were
being legitimized: 'squaws, with neither decency nor cleanliness to
recommend them, are allowed to remain because they wear hoops and
are prostitutes!'[94] Venom, police orders, gunboats, and burnt homes
notwithstanding, Aboriginal people continued to live cheek-by-jowl

with whites. 'There is scarce a street in town but can boast its native residents,' raged the press, and First Nations women persisted in the city's confines and, more seriously, in intimate partnership with white men.[95]

Attempts to address sexual anxiety through racial segregation did not end here, although they did change their form. In December of 1862 a Victoria city councillor proposed a by-law 'declaring it to be unlawful for any person to Harbor Indian women within the City limits excepted always such parties as may be married and their wives are living with them and where such Indian women may be bona fide as servants.'[96] By way of official rationale, he proposed that 'the squaws might all be considered as prostitutes, and that was sufficient grounds for their ejection.' The mayor and magistrate advised that this was beyond the limits of legal justification. The councillor altered his resolution to refer only to 'squaw dance houses,' but this too was rejected.[97] In 1865 Philip Hankin, now Victoria's superintendent of police, again complained of the presence of Aboriginal women in the city and named it as inimical to public health and morality. While he requested that these women be forcibly removed to the reserve, the attorney general asked him to content himself with existing laws.[98] In 1869 Pemberton devised an elaborate plan for a racially separate Victoria. In his envisioned community, 'such Indians as have no visible means of support, & are the associates of thieves, or prostitutes who are disorderly, be treated as vagrants, and be given the option either to remove to the Indian Reserve, or be dealt with under 5 Geo.4.C.83, and be sent to prison.' Racial separation would be further maintained by the erection of a fence around the reserve, police control of the reserve, and admittance fees levied against those non-Aboriginals who dared to traverse this colonial divide.[99]

Arthur Kennedy's appointment as Vancouver Island Governor in 1864 lent palpable support for these ongoing campaigns to develop an effective means of preventing sexual and social contact between settlers and First Nations. His predecessor James Douglas had been at best ambivalent about racial segregation. As Paul Tennant has argued, Douglas's policies assumed assimilation and the possibility of a biracial society.[100] When settlers clamoured for the removal of First Nations people from Victoria, Douglas sternly refused to comply. While he conceded that Aboriginal people were 'a public inconvenience,' he contended their that 'their violent removal would be neither just nor politic.'[101] He explained that Aboriginal people were a useful if lesser component of colonial society. 'Much apprehension is felt by the inhabitants at the close contiguity of a body of Savages double to them in number,' he told the Colonial Office. 'In these apprehensions I do not share, for the object of the Indians in visiting this place is not to make War upon the white man, but to benefit by his presence, by selling their Furs and other commodities.'[102]

Governor Kennedy, in contrast, was a true enthusiast of racial segregation, particularly in its capacity to prevent sexual contact across racial lines. 'I think a great mistake has been made in permitting an Indian settlement to grow up and continue in juxta-position with a city like Victoria,' he reported to the Colonial Office, 'thus mixing the two Races together to the greatest degradation of the one, and the demoralization of both.' He was especially disturbed by the apparent toleration of 'the shameless prostitution of the women and drunkenness of the men who live mainly by their prostitution.'[103] Kennedy also shared these opinions with the relevant Aboriginal authorities, when, in his inaugural address to 'Indian Chiefs,' he threatened to take a firm hand with prostitution and warned them of immoral whites.[104] Presumably with Kennedy's support, the police began to prosecute dance houses as 'disorderly houses,' or, more vaguely, 'nuisances.'[105]

As in other outposts of empire, it was ultimately public health legislation that served as the most effective foot soldier of racial segregation. As Nicholas Thomas points out about Fiji, 'almost anything to do with the organization of custom or village life could potentially be modified in the name of sanitation, since this did not emerge from any interested attempt to impose British or Christian values, but from the state's rational interest in preserving the native race.'[106] A Sanitary Commission was authorized for Victoria in the wake of the 1862 smallpox campaign, relieving Pemberton of the necessity of performing tasks that he felt could only be performed by a board of health.[107] After 1868 city governments passed public health laws that allowed for the wholesale removal of First Nations people. Victoria empowered the Board of Health or mayor to 'from time to time, and at any time, to prevent and remove all or any Indians, not for the time being actually in the service of any person residing in or about the said City, from living within the limits of the said City, and to specify the conditions (if any) under which they, or some of them, shall be allowed to remain there.'[108] This regulation was put to work late in 1868. Pemberton and his men surveyed Victoria's households, ferreting out First Nations sufferers and removing them to the hospital located on the reserve.[109]

Governor Arthur Edward Kennedy, ca 1864.

The persistent object of regulatory efforts – First Nations settlements within the city of Victoria, 1867–8.

It was when public health laws were enacted on a colonial level, however, that implicit connections between gender, race, and disease became especially clear. In early 1869 Victoria's civic government requested that the colony provide some means 'for the removal of the Indians from the City of Victoria.' The governor replied that extending the powers of the Board of Health Bill would most effectively accomplish this end.[110] By July the colony had passed public health legislation further facilitating the removal of Aboriginal people from New Westminster and Victoria.[111] Some thought it an autocratic and arbitrary law that would unnecessarily increase colonial machinery while robbing the municipalities of their powers.[112] Its supporters such as Governor Frederick Seymour successfully argued for the bill's passing on the grounds that it would legitimate actions, like those taken by New

Westminster's city council around smallpox, that had previously been performed without the sanction of the law.[113]

Removing First Nations people from the homes and streets of white British Columbia, it seems, remained as much an elusive goal as it was a compelling one. Efforts to segregate urban spaces by race failed because British Columbians, both Aboriginal and settler, resisted the vision of colonial society which underpinned them. Despite the constant escalation of methods and honing of legal tools, the urban settlements of colonial British Columbia were never successfully segregated. Aboriginal people continued to live among whites and continued to have extensive social and sexual contact with the colonial community. Relations between white men and First Nations women were as much a part of British Columbia society as the fur trade or gold rush. Despite the prevailing construction of mixed-race relationships as agents of white male decline and the various efforts made by missionaries, journalists, and lawmakers to either abolish mixed-race relationships or render them compatible with white visions of appropriate sexual and social behaviour, these relationships persisted both on the British Columbia streets and in the worried, churning minds of reformers and critics.

These resistances, failures, and limitations are as important, perhaps, as are the attempts to prevent or radically reconfigure mixed-race relationships. The issues of mixed-race relationships and reform garnered such intense commentary because they struck at the fragile heart of the colonial enterprise. The many and diverse attempts to force First Nations people, especially women, from white settlements exposed what Ann Laura Stoler identifies as two powerful yet false premises upon which colonialism depends: the notion that Europeans were an easily identifiable and discrete entity, and that boundaries between colonized and colonizer were clear and complete.[114] Mixed-race relationships, rendered so prominent in events like the smallpox campaigns of 1862, made it painfully clear that white and Aboriginal people shared ties, homes, children, and labour. In doing so, they challenged colonialism's foundational fictions. So too did the difficulties that characterized British Columbia's efforts to attract and retain what its promoters deemed an adequate settler population.

Chapter 5

Land and Immigration, Gender and Race: Bringing White People to British Columbia

In 1859 Governor James Douglas explained that British Columbia would never become an adequate colonial society unless it attracted more agricultural settlers. 'The Colony is yet destitute of one highly important Element,' he wrote, 'it has no farming class, the population being almost entirely Comprised of Miners and Merchants.' Douglas contended that it was agriculturalists who 'must eventually form the basis of the population, cultivate and improve the face of the Country, and render it a fit habitation for civilized man.'[1] He was not alone in associating British Columbia's imperial ills with the smallness of the white population and its footloose habits. In their efforts to bring order and respectability to British Columbia between 1849 and 1871, reformers persistently turned to land and immigration policies. Immigration schemes would draw a respectable, British population while liberal land policies would encourage permanence, domestic family organization, and agriculture. Despite their brilliant dreams of free land and cheap passages for the teeming masses of Europe, white British Columbians had to be content with a gradual loosening of land policy and with minor and episodic assistance with emigration. Even in the face of these manifest failures, reformers, journalists, and politicians continued to look to both land laws and immigration policy when attempting to transform British Columbia into an orderly, white settler colony anchored with respectable gender norms and racial identities.

Looking to the Land

Land lay at the heart of British Columbia's colonial project. It was the arena in which the fundamental struggle of colonization occurred.

'Colonization necessarily involves the contact, and practically the colli-
sion, of two races of men – one superior, and one inferior, the latter
being in possession of the soil, the former gradually supplanting it,'
explained the *British Columbian* in 1865. 'The history of every civilized
country illustrates the truth of this proposition. Everywhere, in obedience to what appears to be a natural law, the uncivilized native has
receded before the civilizer.'[2]

From the outset of white occupation, land was the medium through
which colonial society aimed to reconstitute itself. In 1849 Vancouver
Island was established as a colony under the proprietorship of the
Hudson's Bay Company (HBC) who agreed, in turn, to colonize the
Island. HBC land policy not only worked to displace indigenous peoples, but to mould the settler society's racial, gendered, and class character. It was patterned after the ideas of colonial theorist Edward Gibbon
Wakefield, and attempted to reproduce British class relations by using
high land prices to deflect poorer immigrants into the local labour pool.
Wakefield had argued that single immigrants should be rejected, since
if all were married, 'each female would have a special protector from
the moment of her departure from home' and 'no man would have an
excuse for dissolute habits.'[3] In a modified version of these goals,
Vancouver Island's land law mandated that land be sold at £1 an acre,
and purchasers of one hundred or more acres 'take out with them five
single men, or three married couples, for every hundred acres.'[4]

The 1849 scheme clashed sharply with local conditions since, as
Richard Mackie notes, it 'depended on the presence of agricultural
land, on a steady flow of wealthy emigrants in search of land, and on
the presence of landless immigrants willing to engage in wage labour
for the landowners,' none of which prevailed on Vancouver Island.[5]
Throughout the 1850s opponents of company rule, including Governor
Richard Blanshard, argued that the price of land, conditions of sale, and
the HBC monopoly combined to prevent immigration and 'render the
formation of a Colony hopeless.'[6] That the Colonial Office opted to not
renew the HBC grant in 1859 and assert its control over Vancouver
Island did not assuage their concerns. Led by the self-appointed 'reform' paper, the *British Colonist*, critics continued to call for a more
liberal land law. Their demands were motivated by a critique of the
local colonial project and legitimated by agrarian discourse, which, as
David Demeritt explains, celebrated 'agriculture as the source of all
wealth and the wide distribution of land among yeoman farmers as the
source of freedom and democracy.'[7]

Accessible land, its promoters argued, would achieve three particular goals. First, an appropriate land policy was crucial in the basic effort to dispossess First Nations people of the soil and create a white society in its stead. British Columbia, the *British Colonist* argued, had stupendous potential as a settler colony: 'a brilliant future – and not far distant, is in store for these colonies, and those rich valleys and extensive plains, which are now the hunting ground of the red man, will be converted into smiling fields, and the happy homes of a thickly-settled rural population will take the places where now alone are seen the dingy huts of the native savage.'[8] Accessible land, more than simply bringing white bodies to British Columbia, would encourage the adoption of an orderly model of white family organization. 'To every single man, farmer or fisher, should be given 250 acres at least, and every head of a family 500 acres,' the Victoria press demanded in 1859.[9] A liberal land policy would also induce footloose gold miners to become permanent, agricultural settlers. 'Casual rushes of miners, however great, may give a temporary impulse and a transient success to newly settled lands, but until the immigrants sit quietly down to till the soil and build homesteads, there can be no substantial progress,' contended the *Vancouver Times*.[10] British Columbia land policy, agreed Colonial official Herman Merivale, should focus not on drawing population as much as it should deal with the weighty question of how to 'tie down an existing nomad population to the soil.'[11]

These concerns encouraged officials to tinker with land policy throughout the colonial period. Starting in the early 1850s, local officials modified Vancouver Island policy by granting land on more generous or flexible terms. Provisions mandating the importation of male labourers or married couples were among the first to go.[12] In 1858 and 1859 Douglas cut the price of unsurveyed land on the Mainland and allowed aliens to purchase land if they swore allegiance to the Crown. Early in 1860 he further liberalized land policy by allowing men to pre-empt 160 acres of unsurveyed land (not including townsites, mining areas, or First Nations settlements) for a nominal down payment. The land became private property if it was 'proved up' within two years. Douglas hoped this law would 'have the effect of enlisting the sympathies, and letting loose the energy, intelligence and activity, of the whole Emigrant population upon the public domain adding daily to its value.'[13] By 1870 adult men with the correct national affiliations could pre-empt any tract of unoccupied, unsurveyed, unreserved Crown lands under 320 acres north or east of the Cascade mountain range, and 160 acres in the rest of the colony.[14]

These modest innovations did not satisfy local critics, who clamoured for free land throughout the colonial period. Yet the Colonial Office remained too deeply committed to notions of private property to condone free grants. In managing a colony, they were aspiring to design a new society. Through the lens of mid-nineteenth-century mainstream political discourse, private ownership of the land was essential for the construction and maintenance of an adequate society. It was thus with great reluctance that the Colonial Office was even willing to countenance pre-emption. In 1860 Douglas applied to raise Mainland pre-emption limits, burying the Colonial Office in a mound of paper arguing that British Columbia was such a poor, racially plural, and unsettled place that prevailing theories of private property and social development did not apply.[15] Such arguments convinced the Colonial Office that the dangers of accessible land were outweighed by 'the risk of driving away from the Colony the only persons who are likely to bring any part of its soil into cultivation of perhaps several years.'[16] In 1868 the Colonial Office assented to further liberalization, again swayed by the difficulty of increasing the colonial population.[17]

However much the Colonial Office was willing to compromise on the question of pre-emption, they remained firm in their opposition to free grants of land. Not only would free land fail to augment colonial coffers, but it set an improper tone for colonial society. In 1860 Douglas proposed that British subjects be given twenty-five acres of land on Vancouver Island. The Colonial Office objected that this plan could 'offer no temptation to any person above the rank of a labourer.' The expense and time required to relocate to Vancouver Island worked to prevent the emigration of even that lowly group. No working man would opt for this course when, 'for a fourth of that sum they could pay the expense of their passage to, and purchase an equal quantity of Crown land, free of all conditions in Canada, New Brunswick or Nova Scotia.' As much as they would fail to attract settlers from Britain, free grants would draw immigrants from the nearby United States.[18]

London and Victoria came into conflict over the competing claims of race and nation – two related, but ultimately separate categories – within the colonial project. That free land would attract American and not British settlers did not trouble the 'reform' faction of the local elite, who supported *white* colonization regardless of national flavour. Should the colony, the *British Colonist* asked, 'lure away from our doors a moral, orderly, industrious and thrifty foreign immigration, to guard against undefined fears of an improbable international struggle, or even on the visionary grounds of pioneering our virgin soil or our rich miners for a purely British immigration that may never come till we are able to pay their passage?'[19] Yet the Colonial Office had these very 'improbable international struggles' foremost on their administrative minds. They demonstrated little interest in British Columbia other than displaying an episodic desire to ensure that it remained within the orbit of British sovereignty. If a liberal land policy would threaten that political control, it was not worth whatever white settlement it would attract. One historian, adopting the perspective of the Colonial Office, argues that Douglas's grant proposal was 'inane and received short consideration.'[20]

Differing perceptions of land law among metropolitan and colonial elites shows how the imperial enterprise generated not only conflicts between white and Aboriginal, but between different levels of colonizers. Yet few disputed the land laws' chosen place in the effort to render British Columbia a respectable settler colony rooted in orderly gendered and racial identities. Land laws aspired to secure the colony's British identity. In 1859 the Commissioner of Lands and Works argued that 'all theories of Colonization affecting sales of Land I submit must for the present yield the more important point of practically & effectually beyond all peril securing the British Crown in a legitimate and economical matter these Colonies.'[21] It would also work to encourage domestic family formation. After 1861 Vancouver Island explicitly rewarded domestic and legal family formation by allowing married men to pre-empt 200 acres of country land and an additional ten acres for each child under ten instead of the 150 acres available to single men. These bonuses could only be claimed, as one pamphleteer commented, when 'these blessings reside in the colony.'[22]

Land law aimed to punish men who failed to form 'legitimate' families as well as reward those who did. Colonial legislators looked to land laws to limit the mobility of white men in British Columbia. In the 1860s 'homestead laws' were supported on the grounds that they would prevent men from selling the family farm and saddling women with debt. The *Vancouver Times* argued that such a law would not only protect the vulnerable from louts and encourage family migration and a generally moral climate:

> Numbers of men who would gladly bring their wives and children amongst us, and establish themselves permanently in the colony, are afraid to trust the comfort of those whom they love on the chances of trade, or of mining, or on the uncertainly of health and employment in a country where

should their own means fail, there is no limit on the law of distant, and where they cannot expect that assistance should they become victims of misfortune which they would obtain in other places from friends and kinsman. If our legislators are ambitious in winning the good opinion of the permanent population of the country, of earning the gratitude of women and children who are now amongst us or who may hereafter join their relations, if they would encourage sobriety, industry, and marriage, if they will enact a law which will allow every family to acquire for themselves a homestead of some reasonable value, say $1000, and place it beyond the reach of sequestration.[23]

Two years later calls for a protective law were partially answered when British Columbia's Homestead Ordinance was revised to ensure that, if wives were resident in the colony, men could not alienate homesteads without their permission and that widows would automatically inherent this property.[24] Explaining local support for this legislation, Attorney General Henry Crease spoke of the need to reinforce fragile family bonds in British Columbia, telling the Colonial Office 'that it is merciless to sell up *all* a Debtor's property in a Colony where the establishment of families is of infinitely more difficulty than in the Mother Country.[25]

While land laws might shore up domestic families, colonial legislators made clear that their intention was not to empower white women. As Bettina Bradbury has shown, common law was altered over the nineteenth century to increase married women's property rights in other white settler colonies.[26] British Columbia's land policy made no similar concessions, suggesting the profound masculinism of both colonial and agrarian discourse. Yet some white women did manage to pre-empt land, shrewdly utilizing their racial and military status to secure rights denied them on the grounds of gender. Widows claimed their right to the 150 free acres of land promised to Royal Engineers upon completion of their military service, but only after Sarah Brown successfully argued for their inclusion. She started a trend that other women quickly followed, some acquiring relatively valuable tracts of land around the southern shores of the Fraser River.[27]

These exceptions aside, that free land was only for men, and more especially non-Aboriginal ones, was confirmed when legislation was drafted that inadvertently allowed both women and First Nations people to pre-empt land. Paul Tennant points out that the 1860 Land Ordinance allowed First Nations people to pre-empt land like settlers.

Some utilized this opportunity to acquire land, especially along the Fraser River.[28] Their right to do so was removed in 1866, an exclusion reaffirmed a year later when a new land law was drafted that failed to define 'person' in gendered or racialized terms. Such inclusiveness, while probably unintended, deeply disturbed officials. Crease asked the Colonial Office to disallow it on the grounds that it raised the dangerous possibility that First Nations people would be allowed to compete equally with whites. 'In defining "person" it is a question whether room should be made for the Red Man [sic] (who in this Country are far superior in intelligence to the average of the lower class of labourers in the Agricultural Counties at home) to go in and cultivate alongside with the whites.'[29] For Joseph Trutch of the Department of Lands and Works, it was not the racial but gendered implications of the proposed 1867 legislation that were most troubling. He so strongly objected to the possibility of women pre-empting that further condemnation of the proposal seemed unnecessary.[30] Trutch meant business on this point. A few years later, he refused to allow the Sisters of St Ann to pre-empt land at Cowichan, even though this teaching order had previously been informally exempted from the gender-exclusive law.[31] Trutch's vehemence affirms that British Columbia's land policy aimed to foster a certain form of family formation – which included, but was not defined by, white women. White women were necessary ingredients in the reconstruction of the colonial order, but as lesser partners.

Land law's conspicuous place in public debate either masked or mirrored the fact that few white people were even remotely interested in pre-empting agricultural land in colonial British Columbia. Those who did often failed to transform the land in accordance with the goals of mainstream agrarian discourse. By 1868 27,797 acres of mainland land had been sold, but only 20,000 acres fenced and 6,000 acres cultivated. Vancouver Island was not in an entirely better position. There, 75,000 acres of land had been sold, about 8500 acres farmed and 2,500 cultivated.[32] Local officials despaired of these statistics, but took heart in the knowledge that, if nothing else, land law furthered the cause of white supremacy by expressly preventing Aboriginal people from preempting.[33]

Disappointment in the failure of European agrarian practices to take root in British Columbia was widespread. Yet, as Ruth Sandwell points out, this 'failure' primarily reflects the priorities of nineteenth-century European economic discourse, which presented commercial agriculture and capital accumulation as the only viable economic goals. She argues that settlers on Saltspring Island had different aims than Wakefield: 'Land, and the economic flexibility it offered to those living on it, and not capital accumulation, was the goal sought by most families.'[34] Belief in the failure of agriculture in colonial British Columbia reflected this gap between dominant categories of acceptable lifestyles and popular white rural practices which, much to the dismay of observers, more closely mirrored local Aboriginal practices than reflected bucolic agrarian discourse. Reformers thus looked beyond land legislation to immigration. Without the 'combined inducement' of free land and cheap passages, wrote one author, 'it will be in vain for the Colony to bid successfully for immigration.'[35]

Promoting Immigration

Like land, white population lay at the heart of British Columbia's colonial project. The HBC was granted proprietorial rights to Vancouver Island because they promised to colonize it, and its grant was not renewed in 1859 because of their perceived failure in this central enterprise. This political action did not satisfy colonial reformers, who continued to blame the absence of a large white population for a multitude of colonial conundrums. The *British Columbian* argued the colony's poor showing stemmed from the fact that 'we have only a mere handful of population, a few thousand people living upon one another.'[36] Without a large population, wrote the *Cariboo Sentinel*, 'a country may remain forever a barren wilderness, dotted here and there with a few fishermen's huts and a few miners' and lumbermen's cabins, and known only to the world as an inhospitable and poverty-stricken place.'[37] As much as colonial promoters suggested that British Columbia's ills stemmed from the sparseness of its white population, they had a related and almost boundless faith in the potential of white bodies to make it a successful colonial enterprise. But even the most shameless boosters recognized that British Columbia's distance from centres of white population meant mass immigration required active state intervention. 'To have our country filled up we must not only assist people to reach our shores, but we must show them the way to earn a living after they get here,' wrote the *British Colonist* in 1866.[38]

Despite the apparent neutrality of terms like 'population,' the effort to draw peoples to British Columbia was an overtly racialized process pivoting on entrenched notions of 'legitimate' and 'illegitimate' occupants and 'desirable' and 'undesirable' migrants. While the historiography on migration tends to treat the movement of European peoples as apolitical movements to unoccupied spaces – Donald Akenson, for instance, explicitly defines Ontario's Leeds and Landsdowne townships as *'empty,'*[39] – immigration was an imperial as well as a social act, part and parcel of the ongoing effort to displace Aboriginal populations and assert a specific brand of white dominance. As Daiva Stasiulis and Nira Yuval-Davis point out, settler rule aims not only to consolidate control over indigenous populations, but to create and maintain unity with the settler population.[40]

Not all non-Aboriginal migrants were deemed equally desirable. While Douglas encouraged the migration of African Americans associated with the Pioneer Society of San Francisco in 1858, others did not share his enthusiasm. Despite their apparent fit with the colony's putative values of hard work, Protestantism, and respectability, the sizeable presence of African Americans in Victoria was regarded by many white people as a problem.[41] Yet it was Chinese immigration that created the most ambivalence among British Columbia's white commentators. Prefiguring the extravagant anti-Asian discourse and action of the *fin de siècle*, they welcomed perceived industriousness of Chinese people, but feared they would never become adequate members of the colonial project. The Grand Jury of Cayoosh (later Lillooet) told the governor in 1860 that Chinese settlers were a benefit to traders and government alike and asked that the state 'afford them every due protection to prevent their being driven away, wither by attacks from Indians or otherwise.'[42] Yet the conviction that Chinese men were fundamentally incompatible with colonial values and culture more often held sway. The *Cariboo Sentinel* argued that Chinese men could not be colonists for a variety of reasons, all indicating their fundamental difference and many invoking explicitly gendered images. The Chinese were 'aliens not merely in nationality, but in habits, religion'; they never became 'good citizens' or served on juries or fire companies; they never married or settled outside of China, and were 'more apt to create immorality than otherwise'; they dealt 'entirely with their own countrymen'; they hoarded money and evaded taxes; and, lastly, these immigrants were themselves 'inimical to immigration.'[43]

While white settlers railed against people of colour among their number, the state worked to encourage immigration from Britain and, occasionally, British settler colonies and the United States. Between 1849 and 1858, it was the colonial state's merchant proxy, the HBC, that bore the responsibility of coordinating and subsidizing migration. Along with the Puget Sound Agricultural Company, they imported 250 men, 75 women, and 78 children between 1849 and 1852, chiefly to labour on the company's farms.[44] In 1853 the 'annual ship' transported an additional 125 persons from Britain.[45] The 23 miners and their families sent from England to Nanaimo in 1855 constituted what Douglas 'the largest accession of white inhabitants the Colony has received during that period.'[46]

Ironically, funding for immigration became less secure rather than more abundant and regular after 1858. To be sure, colonial governments consistently allocated small sums to disseminate information, publicize the colonies, subsidize mail, and explore territory, and occasionally gave assistance to individual immigrating families. They also repeatedly aimed to devise more systematic efforts. In 1861 a special committee of Vancouver Island's House of Assembly met on the question of immigration and, after a year of meetings, allocated £500 for the 'diffusion of Information respecting Vancouver Island,' of which only £60 seems to have been spent.[47] In April 1864 British Columbia's legislature struck a select committee to consider assisted emigration, only to have the committee re-formed in 1865 and scuttled early in the next year.[48] 'The subject of adopting some scheme of assisted immigration has been under the consideration of the Legislative Council on two occasions,' a local official explained to the Colonial Office, 'but without I regret to say any satisfactory results.'[49] Union did not alter this pattern. In 1867 the Legislative Council reinvented the immigration wheel by calling for the intensification and rationalization of immigration efforts.[50] A few months later, John Helmcken was asking the Colonial Secretary 'whether it be the intention of the Executive to make provision for the encouragement of Immigration?'[51]

This cyclical proffering and abandoning of emigration schemes deeply disturbed those who saw a large white population as the cornerstone to a successful settler society. In 1864 the mainland press commented that excepting 'fifty pounds paid to a parson at Lillooet for an Essay,' the colony had 'not yet expended a single dollar' on immigration.[52] Five years later, the British Colonist moaned that no emigration promotion had occurred, 'although urged again and again, both by Legislative revolutionising and through the Press.'[53] Has the state, asked the British Columbian the same year, 'hitherto assisted directly or indirectly, to bring a single man or woman to our shores?[54] Such inaction was indicative of poor political priorities. 'Amongst the army of officials who absorb the revenue of the Colony, is there one whose business it is to meet the intending settlers, and supply that advice and information so necessary to a stranger? Not one,' they ranted.[55]

Bitter complaints aside, government confusion and passivity on immigration was hardly surprising. The Colonial Office expected British Columbia to be financially self-sufficient. Anticipated revenues from land sales were inevitably less than expected.[56] In this context, raising money for immigration proved difficult or impossible. In April 1861 Anglican Bishop George Hills wrote in his journal: 'Called on Governor. Spoke of Emigration ... He had no plan. All money at present must go for Roads.'[57] Colonial Office disinterest in both assisted emigration and British Columbia did not improve this situation. The Colonial Office thought that given its location, British Columbia could only reasonably expect emigrants from the Australasian colonies, and not from Britain, and announced that they had no intentions of ever assisting emigration to there.[58] When pestered to subsidize steam communication, Colonial Office staff made it clear that they lacked the requisite political will. 'When this Country was supposed to be overpeopled, there was the appearance of a domestic object in schemes for using the proceeds of English taxes to encourage emigration. But that state of things has long ceased to exist,' noted Colonial Office bureaucrat and colonial theorist Herman Merivale.[59] Domestic issues like overpopulation fuelled the various assisted emigration schemes of the 1830s and 1840s and would again motivate major emigration schemes in the *fin de siècle*. But these efforts ground to a near halt when such fears subsided or waned at mid-century, and events like New Zealand's Maori Wars and the Indian Rebellion of 1857 challenged British faith in the imperial project.

In this context, white British Columbians' efforts to disturb what they dubbed 'the lethargy of the Colonial Office'[60] had little success. Faced with a seemingly needy and lacklustre colony and inadequate political resources, the Colonial Office despaired of what to do with the imperial albatross that was British Columbia. In 1865 Thomas Elliot, assistant undersecretary to the Colonial Secretary, responded to a request for additional military assistance against possible Aboriginal resistance with exasperation. 'I am so obtuse,' he wrote, 'that I never could quite understand why we were so anxious to colonise British Columbia & Vancouver, and I certainly always felt that inasmuch as for practical purposes they are the most inaccessible spots on the Globe to either British Forces or Immigrants, they must unavoidably be for us the weakest, if not the most useless.'[61]

Given local difficulties and imperial disinterest, it is hardly surprising that devising and orchestrating a government-sponsored immigration scheme fell largely on the combined shoulders of the local colonial elite and those who earned their living marketing emigration. In Victoria and New Westminster, prominent, middle-class whites gathered together to represent what they construed the interests of the colony to be. Inevitably, this involved white immigration. In 1862, for instance, an Immigration Office worked to match workers and bosses and, in doing so, further colonial interests.[62] One prominent supporter of this office, Gilbert Sproat, turned his voluntary immigration work into something resembling a career, when in the early 1870s he succeeded in having himself appointed agent general of British Columbia. From his ill-funded London office, Sproat wrote copious handwritten reports and managed to publish a few emigration guides. More often, he waited 'for instructions as to the principles and duties of the Government plan for stimulating immigration.'[63] Instructions never came.

While reformers worked to encourage migration, a small army of metropolitan entrepreneurs worked to turn emigration into a business. They published a plethora of emigration guides advising Britons how to get anywhere in the globe, including, especially in the late 1850s and early 1860s, to British Columbia. These pamphlets usually included information on shipping, maps, and other practical advice. Often, they were little more than a peculiar amalgam of clippings from the metropolitan and local press and Colonial Office material. While scholars have lately paid growing attention to travel literature and empire, little work exists on this material, which – given that its authors had often never been to the destination being discussed – may better be characterized as 'not-travel literature.' In British Columbia, not-travel literature had purveyors as famous as Charles Dickens.[64] In the way it constructed and disseminated knowledge about colonies for a metropolitan audience, not-travel literature provides a sleazy and under-developed variation on the Orientalist thought so influentially analysed by Edward Said.[65] Yet it was through such literature that much of the practical work of empire took place, marketed by individuals with distinctly limited experience and a seemingly limitless profit motive. While British Columbia was too far from well-established European tourist routes to be visited by many white travellers, a handful of authors published travelogues of the colony. Aristocratic overlanders Viscount Milton and Lord Cheadle produced probably the best known of these works,[66] and other white men with personal experience in British Columbia also got in on the emigration literature business, parleying their colonial days, however short, into literary currency. All of this work was watched closely in British Columbia, and frequently found wanting by home-town pundits.[67]

In promoting emigration to British Columbia, pamphleteers, travel writers, and autobiographers trotted out many of the same arguments made by state officials. They regaled readers with promises of high wages, cheap land, and easy gold, and warned them of hard labour, false promises, and trying journeys. Like government officials who used land legislation to foster nuclear families, some travel and immigration writers laboured to encourage white men to take up the path of the married farmer. In an immigration pamphlet, Sproat told potential farmers to 'get a wife.'[68] Others were more ambivalent, like 'A Returned Digger' whose much-reprinted emigration guide advised that 'a family is a burden till a man is established.'[69]

Immigration pamphlets were also concerned with representing British Columbia as a suitable place for a white settlement – a somewhat difficult argument given its location and largely First Nations population. A favourite point was the climate. If nothing else augured for this place being a suitable venue for white supremacy, this surely did. While Canada was too cold and Australia too warm, British Columbia's mildness was uniquely suited to the Englishperson's constitution, making it an attractive place especially for married men who benevolently feared for the health of their women and children. Alexander Rattray wrote that a married man would have 'the comfort of knowing that his family is to reside in a country with a climate at least as healthy as that of England, and probably more salubrious than that of any other colony to which he could resort.'[70] For 'the European constitution,' another work argued, the colony's climate was 'one of the finest in the world.'[71]

Others took care to explain that the Aboriginal population was not as large or threatening as prospective settlers might imagine. Emigration Commission surveys presented Aboriginal people as prospective cheap labour and as possessing 'a strong desire to see the white men settled among them.'[72] Others took care to distinguish First Nations from the threatening 'Indians' of popular European lore. 'The Indians are not of the same tribes that the American backwood's man has to encounter in the United States, but a peaceful and well conducted set,' wrote one pamphleteer. As something of an added bonus, they were dying out. 'They number considerably less than 100,000, and their numbers are decreasing yearly, so that in a quarter of a century more, an Indian will be considered almost a novelty in this fine colony.'[73]

Not-travel and travel literature also peddled a package of more spec-tacular half-truths. Stories that probably began with a single author were picked up and repeated by subsequent writers. Among the more bizarre yet telling examples of this was the claim that First Nations widows threw themselves on their husband's funeral pyres, a story reprinted in a number of works. One suggested that 'this custom comes from Hindustan, that the widow or widows lie on the funeral pile, and are only permitted to leave it after the fire has been applied, and their bodies have become more or less honorably blistered.'[74] This is surely an overt example of the process where by profoundly different peoples – here those of the Indian subcontinent and northern part of North America's Pacific coast – were collapsed into one single menacing and bizarre 'other.' The *British Colonist* made note of the circulation of this story, noting that 'of all the heavy yarns we have heard, we believe it to be the heaviest.'[75]

The difficulty both local and colonial officials had in executing large-scale immigration schemes, however, did more than create space for the entrepreneurial and authorial. It led some to fundamentally challenge British Columbia's ability or, more profoundly, its need to attract a large white immigration. In 1861 the *Victoria Press* argued that mass immigra-tion was an impractical goal cooked up by those unaccustomed to colonial labour, race politics, and labour relations. 'It may suit a number of lackadaisical beings who are entirely unfitted for Colonial, or in fact any practical useful life, to be enabled to obtain, by a superabundant supply of immigrants, civilized *servants* at the same price they now pay for Indians,' they wrote.[76] There was no point, they thought, to seeking immigrants when the existing colonial population lacked work. Their anti-immigration position, indeed, became this newspapers' chief edi-torial plank, evoked frequently to distinguish them from the competing and relentlessly pro-immigration *British Colonist*. The *Victoria Press*'s position was shared by Helmcken, who in 1869 went so far as to argue that 'immigrants were mythical beings.[77] Years later Helmcken would replicate this view in his memoirs, deeming those bent on massive immigration patently unrealistic. 'The grumblers,' he opined, 'did not heed that the length and expense of travel and unwillingness to come to an unknown country were great drawbacks – they wanted to see the country made populous at once.'[78]

Yet those who questioned the merits or feasibility of mass white immigration never captured the mainstream of public discourse. The *Victoria Press* claimed that they had been accused of 'libelling the fair fame of these progressive depencies [*sic*] of the British Crown' for criticizing those they dubbed 'ardent immigrationists.'[79] Ultimately, British Columbia's apparent inability to attract white, especially British, immigrants served not as a reason for challenging the viability of colonialism, but rather as a rationale for the colony's entry into Confederation.[80] That Confederation was acceptable because it would solve British Columbia's immigration woes was a widespread enough view to lead the *British Colonist* to caution against it.[81] In this sense, the failure of land and immigration policies to work their intended miracle resulted not in the questioning of colonialism, but merely in a shift in the particular shape of the local colonial project, a fine-tuning, as it were, of the imperial machine.

Journalists, politicians, and travel authors looked to immigration for much the same reason they called for an activist and liberal land policy in British Columbia. Throughout the period 1849 to 1871, assisted immigration and a liberal land policy were widely considered to be capable of reshaping British Columbia's languishing colonial fortunes. A new land policy would not only draw white settlers, but also encourage them to adopt nuclear families and become permanent, agricultural settlers. An effective program of assisted immigration would provide the white bodies upon which any orderly settler society was premised. While an accessible land policy and mass immigration program were repeatedly called for, neither were really implemented. Ultimately, it was only in the specific area of female immigration that these efforts paid off. Here, the sheer ideological weight of the conviction that white women were a necessary component of any adequate society provided the necessary motivation to transform vague desires and schemes into concrete action.

Chapter 6

'Fair Ones of a Purer Caste': Bringing White Women to British Columbia

In 1862 a letter to the editor of New Westminster's *British Columbian* explained that only the immigration of white women could redeem the colony. Its author was especially concerned with white-Aboriginal relationships, dubbing them an 'evil' that could 'only be remedied by the introduction of fair ones of a purer caste into the Colony.'[1] In turning to the well-worn imperial panacea of white womanhood, this writer joined a chorus of voices associating white female immigration with local imperial fortunes. They hoped that under the influence of their collective better halves, white men would forsake rough, homosocial culture and the company of First Nations women and become productive, settled, and responsible colonial subjects. At last, they would give up the gambling table, the bar-room, the dance house, the Aboriginal home, and their mixed-race families for identities and behaviours befitting an outpost of British civilization. The notion that white women could reconstruct individual white men and, in doing so, transform British Columbia's colonial society as a whole was strong enough to fuel four assisted immigration schemes between 1849 and 1871.

White Women and Colonial Discourse in British Columbia

Why did white women emerge as something of a generic social panacea in colonial British Columbia, as a solution to myriad gendered and racialized dilemmas? On the one hand, they were thought to bring the qualities of gentility, morality, and piety so routinely connected with white women throughout the imperial world.[2] In 1859 Governor James Douglas commented: 'the entire white population of British Columbia does not probably exceed 5,000 men, there being, with the exception of a few families, neither wives nor children to refine and soften, by their presence, the dreariness and adversity of existence.'[3]

Commentators assigned white women three additional and specific roles within British Columbia's local colonial project. First, white women would compel white men to reject the rough homosocial culture of the backwoods in favour of normative standards of masculinity and respectability. White women, an emigration writer explained at length, were necessary if white men were to be drawn away from the rough ways of the mines: 'One thing has yet to be mentioned in connection with the gold diggings of this colony, and that is the *scarcity of women*. The emigrant from Europe will be greatly surprised to find himself among a class of individuals that know not the value of "better halves" or to whom the definition of "sweetheart" is as new as to read to them the names of some great Roman orators. And this generally accounts for the gambling and drunkenness that the diggings are plagued with. If every man, or say every other man, was provided with a wife, or sweetheart, or sister, he would find in their company much greater pleasure than by associating with groups of Californian miners whose policy is to become the dupes of clever "Jews" of the diggings – those men that keep the gaming tables, and the pipe and glass.'[4] Here, white women are represented as the only real solution to the hallmarks of backwoods male culture – gambling, drunkenness, and ethnic plurality under an odious American cast. Missionaries added a religious spin, arguing that white women would Christianize men in a context where religiosity was profoundly lacking. 'Dissevered from the softening influence of women,' wrote Anglican R.C. Lundin Brown, 'men become more or less rough ... To many men the Son of Mary still reveals Himself through woman, and through her puts forth His healing and civilizing grace.'[5]

Notions of respectable masculinity were in many ways consistent throughout much of nineteenth-century Anglo-American culture, but took on particular contours in specific settings. In British Columbia permanent settlement played an important role in defining male respectability, and white women were accorded a special role in the ongoing effort to make footloose men permanent colonists. A local journalist argued that 'the society here and throughout these colonies will prove *shiftless* for a long time, except Government or someone else provides wives for our young men.'[6] White women's stabilizing presence was assigned an economic role since without them, men would roam, 'their industry as producers and expenditures as consumers being lost to the colonies.'[7] In 1869 Acting Colonial Secretary Charles Good wrote, 'a terrible disproportion exists between the male and female population, the former exceeding the latter by some 277 per-cent.' Like many other commentators, Good assigned this demography serious social weight. 'It is impossible,' he continued, 'to lay too much stress on this evil which does more to retard the advance of the Colony than any other.'[8]

The second service white women would perform for colonial British Columbia was to simultaneously address the local labour market and relieve overpopulation in Britain. It became axiomatic to argue that British Columbia lacked a sufficient number of domestic servants. With-out an adequate supply of white women to labour in the colony's households, supposedly normal gender, racial, and class relations were disrupted. Men were forced to assume unfamiliar domestic chores, most notably the care of children. Sophia Craycroft, travelling compan-ion of Lady Franklin, noted that 'it is quite common to see gentlemen carrying the children,' since even ladies lacked servants.[9] This predica-ment was represented visually by William Crickmer, Anglican mission-ary to Derby (later Fort Langley). He sketched a series of pictures of his family in 1859, where his wife was the 'head nurse' and he the unlikely and ironic 'under-nurse.'[10]

Racial as well as gendered divisions of labour were unsettled by this colonial context. Without white female labour, colonists were force to rely on 'Indian labour and native or half-breed servants,' who, one writer thought, 'are often too obtuse, dirty, and untidy, to be of much use.'[11] By the late 1860s and early 1870s, Chinese men would fulfil the role that white women did not in British Columbia.[12] White women's scarcity also forced the bourgeoisie to perform labours normally re-served for their lessers. 'Gentlemen clean their own boots cut their own fire wood, and do other similar work: ladies are their own cooks and housemaids, dressmakers & almost everything else,' wrote a perplexed missionary in 1859.[13] Even when ladies found servants, normal power relations were disrupted by the domestics' choice position in the understocked labour market. Scientist Robert Brown, reflecting on the unlikely predicament of having to clean his own boots, complained that servants 'dictate to the "missus" entirely.'[14]

Arguments about British Columbia's need for white women were neatly matched by metropolitan fears of surplus women. Especially after the release of the 1851 census showing disproportionately high rates of unmarried women, the 'surplus woman' became a flashpoint in

Reverend W. Burton Crickmer pictured the gendered and class disruption
caused by the absence of white female servants.

Chinese male labour gradually replaced First Nations help. Chinese male servants employed by Victoria's Government House, ca 1860s.

British debate.[15] While feminists like Jessie Boucherett and conservatives like W.R. Greg struggled over the meaning of unmarried women, both constructed colonial emigration as an expedient way to resolve crises in British gender relations.[16] A British author saw British Columbia as an ideal receptacle for surplus women. While ten thousand women could leave Britain weekly without effect, in British Columbia, 'such an accession would transform an unsettled multitude into an organized community and lay the foundation of a nation[']s life.'[17] British Columbians easily appropriated the language of surplus women for their own purposes. Quoting Greg, the *British Columbian* presented the colony as a wonderful remedy to the 'redundancy of women.' 'There are in British Columbia hundreds of respectable men,' they wrote, 'who would be all the better for having wives and who would make excellent husbands; but there are no wives for them.' It was, they continued, 'no credit to our nation that while thousands of her daughters are withering under enforced celibacy at home thousands of her sons are pining in the colonies for want of wives.'[18]

Third, white women would address the other central 'problem' of British Columbia's gender organization, namely, the widespread practice of white-Aboriginal conjugal relationships. As early as 1851 naval official Fairfax Moresby suggested that only a change in immigration policy would address what he saw as the problem of mixed-race relationships. 'I would earnestly recommend the Hudson's Bay Company to send a larger proportion of married men,' wrote Moresby in 1851, 'of the labourers who arrived in the "Tory" 75 in number, only 9 bought their wives – the single men scatted amongst an Indian population will cause results not necessary to dilate on.'[19] Others agreed that mixed-race relationships would reign until white men's 'natural' object of desire – white women – were available. Naval man R.C. Mayne saw white women's ability to halt white-Aboriginal relationships as their primary use in the colony: 'If nothing else pleads for the introduction of Englishwomen to British Columbia, this fact surely does.'[20] 'Colonista,' a woman who claimed local experience, wrote that 'there are hundreds of men, well able to marry, who, if they be particular to a shade of colour, cannot get wived. Surely there is something rotten in the state of' society which sadly requires putting to rights.' Saving white men from dubiously coloured women could only be accomplished, she continued, if white women could be persuaded to migrate.[21]

This discourse presumed the 'naturalness' of same-race desire but betrayed a deep fear of its fallacy. It was also premised on the belief that, in saving white men from Aboriginal women, white women would save the colony as a whole. It was not simply that individual white men cleaved themselves too closely to those of lesser race when white women were absent. Rather, the practice of mixed-race relationships was thought to damage and imperil the colony as a whole. 'That many of the native women are cleanly, industrious, and faithful, we do not pretend to deny,' wrote New Westminster's *Mainland Guardian*, 'but, we regret to say, they are the exceptions. With the increase of our white female population, we look for new life in our agricultural pursuits and we hope that every inducement will be offered to healthy industrious women, who are desirous of finding good husbands and comfortable homes, in this province, to come out to us.'[22] Samuel Wilberforce, the Bishop of Oxford, speaking at an 1861 meeting of the Columbia Mission, associated inappropriate racial mixing with white women's absence:

> And, then, I need not dwell upon those degrading moral abominations which will be introduced into the population of that young state, unless you bring about an equality of the sexes. You first make any true relation between the aboriginal people and the settlers an impossibility. I am not going to dwell upon it, but I know, from letters I have myself seen, that the great hinderance [*sic*] to Christianizing the natives of that country arises from abominations which from this cause have spring up in the colony. And how can it be otherwise? With a degraded people to deal with, with people used, under their heathen system, to a low, 'squaw' estimate of woman, how is it possible but that, in pouring forth from this country a mass of men, not governed by high moral or religious principles, you should be doing to that native race the most deadly and the most irreparable wrong? It must be so.[23]

Thus, white women would ensure that proper – namely, European – gender roles would hold sway over the inherently degraded First Nations notions of manliness and womanliness that threatened to engulf the nascent colonial society of British Columbia.

Colonial promoters thus envisioned a particular role for white women in the process of transforming British Columbia from a rough, racially plural resource settlement into an orderly settler colony. This discourse did not emphasize those women who occupied a formal role in the imperial project, but rather privileged ordinary, working-class white women who would marry miners and farmers and perform domestic and agricultural labour. Making this point clear, 'A Returned Digger' wrote: 'They want no governesses or ladies' companions ... but women who can look after families and houses, who can brew, bake, do all other domestic offices, and meet the husbands, brothers, and employers with smiling faces when the men return from the day's work.'[24] White women's importance lay not as autonomous political subjects but rather in their ability to shape and control white male behaviour, as *objects* that would shape the behaviours and identities of the true *subjects* of colonization, white men.

This discourse about white women and colonialism ultimately provided the necessary motivation to transform the constant demands for assisted immigration into concrete action. While reformers, journalists, and officials called for an activist land policy and a program of general assisted immigration from 1849 and 1871, it was in the area of female immigration that these calls were most substantially answered. Here, the sheer ideological weight of the conviction that a society lacking white women could not be a moral or even adequate one provided the motivation necessary to orchestrate, as opposed to merely call for, large-scale assisted immigration. Four times – in 1859, 1862, 1863, and 1870 – British Columbian reformers and officers worked in concert with British parties to coordinate the movement of white women.

Assisted White Female Immigration to British Columbia

Family migration was first evoked as part of the effort to transform a fur-trade settlement to a white settler colony with the establishment of Vancouver Island as a colony in 1849. The Wakefieldian land system initially encouraged landowners to sponsor the passage of married couples.[25] Especially around their coal mines in Nanaimo and Fort Rupert, the Hudson's Bay Company (HBC) encouraged working-class, white family formation by directly importing English and Scottish families and providing them with housing. The Muirs of Fort Rupert, like the thirty-six married colliers sent on the *Colinda* to work the Nanaimo mines, represented a significant effort to transform Vancouver Island into a colony rooted in European domestic families.[26]

Just as the appearance of family migration marked the transition from fur-trade to settler colony, the appearance of female emigration schemes punctuated the onset of sustained colonization on the mainland. The emigration of white women was piggybacked on the arrival of the Royal Engineers, the solider-settlers sent to assure British military authority over the mainland and colonize it. Putting it plainly, the Colonial Secretary Lord Bulwer Lytton told them 'you are to be the Pioneers of Civilization.'[27] Women were given a modest but key role in this civilizing mission. The initial detachment of 121 Royal Engineers was accompanied by thirty-one women and thirty-four children, and at least another nine children were born on board the *Thames City* as it travelled via Cape Horn.[28] In their shipboard newspaper, the engineers inscribed themselves into overlapping narratives of colonialism and agrarian familialism. They dreamed of a colony where there were 'settlers from old England to cultivate the country, whose bright and happy faces will form a delighted contrast to the care-worn, dissipated, and scoundrelly physiognomies of the gold diggers in general,' joined by 'many of the detachment, with their wives and families, comfortably settled on comfortable little farms.'[29] That the Royal Engineers had a familial, as well as military and colonial mission, was reconfirmed when the detachment was disbanded in 1863. Each man committed to remaining in British Columbia was awarded 150 acres of free land, a grant that was, in response to requests, later extended to their widows.

The women and children accompanying the Royal Engineers were soon joined by more. In 1860 Commander Richard Moody inquired about the possibility of assisting the passage of non-commissioned soldiers' wives and partners who had not joined the initial detachment. Enclosing a list of seven women and six children, Moody wrote that his men were 'most anxious for their wives and "promissi sposi" to join them.'[30] In a fit of unusual enthusiasm that would never again be repeated, the Colonial Office immediately pledged their support.[31] Their patronage was premised on a rationale that would be evoked again and again in future discussions of colonialism and gender: female immigration was desirable because it was both indicative and generative of respectable male behaviour, here represented most potently by permanent settlement. A marginal note by a Colonial Office staffer remarked: 'The men sending for their wives is so strong an indication of an intention to stay' that elaborate repayment schemes were not necessary.[32]

By the autumn of 1860 the Emigration Commission had coordinated the passage of the women on board the *Marcella*. Initially, all but one of the women accepted the offer of a free passage. On further rumination, three declined to go to British Columbia for a variety of reasons relating to the precarious circumstance and proud culture of working-class women in 1860s' Britain: one was seriously ill, one insulted by the suggestion that she would be considered an 'emigrant' or object of charity, and another lacked the necessary money to reach the port. The *Marcella* ultimately carried only three women and four children, their passages sponsored by the Emigration Commission.[33]

Anticipating the hullabaloo that greeted the arrival of later immigrations, Victoria excitedly awaited the docking of the *Marcella* in the spring of 1861. Rumours flew about the number of women on board, causing 'quite a flutter visible for a time among the young bucks, who spruced themselves up with a view of "doing the agreeable" towards the "forty young Ladies" said to be aboard.'[34] When the *Marcella* arrived with her cargo, men attempted to infiltrate the ship in the harbour, and a crowd met the women as it docked. The male mass was distinctly disappointed when it was discovered that only four women were aboard. A 'large number of citizens,' wrote the *British Colonist*, 'had gathered to obtain a glimpse of the pretty faces and symmetrical figures of the forty blooming English lassies some time since reported to be aboard. Some could not curb their impatient longings till the vessel reached the dock, but procuring small boats boarded her in the channel. When it was found, however, that instead of forty, there was only *four* ladies aboard, a general desire to return to the shore was manifested ... The hoax was a cruel one; and the wretch who could thus wantonly trifle with the affection and feelings of our young bachelors deserves to pass a month in the chain-gang.'[35] Here, the disappointment between the romantic construction of white women – 'pretty face and symmetrical figures' of 'blooming English lassies' – is contrasted with the generalized male disappointment which the four soldiers' partners actually produced.

The confusion, excitement, disappointment, and mismanagement that characterized the arrival of the *Marcella* proved a harbinger for the female immigration projects of 1862 and 1863, remembered in popular British Columbia lore as the 'brideships.' These efforts were the result of the combined activity of British feminists, missionary agencies, and, to a lesser extent, British Columbia's elite. In London, a small group of well-to-do women known as the 'ladies of Langham Place' launched a multifaceted effort to broaden the acceptable sphere of activity for women, especially middle-class ones. They worked to expand women's employment opportunities by challenging the gender-typing of jobs through the Society for the Employment of Women and opened a law-copying office, a registry office, a printing press, and a telegraph station to provide work for middle-class women.[36]

It was this desire to expand middle-class women's possibilities that led these feminists to assisted migration. Throughout 1859, 1860, and 1861, their mouthpiece, the *English Woman's Journal*, carried a series of stories promoting emigration to British settler colonies as a useful option for both individual women and the feminist movement. In doing so, as James Hammerton argues, they took advantage of the positive view of female immigration that emerged after the scandals of the 1830s and 40s.[37] Reaping the benefits of shifting public opinion was not without political costs. Speaking to the Association for the Promotion of Social Science in 1861, Maria Rye explained that female emigration was a political compromise between the feminist conviction of the need for women's independence and popular opposition to women's waged work:

> I believe that all present must remember the fact, that soon after the establishment of the 'Society for Promoting the Employment of Women' remonstrances were made by no inconsiderable portion of the press against the movement. To this we replied, 'Are women to perish simply because they are women?' and when it was proved, as unfortunately it was proved only too clearly, that there were thrown upon their own resources hundreds of educated women – women of unblemished character, and, in many instances, women of capability and power – but who could literally find no employment whatever – and this in London alone, the unanimous advice from all quarters, from papers of the most opposite political opinions, and from pens the most antagonistic on every other subject, was invariably 'Teach your *protégés* to emigrate; send them where the men want wives, the mothers want governesses, where the shopkeepers, the schools, and the sick will thoroughly appreciate your exertions, and heartily welcome your women.'[38]

Female emigration let Rye navigate the muddy waters separating feminist goals and prevailing anti-feminism. Like the British feminists studied by Antoinette Burton in *Burdens of History: British Feminists, Indian Women, and Imperial Culture, 1865–1915*, Rye exploited colonial sentiments and utilized the prevailing politics of imperialism to argue for the expansion of white women's roles and possibilities.[39] Inserting white women into the rhetoric and geopolitics of empire proved easier than challenging the British gendered division of labour or even the more modest goal of finding women paid work in London.

When metropolitan feminists searched the globe for colonial realms where white women could acquire independence and rights, they soon looked to British Columbia. In London, the colony received a good deal of popular press in the late 1850s and early 1860s and acquired a small but influential cabal of boosters with significant ties to reform and missionary circles. It was this group that came together in February 1862 to sanction the creation of the Columbia Emigration Society (CES), an offshoot of the Anglican Columbia Mission 'founded in the first instance to facilitate the Emigration of Industrious Women to the Colony of British Columbia.'[40] Overseen by the Lord Mayor of London, the founding meeting of the CES represented a substantial block of improving, Evangelical, bourgeois circles, and garnered a substantial amount of attention in both metropole and periphery.[41] Here is a fine example of what Burton dubs the imperial public sphere, that 'imagined and contested space where unseen communities were drawn together through a shared public spectacle that transcended boundaries of "Home" and "Away" precisely because it brought colonial "domestic" matters directly to the sightline of metropolitan readers.'[42]

The founding meeting of the CES was a dramatic affair that set the sensational tone for the assisted immigration that followed. Missionary John Garret read an allegedly private note from a local source, portraying it as a juicy secret he felt compelled to share. 'Though this note is confidential, and not intended for the public ear,' he said, 'there is one thing which you may make public – nay, even proclaim from the housetops. It is this – the cure for what, if left alone, will ultimately ruin religion and morals in this fine country – I mean an emigration of white women from Great Britain.'[43] Not to be outdone, Wilberforce regaled the London Tavern with tales of workhouse girls bred into a life of crime and wild young colonial men who, unless tamed by woman and church, would ensure British Columbia's quick descent into massive immorality. Member of Parliament Arthur Kinnaird took the voice of moderation and foresight, marshalling support and planning the execution of this remarkable emigration.[44]

From the outset, the CES accorded white women a special role in the imperial project in British Columbia, an assertion feminists loudly applauded. 'Think of the 600,000 more women at home than there are men,' Garret bade the audience, 'and then think what society must be here. Churches may and must be built, our faithful witness must be borne for holiness and virtue, but where there is no wedded life, churchgoing must be difficult, because morality is almost impossible.'[45] While women committed to expanding the parameters of female experience might have objected to the construction of woman as synonymous with wife and mother, they found common ground with the missionaries in the representation of white women as powerful imperial agents. Discussing British Columbia, the *English Woman's Journal* agreed that 'religion and morality would be altogether ruined unless an emigration of white women from Great Britain took place.'[46] Missionaries' returned this support by recognizing the importance of middle-class women in the imperial effort. Wilberforce applauded bourgeois women who gave their attentions 'which have been wasted upon lap-dogs' to the 'salvation of souls,' suggesting that they superintend the passage of working-class girls to British Columbia.[47]

This convergence between mid-century metropolitan feminists and imperialism was further entrenched when the Female Middle-Class Emigration Society (FMCES) was founded in May 1862. With a retinue of influential patrons, the FMCES was effectively managed by Jane Lewin and Maria Rye, its 'secretaries.' Their stated goal was to relieve the problem of surplus women by recasting assisted female emigration in the guise of middle-class respectability.[48] While emigration schemes had too often sent 'the half-savage and wholly untaught and unskilled population of the wilds of Ireland and Scotland' to the colonies, the FMCES would cater to educated women and ensure their moral regulation.[49] In practice, the FMCES organized and sponsored women's passages so long as they agreed to repay all they owed within two years and four months. In its first year, they claimed to have been deluged with applicants, and to have officially assisted some 54 women and unofficially aided another 315.[50]

The FMCES's first large-scale immigration was directed to British Columbia. This effort tested the boundaries not only of their organizational abilities, but of the FMCES's claim to be a respectable, middle-class organization. Early attempts to establish a committee in Vancouver Island were thwarted by the unwillingness of local contacts to support middle-class female immigration. In 1861 Sarah Crease, wife of the attorney general, told the FMCES: 'I regret that I cannot give you any hopes of being able to benefit educated women by sending them out here.' Crease thought a few servant women were needed, but worried about their morality in the perilous, rough environs of Vancouver Island. 'The bane of the country is drink; assisted much by the removal of the pressure of that portion of public opinion consisting of social and family influence, which at home has so powerful an effect in helping to keep things straight,' she continued. 'Personal character comes out here, sharply and clearly defined.' Given local labour needs and moral climates, Crease considered family migration more suitable.[51]

The establishment of CES in the spring of 1862 provided the encouragement that correspondents like Crease had explicitly failed too. In September 1862 Rye commented that British Columbia would likely be as important a destination for assisted female migrants as Australia.[52] FMCES set about establishing local contacts among Victoria's and New Westminster's elite, but it was their connections with CES that gave them the support and backing they required to organize an emigration to British Columbia. Initially, Rye merely asked if she could attach a party of twenty women to the forty women chosen from public institutions to travel on the *Tynemouth* sponsored by the Columbia Emigration Society.[53] Building on this alliance, CES requested that Rye coordinate its entire female emigration effort.[54]

While FMCES continued to publicly represent itself as dedicated to assisting middle-class women, Rye admitted that the British Columbia migration would focus on working-class women. 'I am fully aware,' Rye told Hills in May of 1862, 'that none but *working* women are wanted in British Columbia.'[55] In July of that same year, Rye reprinted what she called an 'admirable letter' from Colonel Moody in the *London Times*, which contended that middle-class women had no place in the colony of British Columbia. 'I am sorry to say the opening for educated women here is at present very slender,' Moody contended. 'Household work is what is demanded. Our wives, the ladies of the colony, from the highest to the humblest, have to labour in the kitchen, the nursery, and the washhouse.' He added that his family would like a nursemaid and a washerwoman, a request his wife, for one, had occasion to later regret.[56]

That FMCES did not fight local correspondents on the point of class was partially a response to the particularities of British Columbia and partially a result of a meaningful policy shift. In November 1862 Rye told a meeting that FMCES had began by 'sending out governesses only, but they soon found out that if they adhered to that principle the whole scheme would fall to the ground.' They resorted to what they called an 'amalgamated system of emigration' that combined working women with a smattering of their bourgeois counterparts. FMCES's thin veneer of middle-class respectability faded quickly thereafter. There were only forty governesses among the four hundred women aided by FMCES by 1862.[57] In 1871 Rye privately explained that her efforts were dogged by the political conundrum she described as 'the removal of high class women creating indignities at home – or the removal of low class women ... creating an equal indignation abroad.' Rye gave up altogether on adult women, arguing that 'the removal of children although of the pauper class – is the best way to over come all objections & all differences.'[58] These shifts have not stopped historians from continuing to refer to FMCES as an organization dedicated to middle-class women or, more often, 'gentlewomen.'[59]

The productive alliance formed between British missionaries and feminists came as something as a shock for the local elite in Victoria. Local reformers had long called for an assisted female migration, arguing that only white women could ensure British Columbia's entry into the exalted status of respectable, prosperous, white settler colonies. A member of the Vancouver Island House, Selim Franklin, made something of a career of promoting female migration as a panacea for the colony's many ills. In 1859 his election platforms included exploration, road-building, a new land policy, and assisted immigration of 'respectable females.'[60] In 1861 he told the house that female migration would render the colony's migratory population permanent, and he 'canvassed the electors with a promise to bring out from England or somewhere a cargo of damsels.'[61] While people might object to other aspects of his platform, they thought that if 'he had fulfilled his promise he would have proved a father to his country,' an interesting comment given Franklin's status as a Jew and a bachelor.[62]

This history of agitation did not prepare Victoria's elite for the inauguration of the long-sought-after immigration. 'This London "Columbia Mission Meeting" has taken us quite by surprise,' wrote New Westminster missionary H.P. Wright in a private letter to the Society for the Propagation of the Gospel in Foreign Parts in April 1862. While he had told metropolitan friends of British Columbia's desire for white female immigrants, he expected neither the pace nor the form that the emigration took. 'The Bishop is as much puzzled as I am,' Wright added.[63] It was not until June that a 'local committee' was formed in Victoria to cooperate with CES. This committee looked much like the other manifestations of the local, improving elite, constituted, as it was, by a potent mix of Anglican clergy, improving businessmen, colonial officials, and naval officers.[64] Yet communication between London and Victoria remained limited and unclear, and efforts to form a committee on the Mainland failed altogether.[65]

Limited communication hints at a deeper conflict between the intentions of the metropolitan female emigration movement and the settler community. FMCES embraced emigration as a means of fostering female independence. A contributor to the *English Woman's Journal* noted that 'the promoters of female emigration look upon it as anything more than one among many means of improving the condition of women.'[66] Distancing themselves from those who equated female emigration with the marriage market, FMCES warned women to never look upon immigration as a mere means to marriage: they must 'fully understand that they go for *work for independence,* not to marry, and be idle.'[67] From the outset, white British Columbians made clear that their reasons for supporting the assisted migration of white women were different. They wanted female immigrants to be wives for working-class white men, especially miners. The *Victoria Press*'s London correspondent interpreted female emigration as an effort to 'supply the market with that most desirable of all commodities – wives for the diggers.'[68]

White working-class female independence was not ultimately compatible with the colonial project. The ability of colonial discourse to subvert the possibility of women's independence in this realm suggests the extent to which the feminist intentions of the female migration movement were modified in colonial contexts. Upon receiving news that British Columbia was to be an object of FMCES's benevolent intentions, the local press made clear that the colony would accept the assisted migrants only on explicitly anti-feminist terms: 'We never knew a man with matrimony in his eyes who expressed any affection for "bluestockings,"' they explained. 'The women we want in this and other colonies are women prepared to rough it as well as ourselves, women who, while acting as domestic servants, the class we particularly lack, will possess all the fair graces of womanhood and the virtues which will make them an ornament to their sex, at once model servants as well as model wives.'[69] Like Greg, this journalist saw female migration as a means of fortifying the binary status of nineteenth-century gender. Feminist approaches to emigration were undermined by existing colonial discourses and the unwillingness of metropolitan feminists to provide a substantive critique of them.

Divergent political goals did not dampen local excitement about the boat-load of young white women. As the *Tynemouth* neared, local journalists kept track of her movements, the cargo she carried, and her staff.[70] They worked hard to build anticipation about the ship's arrival. 'Sixty single ladies – think of it, ye single, bald-headed, and a-little-on-the-grey order, and build your habitations larger!' bid the *Victoria Press*.[71] The *British Colonist* thought the arrival of the *Tynemouth* a cause for real celebration: 'A general holiday should be proclaimed; all the bunting wave from the flagstaffs; salutes fired from Beacon Hill; clean shirts and suits of good clothes brought into requisition.'[72]

The *Tynemouth* rolled into James Bay on 19 September 1862, bringing a formidable mixture of scandal and thrills to Victoria. The three-month passage around the cape was eventful: the coal-passers struck, some twenty sailors deserted, the crew broke into open mutiny twice, and passengers were forced to serve as sailors between the Falkland Islands and San Francisco. The conditions of the female immigrants was another cause for rumour and outrage. The women were kept entirely separate from the other passengers, which may have protected them from male attention but did not shelter them from dark and poorly ventilated accommodations.[73] Another passenger, artist Frederick Whymper, remarked that 'they must have passed the dreariest three months of their existence on board, for they were isolated from the rest of the passengers and could only look on at the fun and amusement in which everyone else could take a part.'[74] The young women, reported Hills, had indeed 'objected to being restrained.'[75]

The troubled voyage did not prevent Victoria from transforming the arrival of all these white female bodies into a spectacle unlike any seen before. The small city was abuzz with news of the nearing of the *Tynemouth*. Miner and observer John Emmerson wrote: 'The arrival of those girls was anticipated several months, and formed the main topic of conversation: and on the first intimation of the approach of the vessel with its fair freight the inhabitants were at once on the tip-toe of expectation, and turned out *en masse* to witness the disembarkation.'[76] Charles Hayward's diary entry for 19 September read: 'Excitement in town owing to girls' arrival.'[77] The hype extended well beyond the city limits. On the road between the Cariboo and Yale, missionaries 'heard of the arrival of the Tynemouth steamer from England.'[78]

The spectacle escalated when the *Tynemouth* entered Victoria's harbour. Five men tried, without success, to board the ship to 'catch a glimpse of the rosy-cheeked English beauties.'[79] The women were eventually brought from the *Tynemouth* to James Bay on the ultimate symbol of colonial authority, the gunboat *Forward*, watched, as one newspaper noted, 'before the admiring gaze of some 300 residents.'[80] So thick was the crowd watching the women move from gunboat to their accommodations at the Marine Barracks that 'it required the united exertions of four policemen and the same number of stalwart marines to obtain a passage for the fair immigrants.'[81] 'Every available inch of ground from which a view could be obtained,' wrote the *British Columbian*, was 'occupied by men of all ages and colors, eagerly looking for a sight of the long looked for and much talked about cargo.'[82] The 'large and

Local Intelligence.

ARRIVAL OF THE TYNEMOUTH.

The emigrant steamer Tynemouth, 1700 tons, Capt. Hellyer, arrived at 8 o'clock last evening off Esquimalt harbor and anchored in the channel. She left San Francisco last Friday, where she had stopped two days to coal.

She started from Dartmouth with 246 passengers in all. One female died on the passage, and about twenty men left the ship at San Francisco, in consequence of representations made to them by the people there.

Her voyage occupied 99 days from Dartmouth to Victoria; and she was in port 13 days at the Falkland Islands and two days at San Francisco coaling.

The accommodations for the emigrants are represented to be very defective, the place apportioned to the single females being dark and much in want of ventilation. There was much discontent expressed, and the crew broke into open mutiny twice on the passage. At San Francisco, half the crew deserted; of the remainder, four were brought to this port in irons.

She brings 60 female immigrants, under the charge of the Rev. W. R. Scott and lady, 50 of whom obtained free passages from the Female Emigration Society, and the remaining ten availed themselves of the protection afforded by the Society, paying their own expenses.

The following are their names.—

M King, S M Duren, F M B Wilson, J E V Ogilvie, E H Cooper, M Cooper, H Holmes, G J Holmes, M Faussett, T Hirch, L Townsend, C Townsend, J Macdonald, M Macdonald, L Macdonald, G Macdonald, S Macdonald, J Macdonald, A J Morris, E A Morris, E B Abington, O A Abington, S Picken, C A Kendrich, M Dwilly, M Crawle, E Quina, S Gowing, M Hales, A Egginton, E Evans, E J Evans, E H Tammage, B R Wilson, E Reynolds, J A Saunders, F Curtis, I Curtis, E Berry, H Barnett, M L Chase, S Shaw, J Sentzenich, J L Hurst, E McGowen, K McGowen, S Baylis, M Gillan, J Fisher, A Joyce, S Lovegrove, M Hodges, M A Hack, M T Coates, J Robb, M Robb, J Robb, J Robb, M Renen.

Victoria's local press disseminated information and excitement about the *Tynemouth*. From *Victoria Press*, 18 September 1862.

anxious crowd of breeches-wearing bipeds'[83] followed the women to the Marine Barracks and continued their surveillance project. The 'young women,' a journalist remarked, 'were unable to enjoy a walk in the enclosure without being subjected to the gaze of a rabble of some forty persons, who hung about the premises, and leaning on the fence, scanned the inmates in a manner that was disgraceful.'[84]

This spectacle was organized primarily around the right of men to access the migrant women as the cargo that they were. And judge them they did. The *British Colonist's* journalists managed to get aboard the steamer, and they took 'a good look at the lady passengers.' They found them acceptable and remarked on their suitability as wives. 'They are mostly cleanly, well built, pretty looking young women – ages ranging from fourteen to an uncertain figure; a few are young widows who have seen better days,' was their evaluation. 'Most appear to have been well raised and generally they seem a superior lot to the women usually met with on emigrant vessels. Taken altogether, we are highly pleased with the appearance of the "invoice."'[85] The competing *British Columbian* was more ambivalent. 'Altho' in the lot there are perhaps few that might be called good-looking,' one wrote, 'as a whole, they were neat and tidy, and presented a very creditable appearance.'[86]

After negotiating the crowds of men, the women were sequestered at the Marine Barracks, while the committee worked to place them as domestic servants. With the bishop away and the government providing no support beyond authorizing the temporary use of the barracks, this task fell on a disorganized group of local elites.[87] Edmund Hope Verney enumerated the many ills and disadvantages that plagued the committee's efforts:

> Until three days before she came in, no preparations had been made for the reception of the females beyond plenty of discussion at committee meetings: we concluded that we could do nothing because, as a committee, we had received no information that such a ship as the 'Tynemouth' was on her way out, nor did we know, as a committee, on what terms she was bringing out female emigrants: so when ladies came to us to engage servants we could not answer what wages they would expect, nor whether they had made any agreement to accept such situations as the committee should procure from them: in addition to this, we could procure no official recognition of our existence as a committee from the governor or any one else ... an official recognition of our existence as a committee, was sent to us by the Colonial Secretary *after* the women were landed: add to this that

the Bishop is at Cariboo, the Governor in British Columbia, and the Arch-deacon at New Westminster, and you will divine how aghast the Commit-tee looked, when they were told that their sixty young ladies might be expected in two days or less.[88]

In a defensive and detailed report, the committee explained how they borrowed food, supplies, and labour to transform the Marine Barracks into accommodations considered suitable for the young white women. Sketches of their quarters illustrating the fence surrounding the bar-racks and the police presence suggest the committee's interests in both protecting women and creating a space that, like the panopticon, fa-mously analysed by Michel Foucault, would facilitate surveillance of the women.[89]

A committee constituted by prominent wives of the colonial elite was formed after the arrival of the immigrants and seems to have per-formed much of the work involved in despatching the young women.[90] Despite initial praise, the Ladies Committee was later criticized for con-fining their work to 'keeping down the price of wages by combination than to doing the best in their power for the benefit of their charges.'[91] Such charges suggest that the bourgeois ladies' class interests over-whelmed their gender solidarity. These committees were controversial because of their responsibility for the task of protecting the women from that very thing that justified their importation – male attention and desire. Their dilemma is one that underwrites much of the history of modern sexuality, namely, the difficult necessity of simultaneously en-couraging heterosexuality and limiting and shaping heterosexual prac-tice. Verney told his father that the few women who 'straggled away' were 'brought back by the vigilant police.'[92] When a young woman 'engaged in an animated conversation with a young man on the outside of the enclosure,' two clergyman and a naval officer quickly intervened. The *British Colonist* mocked their prudishness by suggesting that a guard of marines be placed around the barracks and that interloping men be bayonetted.[93] Ideology went hand in hand with more overt surveillance. A week after their landing, the *Tynemouth* chaplain Rever-end Scott gave a highly publicized sermon to the women, bidding them to remember their role as colonizers and representatives of English womanhood. Scott admonished them 'always and under any circum-stances to shape their conduct so that they might prove a credit to their English mothers, from whom many were now departed forever.'[94] These efforts aimed to ensure that the brideships would produce respectable heterosexuality, and not easy, expressive, working-class sexual contact.

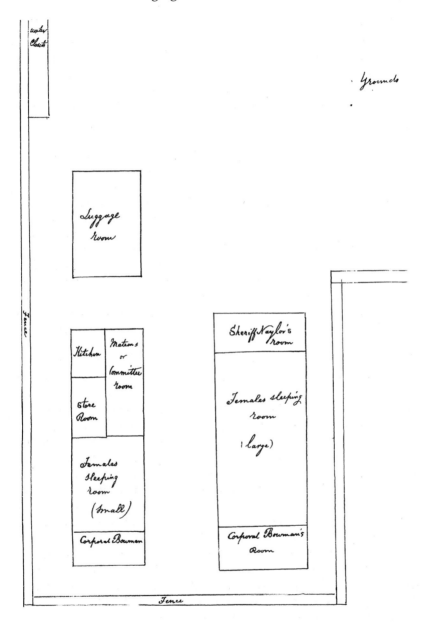

A sealed and ordered space: Gilbert Sproat's 1862 sketch of the female immigrants' quarters complete with the fence separating them from the community.

The excitement, confusion, spectacle, and challenge of the *Tynemouth* was replicated in the voyage of the *Robert Lowe*. This ship reached Victoria four months later, in January 1863, with thirty-six or thirty-eight women, mostly from Manchester and Lancashire.[95] These women were again endorsed by the mission but coordinated by Rye, who referred to them as 'My 40 women.'[96] The *Robert Lowe*'s long, 114-day voyage was again the object of careful attention in British Columbia.[97] When she arrived, on 12 January 1863, Victoria's crowd put on a another spectacular performance. The *British Colonist* took care to dampen fears about poor or amoral shipboard conditions, claiming that 'Everything, in fact, that a tender parent could do for his daughters' [*sic*] house and welfare' was performed by the captain and chaplain.[98] They also bade the receiving committee to develop more effective ways of protecting the women from the diabolical attentions of aimless working-class men: 'There is not the slightest necessity for any parade about so simple a matter as the landing of a few passengers, and we cannot conceive anything more heartless or ill considered than to have these poor young strangers, we don't care of what sex, but jeered to the rude gaze of a motley crowd of roughs who, instead of running about idle, should be engaged with the shovel or the axe earning an honest living.'[99]

Despite such warnings, a 'vast crowd' assembled to watch the women land. While the *Robert Lowe*'s regular passengers were brought to shore by civilian steamboat, the assisted female migrants were again given official imperial status and protection, this time by the gunboat *Grappler*. A special footpath between James Bay and the Immigration Barracks was created and lined by prominent bourgeois women, including Mrs Harris, wife of the mayor, and Mrs Mary Cridge, wife of Anglican minister and Immigration Committee member Edward Cridge. Despite the attempt to imbue the landing with civility and gentility, represented most notably by the conspicuous presence of elite white women, the rough culture of British Columbia again prevailed. By the time of landing, the crowd reportedly numbered one thousand. 'The girls,' according to the *British Colonist*, 'had to run the gamut through the utterance of coarse jokes and personalities.' A significant police presence did not, the newspaper thought, make sufficient use of their authority to control the rough and disorderly male crowd.[100] Despite efforts to sanitize the process, the white women's arrival again tested colonial British Columbians' claim to respectability instead of, as was promised, ensuring it.

The women of the *Robert Lowe* were judged as their predecessors had been. In Verney's view, they were 'evidently of a lower class than those who came in the "Tynemouth"; and perhaps better suited for the colony as a whole.'[101] The discovery that at least two women arrived 'almost in a dying state' further blunted enthusiasm. The need to care for these women led a group of elite white women, led by Harris and Cridge, to form an organization dedicated to relieving indigent white women and, in late 1864, Pandora Street's Female Infirmary was opened.[102]

After the *Tynemouth* and the *Robert Lowe*, interest in assisted white female immigration waned but never ceased in British Columbia. At an 1864 mass meeting, Congregationalist minister Matthew Macfie called for a renewed effort:

> Last but least, he would refer to a subject now rather hackneyed, both in the House and out of it – 'Female Immigration' – (laughter). He (the speaker) had talked with many families here, and he was sure that 500 respectable girls, brought out in small detachments, would be immediately absorbed. He would not lead these girls to believe that husbands were waiting for them on the wharves, and that proposals of marriage would be made to each of them in a few hours, but that they might get respectable places at a high rate of wages. He knew of many well-to-do mechanics who were obliged to go to California to secure partners for life because they could not find them here. (laughter) He attached the utmost importance – not to talking about this subject, as had been done for the last two years, but to active energetic movement in the matter.[103]

Macfie's vision of white female immigration combined an older belief in the political instrumentality of white women with a new scepticism about its practicality. Such ambivalence also informed the Mainland government's ultimately unexecuted decision to fund female immigration in 1865, which one member declined to support because 'he understood it was to be a repetition of the *Robert Lowe* affair.'[104]

By 1868 and 1869 memories of earlier, scandal-ridden efforts had faded sufficiently for another female immigration movement to begin anew. The local press suggested that the governor ask Maria Rye to again turn her attentions to British Columbia and commented that 'we should import not only able household servants, but thrifty wives for our setters, and secure the means of rapidly filling the country with a permanent population.'[105] While the assisted female immigration efforts of 1862 and 1863 were conducted with minimal state involvement, this movement was, from its onset, a government affair. In March 1868 Governor Frederick Seymour agreed to the legislature's proposal of appointing 'a Local Board for the furtherance of Female Immigration.'[106] A Select Committee of the House, struck in early 1869, recommended a limited scheme targeting some forty female servants between the ages of eighteen and thirty. Government and prospective employers would each pay part of the women's passage, as would the servants themselves over the two-year period that they were bound to service.[107] When Anthony Musgrave was appointed governor, he easily assented to this plan and allocated an impressive $5000 to it.[108]

This Immigration Board was a highly organized body that met regularly, developed a detailed application form for prospective employers, and widely advertised its work. The board tried to guarantee the women's regulation after landing, recommending that their wages be no less than ten or twelve dollars a month, and that they be bound to two years service. More radically, the board suggested that the women's employment contract be governed by a specially enacted labour law.[109] Much of their strategy centred on implicating local families in the scheme by having them commit to a servant and pay for part of her passage. The local middle class, however, proved less than enthusiastic about the immigration effort.[110] The board responded by modifying their scheme to include only twenty women, reduced the amount of money both servant and employer would be compelled to contribute, and later allowed servants to submit promissory notes in lieu of cash. They empowered Bishop Hills, who was visiting England, to seek servants there and gave him £400 and encouraged local bourgeois families to select their own servants or have British friends do so.[111]

While the Immigration Board emphasized the women's perspective roles as servants, settlers in British Columbia again saw female immigration as a handy means of procuring white spouses. The *British Colonist* worked hard to present service as compatible with working-class domesticity. 'Let them be plainly told,' it insisted, 'that if our families want servants our settlers want wives; and that the manner in which they may fulfil their agreements as servants shall be the best test of their fitness to enter woman's highest and holiest sphere of action.'[112] Service was thus little more than a prelude to marriage. 'Fidelity and capability in service should for these girls be understood tests of fitness for matrimony – the great end and aim of all their exertions,' the *British Colonist* later explained.[113] In the *Cariboo Sentinel*, a poet described

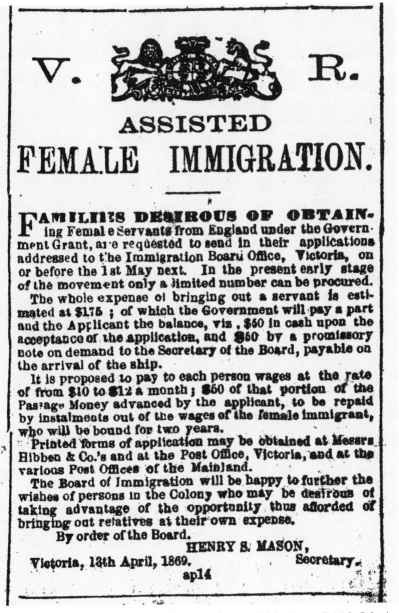

V.   R.

ASSISTED
FEMALE IMMIGRATION.

FAMILIES DESIROUS OF OBTAIN-ing Female Servants from England under the Government Grant, are requested to send in their applications addressed to the Immigration Board Office, Victoria, on or before the 1st May next. In the present early stage of the movement only a limited number can be procured.

The whole expense of bringing out a servant is estimated at $175 ; of which the Government will pay a part and the Applicant the balance, viz , $60 in cash upon the acceptance of the application, and $50 by a promissory note on demand to the Secretary of the Board, payable on the arrival of the ship.

It is proposed to pay to each person wages at the rate of from $10 to $12 a month ; $50 of that portion of the Passage Money advanced by the applicant, to be repaid by instalments out of the wages of the female immigrant, who will be bound for two years.

Printed forms of application may be obtained at Messrs. Hibben & Co.'s and at the Post Office, Victoria, and at the various Post Offices of the Mainland.

The Board of Immigration will be happy to further the wishes of persons in the Colony who may be desirous of taking advantage of the opportunity thus afforded of bringing out relatives at their own expense.

By order of the Board.
HENRY S. MASON,
Victoria, 13th April, 1869.   Secretary.
apl4

The Immigration Board advertised their scheme widely. From *British Colonist*, 14 April 1869.

waiting for the female immigrants, comparing his solitary life to the female-filled days of Mormon leader Brigham Young:

> Would I were a Mormon,
>   With four-and-twenty wives,
> With twice a hundred children,
>   And twice ten human lives!
> I'd raise me up a kingdom
>   All of my kith and kin,
> And make me a little paradise
>   For all that dwelt therein,
> And is it well, Oh, Brigham Young,
>   Or is it rightly done,
> That you have over forty wives,
>   And I have nary one?
> And is it well your children
>   Count above five score and three,
> And not a single child can trace
>   His virtues down to me? ...
>   No sewing buttons on for you,
> No rents are wanting stitches,
>   You have a spouse for everything.
> One for each pair of breeches
>   And then, when weary day is over,
> Each evening of your life
>   You have a home to visit,
> And a new and blooming wife;
>   My love is boundless as the sea,
> As certain to endure,
>   Enough for four young loving wives
> I'm feeling very sure.
>   Then what a shame. Oh, Brigham Young,
> You've one for every day,
>   While I, in lonely cabin,
> Must mine my life away.[114]

Whatever the intentions of the female Immigration Board, the poet 'Slum Gullion' saw the arrival of white women as a way to get partners for poor white men, not servants for their wealthier counterparts.

Confusion, excitement, and spectacle, marked the arrival of 1870s assisted immigrants, as it had earlier efforts. A drunken, ill, and miserable Governor Seymour neglected to inform the Colonial Office about British Columbia's immigration plan, an oversight apparently revealed when Hills arrived asking for money.[115] The local press again kept track of the female immigration effort, especially noting Hills's progress in Britain.[116] The arrival of the *Alpha* on 15 June was greeted with a dampened and cautious enthusiasm. Twenty-two women, including the matron, were on board. The local press took care to portray the voyage as safe and well-regulated, writing that the immigrants were 'all cleanly, healthy, and well behaved' and that there was 'not an accident; not a storm; not a case of sickness.' They urged the community to care for the women, adopting the language of cross-class female benevolence, and suggesting how colonial contexts could sometimes blur class boundaries: 'Need we ask those in this community to whose charge these girls have been confided to think of their lonely and trying position, and, as far as circumstances may permit, act as a maternal part towards them? Do not quite lose sight of the sister in the servant.'[117]

While the female Immigration Board and some observers expressed happiness with this efforts, their satisfaction rung hollow. The suggestion that the government shift its monies and attentions to the 'assisted passages of Families, and relatives of Farmers, Mechanics, and others settled in this Colony' suggests a profound dissatisfaction with this female immigration scheme.[118] In working for the importation of *families*, and not *women*, they endorsed the approach long supported by John Helmcken and others that presented the immigration of entire families as the only feasible means of introducing white women to the colony.[119] Yet their appeals for family migration again received a limited response, and this and the imminence of Canadian confederation led them to recommend that further plans not be undertaken.[120] Like earlier efforts in 1860, 1862, and 1863, this immigration left its supporters more ambivalent than assured.

White women loomed large in the effort to recast British Columbia's colonial society. They would, colonial discourse promised, encourage white men to conform to normative standards of whiteness and masculinity, meet the needs of the local labour market for servants, and help resolve demographic distortion in Britain, and compel white men to reject mixed-race relationships and in doing so, help to save British Columbia from imminent moral peril and imperial disgrace. It was the power and prevalence of this discourse in both Britain and British

Columbia that motivated the four white female immigration efforts between 1849 and 1871. The *Marcella, Tynemouth, Robert Lowe,* and *Alpha* were each informed by the conviction that white women would transform British Columbia from a transient, racially plural resource frontier to a stable white settler colony.

That these immigration efforts created more problems than they solved suggests some of the ways that female emigration reveals the always abiding and sometimes awkward connections between empire and gender. 'The imperial discourse concerning women's emigration to the colonies and dominions,' writes Rita Krandis, 'exposes the problems of gender in the context of the nation and comments on the emigrant women's "place" in the imperial context.'[121] Each boatload of white women brought to British Columbia's shores raised serious conflicts between competing visions of colonialism and was heralded as a failure by the local elite. Their dissatisfaction reflected the conflicts built into the colonial system and the deep chasm that separated imperial discourse from imperial practice. This gap was rendered especially obvious by the failure of working-class white women to behave in ways consistent with colonial discourse.

Chapter 7

'An Unspeakable Benefit?': White Women in Colonial Society

In 1862 Anglican missionary John Garret read a letter urging a well-heeled London audience, once again, to support a mass movement of white women to British Columbia. It argued that an 'emigration to this Colony of some good respectable young women' would 'confer an unspeakable benefit upon British Columbia.'[1] White women's experience in colonial society betrayed such grand promises. Their lives were characterized by an uneasy balance of work and dependency, their special role in the local colonial project, and by their experience of moral regulation. White women's ambiguous imperial performance led even the most stalwart supporters of female immigration to reconsider its relationship to the colonial project. While white women did not challenge the prevailing politics of racism, their experience does hint at the limits on the representations of white women as an unmitigated 'unspeakable benefit' to the colonial project. White women's experience in British Columbia, like so much else, demonstrates the sharp disjuncture between colonial discourse and colonial practice on this edge of empire.

Work and Dependency

Despite the prominence of images of genteel colonial womanhood in discussions of nineteenth-century British Columbia, life for many white women was characterized primarily by labour and dependence. White women's opportunities for wage work were sharply limited. The colony's economy was anchored in resource extraction, which, by the mid-nineteenth century, was gendered male throughout the Anglo-American world.[2] When American feminist Susan B. Anthony visited Victoria on an 1871 speaking tour, she was struck by the limited employment opportunities for women: 'Go and look at your Victoria dry goods stores where great, big six-foot men are measuring off tape,' Anthony said, 'You ought to be ashamed of yourselves for crowding women out of work.'[3]

White women's paid labour was largely confined to a handful of characteristically female areas. Middle-class white women were employed as teachers in private 'dame schools,' the female departments of urban public schools, and one-room schoolhouses. Apparently working conditions were less than ideal in the public schools, and in 1869 female teachers complained of their poor salaries to the governor.[4] If they had access to capital, white women could carve a niche in British Columbia's commercial economy. A handful of white women became players in male-dominated businesses. In 1863 and 1864 Lizzy Roddy was a partner in at least two mining companies.[5] Amelia Cooperman operated an Indian trading depot in Victoria and was one of the few women to be taxed for a trades licence.[6]

Usually, white women's businesses parleyed traditional female tasks into small-scale enterprises. Dressmakers, milliners, midwives, and others served white women. Yet, as Sylvia Van Kirk points out in her study of the Cariboo, women's businesses usually catered to white men. 'If the mining frontier did not provide an opportunity for women to step out of traditional sex roles,' she has observed, 'it did occasion rather exceptional opportunities to commercialize these by providing a range of services for a large male population.'[7] Some worked as washerwomen, while Mrs Landvoight, arriving in Hope 'flat broke and amongst strangers,' sold her homemade tarts and pies until she had earned enough to open a store.[8] Others combined traditional female tasks with the local penchant for drink. When Barkerville burnt down in 1868, at least five women, among them Fanny Bendixen, lost saloons or hotels.[9] White backwoods female publicans were supported because communities recognized their limited opportunities for self-support and, perhaps, felt that their race and gender merited patronage. The *Cariboo Sentinel* urged the community to support one female publican since 'she is a poor hard working woman, with a large family of helpless children to support, and is deserving of the patronage of the community.'[10]

Other white women sold sex and sociability instead of washing or food. Some prostitutes went to the Cariboo for a season and 'made fortunes.'[11] Professional dancers known as 'hurdy-gurdies' were a sub-

Hurdy-gurdy dancers in Barkerville, 1865.

ject of bawdy doggerel, a focus of public attention, and ultimately an icon of regional identity. 'No mining town with money about it on this coast seems complete without a "hurdy-mill,"' thought the local press.[12] Hurdies specialized in the highly physical 'mazy dance,' where, to the tune of a fiddle and after the payment of a dollar, the man threw his partner 'up a foot or two from the floor at the end of every figure.' Mazy dances were also something of a spectacle, where men 'crowded around in a circle, and applauded their efforts in a most demonstrative matter.'[13] The small numbers of hurdies belies their massive presence in lore: the 1871 directory found only three women – Elizabeth Ebert, Kate Scwaitzer, and Emma Scwaitzer – working in dancing houses.[14]

Images of hurdy-gurdies were deeply contradictory. Some thought them heartless exploiters of male gullibility. As James Anderson put it: 'The Dollar was their only love / And that they lo'ed fu' dearly, O / They dinna care a flea for men / Let them coort hooe'er sincerely, O!'[15] Yet, as white women, hurdies were generally exempt from the moral condemnation that was so often heaped on the First Nations women who patronized Victoria's dance houses, although their roles seem to have been similar. A photograph depicts them as fine representatives of respectable femininity, complete with severe hair, high necklines and hoop-skirts. Some observers explicitly defended the moral reputation of hurdies, as when one wrote, 'They are unsophisticated maidens of Dutch extraction, from "poor but honest parents" and morally speaking, they really are not what they are generally put down for.'[16] The challenging sexuality of hurdies was accepted because they functioned as a rare vehicle for white miners to participate in same-race heterosexual sociability. They ensured, wrote the *British Colonist*, that 'miners have a chance of indulging in that rarest of mining luxuries – a dance, with a *real* female for a partner.'[17] That their company had to be bought did not lessen the value attributed to it because it allowed men to avoid mixed-race and same-sex sociability.

Most women who worked for wages in British Columbia, as elsewhere in nineteenth-century British North America, were probably domestic servants. The constant promises of high wages for domestic servants apparently had some effect on women considering emigration. In 1862 Mary Norman wrote to Bishop George Hills from Australia about the prospect of immigrating as a single woman to British Columbia. 'Is it true,' she wondered, 'that domestic servants even are making from twenty to thirty-five dollars a month, and some even more?'[18] It is difficult to know if such promises were borne out. The histories of servant women who migrated on the *Tynemouth* and *Robert Lowe* are especially oblique. The papers of the Female Middle-Class Emigration Society (FMCES) curiously include no letters from women sent to British Columbia. When FMCES occasionally reprinted letters from emigrants, in keeping with nineteenth-century philanthropic discourse, they almost inevitably told of happy experiences and sincere gratitude towards their betters.[19]

Evidence suggests that the experience of domestic servants was less positive than these cheerful publications would have it. In 1863 Governor James Douglas told the Colonial Office that 'with very few exceptions,' the women of the *Tynemouth* and *Robert Lowe* had 'been comfortably provided for.'[20] Others felt compelled to distinguish between the middle- and working-class women, noting that the 'servants were instantly provided with situations,' while the 'governess class, for which the Bishop did not apply, are a difficulty.'[21] FMCES kept track of four British Columbia immigrants in their annual reports. One became a schoolteacher and married in two years; another, dubbed 'not very successful,' found employment as a needlewoman; a third 'left [her] situation rashly, and afterwards found difficulty in obtaining employment,' while the fourth was described as having gone to her sister.[22]

Even if quickly placed in service, the emigrants did not necessarily gain stable employment. Sarah Marsden of the *Robert Lowe* was quickly rejected from her post, Hills approvingly wrote, because the American family she laboured for would not permit her Sunday churchgoing.[23] Others proved a disappointment to their mistresses for more conventional reasons, a judgment they no doubt reciprocated. Mary Moody made an application for a young servant since she would be less likely to marry and require smaller wages. Yet Moody was outraged with the young woman she received: she was 'only *14* & *very* small for her age, neither fit for Nursery Maid or [*sic*] housemaid & can't sew at all ...' 'I am *disgusted*! & w:d much prefer being without her,' raged the first lady of the mainland.[24] Sarah Crease, daughter of the attorney general, argued that dreams of dutiful servants were but vain hopes. Some of the assistant migrants, she remembered, were 'carried off and married a few days after arrival,' and only two laboured for the duration of their indentures.[25]

These poor conditions and limited opportunities both reinforced and reflected the fact that wage work was not central to most white women's lives. Most depended on men for support. Even in Victoria, where opportunities for wage work were probably higher than elsewhere, female-headed households were uncommon. Of 1,025 households canvassed in 1871, only 32 were occupied by a sole adult white women. Another 404 white women lived with white men, and a tiny minority lived in less racially conventional households – 4 with Black men, and another with an Aboriginal man.[26]

Marriage and white womanhood became virtually synonymous. Marriage was represented as a state that was easily available to and desired by all white women. 'No sooner do they arrive,' argued one commentator, 'than they receive substantial offers of matrimony and future happiness.'[27] Tales of white women's upward mobility through marriage circulated throughout colonial British Columbia. Hills privately relayed 'a very funny thing' that he deemed 'illustrative of that early stage in a Colony where ladies are few & in great demand.' A respectable young woman asked if he would like to wed her, saying that 'I should have been unhappy if I thought you would like to marry me & I had not given you the opportunity of saying so!!'[28] Assisted female migrants were famed for their 'good matches' and speedy nuptials. In 1863 Sophia Shaw of the *Tynemouth* married a wealthy Cariboo miner. Their wedding, according to Edmund Hope Verney, was a pinnacle of backwoods excess. Everything was 'carried out in tip-top style,' and everyone was drunk. Jane Ann Saunders, another *Tynemouth* emigrant, married Samuel Nesbitt, 'a well-to-do baker,' while shipmate Emily Berry, after a difficult first winter became engaged to Nanaimo's catechist Mr Cave.[29]

Such tales of colonial marriage were more a staple in immigration propaganda than a reflection of female experience. Susan Nagle's diary provides vivid testimony of the failure of British Columbia's lauded marriage market to work for at least one middle-class white woman. Nagle was the daughter of a proverbially impoverished bourgeois family, her reformer father having been disgraced from his position as harbour master.[30] She worked as a teacher, did charity work, and obsessed about her unmarried state. On her twenty-fifth birthday in 1865, she wrote, 'I suppose people will soon begin to call me an *old maid*. Dear me. *How dreadful!!!*' A few years later, Nagle began a long engagement to a naval officer, during which time two of her younger sisters married, much to her anguish. When it became clear that her engagement might never end in marriage, Susan broke it off and opened a school in Yale where David Holmes, an earnest Anglican missionary, began to woo her. In January 1871, she promised 'to try for the next two months to like him'; by mid-February, she had reluctantly accepted his offer of marriage.[31] It is hard to reconcile Susan Nagle's sad marital history with boosterism about white women's choice spot in the marriage market. Commonly held assumptions about marriage ultimately belied the real power of heterosexual coupling.

But most white women in British Columbia did marry, and limited evidence suggests that they married young. In the sixty-six marriages identified in five Anglican church registers, grooms averaged 30.4 years of age and brides 22.6. Almost half the grooms were between 28 and 32, while over 40 per cent of the brides were still in their teens and another 50 per cent were between 19 and 23.[32] Such age gaps are consistent with white-Aboriginal marriages and the experience of other colonial contexts. Yet they are considerably larger than those generally associated the Western European marriage pattern which, by mid-century, was evident in the Canadas.[33] Such significant age differences between men and women tended to reinforce broader patterns of gendered power relations. As David Peterson del Mar points out in his study of Oregon, women entered marriages to older men 'long before they had the emotional or physical resources to assert themselves.'[34]

That marriage usually meant financial dependence for women was rarely in doubt. The state affirmed it when they gave women pensions after their men were slain, especially in government service. Legislation designed to protect women's wages, investment in homesteads, or other property from their husbands also affirmed women's fundamental reliance on male wages and tried to shelter them from some of the worst excesses of male power.[35] Communities affirmed the dependence of women when they raised money for the widows of men killed in military endeavours, in boating or mining accidents, and sometimes for women who had simply been abandoned.[36] White women also spoke loudly about their own dependence. In 1866 Ann Porteous was charged with attacking her husband while he worked at a saloon. When a weeping Porteous, holding her young child, was unable to raise sureties, the magistrate asked if no provision was made for her support. She replied, 'Not a cent! My husband comes to me sometimes and throws down half-a-dollar, as if I were a dog.' Unable to pawn her off on either the Catholic church or friends, the magistrate brokered a deal between Porteous and her husband, who, he ruled, must support his wife.[37] Catherine Edwards too appropriated the language of female vulnerability when she complained about the government shifting a planned wagon road away from her house, protesting that 'even a woman is liable to lose her whole investment and go away in want through their Agency.' Referring to herself as 'even a woman,' Edwards evoked the colonial government's chivalric responsibility to protect its weakest subjects.[38]

Male violence suggests some of the parameters and the shape of white female dependency. Anthony contended that 'there was no town in America in which wives got so many floggings as in Victoria.'[39] The colonial community had an ambiguous attitude about male violence directed against white women. Conjugal violence was sometimes neutralized as a male prerogative or dismissed as a private matter. Gruesome testimony described how Edward Witney beat his common-law partner Joanna Maguire to death in 1864. While Witney beat Maguire severely over a prolonged period only occasionally punctuated by community intervention, the charges against him were dropped when a physician testified that she had taken responsibility for her own wounds.[40] One Victoria man used 'the principle that it is not right to interfere between man and wife' to justify his unwillingness to help a woman being choked by her husband in front of their children, while at another time, a magistrate declined to punish a batterer on the grounds that the family should not have 'their prospects blasted by having any scandal.'[41]

The white community also publicly condemned male violence with some regularity. Men were routinely convicted in the colony's courts for beating their partners, usually receiving small fines and being bound over to be of good behaviour. 'The practice of woman beating, we are sorry to say, is becoming very common in this town,' judged the *Victoria Press* in 1861. 'Some brutal men will attack their wives on the very slightest provocation, and abuse them shamefully. We only wish that those so treated would lodge complaints against these characters, and then publicly expose them.'[42] The language of respectable masculinity was harnessed to construct violence against women as inimical to true manliness as when the word man was placed in inverted quotes when referring to male batterers.[43] At other times, officials informally provided women with the practical assistance they needed to rid themselves of violent partners. When Mrs Gullion told the court 'that her husband always treated her well when sober, but that he knocked her and the children about time after time, and she could stand it no longer – her desire was to be separated from him, as she could support herself and children very well,' the Magistrate remanded her husband 'to give him a chance to leave the country.'[44]

However ambiguously it was received, male violence suggests how white women were dependent upon and thus vulnerable to their men. White women's opportunities for economic independence were slim. The narrow confines created by white women's experience of work and dependency were reinforced by their role in the colonial project. White women were expected to serve as symbols of imperialism and racial separation. While white women reaped power and satisfaction from this special role in the colonial project, their ability to claim its privileges was dependent upon their willingness to personify a narrow vision of respectable white femininity.

White Women in the Colonial Project

White women were invoked as evidence of British Columbia's transition from savage to civilized. Their presence legitimated the symbolic work of empire. New Westminster women, addressing each other as 'sister colonists,' raised funds and created regalia for volunteer rifle and artillery corps.[45] While Governor Douglas's mixed-blood wife Amelia

Connolly Douglas made few official public appearances, the white wives and daughters of subsequent administrations were key to the construction of public authority in colonial British Columbia. Their appearances at legislative functions was more than incidental: the 'private' virtues of Governor Arthur Kennedy were considered sufficient to compensate for his public failings.[46]

White women's work of empire was individual and social as well as political. John Helmcken remembered the arrival of 'English ladies – *rara avis*' in Victoria. He found them 'very pleasing and nice,' but noted that life quickly 'became more extended, more artificial and more expensive.'[47] A white female face was said to transform the rough and hybrid space of the backwoods. 'Especially at the gold fields, men stand up to look at a woman go past, and I have known the arrival of a fresh female face in a gold digging district create such a stir that the miners have knocked off work for the day,' one author argued.[48] White women were widely touted as evidence of the successful construction of a white society. A Lytton correspondent was pleased to 'see so many of the fair sex arrive in one day,' since it demonstrated 'that this upper country is going ahead fast, and about to be populated.'[49] White women's child-bearing was closely monitored and celebrated as additional evidence of the march of white supremacy. The birth of the 'first perfectly white child' on the Fraser was proudly announced in 1858.[50] The slippage upon which these racially bound definitions of gender and reproduction were built was sometimes rendered explicit, as when a child was dubbed 'the first ... of her sex born in Cariboo,' erasing the very fact of First Nations existence.[51]

White women were expected to shore up white society and to serve as what Anne McClintock dubs 'boundary markers of empire' between the white and the majority Aboriginal population.[52] White women were said to be uniquely offended by the presence of First Nations bodies. Their very 'appearance in the midst of civilised society' was 'little short of an insult offered to female modesty.'[53] Critics seized on the use of gender as a justification for white supremacy by arguing that First Nations people would have to be removed from colonial settlements before white families would migrate. Complaining about 'ladies, with their daughters' being forced to 'make their way through the crowd of lousy "bucks" and hooped prostitution,' one New Westminster commentator asked, 'Is this such an atmosphere as respectable people would chose in which to bring up a family?'[54]

Such ideas were reinforced more by images of dangerous Aboriginal

Officials and their families were key in the public representation of empire. Here one presents flags to New Westminster's volunteer militia, 1868. The audience itself was an imperial spectacle: those in the foreground are First Nations, while those in the background are white.

women than by the spectre of sexually threatening men of colour. But an occasional tale of dangerous First Nations manhood and threatened white womanhood was put to work in the service of racial separation and hierarchy. One prominent captivity narrative described the young wife of the *John Bright's* captain being murdered on Vancouver Island's west coast. Later, it was his daughter who was said to be captured and 'anxiously awaiting deliverance from a fate *worse than death*.' The threat of racialized sexual violence, it seems, was sufficient to merit the dispatch of the gunboat *Sparrowhawk*, which found, much to the disappointment of the *British Colonist*, that 'the girl is a half-breed,' or as another tellingly put it, 'not our child.'[55] At least one First Nations man was given an unusually punitive sentence reminiscent of the draconian legal measures taken against Papuan men. In 1865 Yak, a domestic servant in Nanaimo, received six months hard labour for forcing 'an entrance into the bedroom' of his mistress even though he normally slept in her kitchen.[56]

More often, the notion that white women were boundary markers between races meant that sex of any sort between white women and First Nations men was constructed as literally impossible. Lady's companion and travel writer M. Stannard went to great lengths to argue that Aboriginal men were not a menace to white women, stating that 'in visiting them, they showed me every kindness, never molesting me, although I went alone.'[57] Stannard's willingness to entertain the possibility of sexual contact – consensual or coercive – between First Nations men and white women was not widely shared. When Matthew Macfie devised a list of twenty-three racial crosses, none involved white women.[58] It was this assumption that was later codified in Canada's 1876 *Indian Act* which, while carefully planning for relationships between First Nations women and settler men, does not imagine the possibility of intimacy between Aboriginal men and white women.

White women's special role in the colonial project was practical as well as iconographic. The prevailing discourse of white femininity gave women a language to defend their persons against assaults. When Teresa Wade, a sailors' wife, charged Thomas O'Connor with rape in 1862, much of the trial hinged on Wade's ability to marshall the role of a respectable white woman. While giving her a ride from Esquimalt to Victoria, the two had stopped to drink at two wayside houses, and O'Connor allegedly raped Wade. Witnesses concentrated on the weighty question of whether Wade was drunk, and repeatedly mentioned her status as a married women. While observers and officials sometimes dismissed First Nations women's complaints of sexual assault, nobody challenged Wade's basic right to name coercion or seek redress for it. However much the discourse of white womanhood gave women like Wade meaningful protection, their right to claim it was never assured. The extent to which they were protected by the privileges of white womanhood could be, as in the case of Wade, challenged by their participation in disrespectable behaviour like drinking. Certainly Wade's attacker, O'Connor, justified his behaviour with the claim that 'Mrs Wade had conducted herself as a lady but where parties were drunk there must be allowances made for circumstance.'[59] A similar argument could be made for the social assumptions about white women in colonial British Columbia.

An 1864 trial suggests some of the common ways working-class women challenged prevailing images of white women and respectability. Shopkeepers Herman Schultz and Jasper Newton Trickey were charged with raping Esther Meiss, who had immigrated on the *Tynemouth* two years before. Meiss testified that both Schultz and Trickey 'had connection with me while I was under the influence of the drink which Mr Shultz had given me.' The court testimony revealed a life which departed sharply from the images of white femininity pedalled by the female immigration movement. The defence lawyer suggested Meiss had a continuing and consensual sexual relationship with various men, including Trickey. Meiss herself was willing to admit to having been around the sexual block, acknowledging that 'I was intimate with Mr Jacob before I was married' and to patronizing a 'dancing room.' Her marriage was not a happy one. Defence witnesses testified that Meiss had said her 'husband had gone away and left nothing but bread in the house' and that he would not give her 'a "bit" to buy cheese with.' In response, she reportedly threatened to leave her husband, telling him: 'You have driven it so far that I will have to turn bad.' She looked to Trickey, saying that her husband 'feeds me on nothing but dry bread and fish, but I've got a key to Mr Trickey's room where I can get anything I want.' While Meiss denied all of this, she admitted to stealing money from her husband.[60]

Meiss also suggested some of the ways that working-class women manipulated the female immigration movement to their own ends. In court, she revealed that she had arrived under a false name, probably in an effort to hide her Jewishness and thus reap the full privileges of whiteness, saying she 'came to this country in my stepfather's name, my maiden name is Hurst; I came out in the Tynemouth [*sic*] as Mary

Hodges; I was married as Esther Hurst; my sister wrote me my name, she said I was not born a christian, and I changed the name of Mary Hodges to Esther Hurst.' Yet on arriving in Victoria, Meiss seems to have joined the local Jewish community; her husband was attending synagogue when the alleged rape occurred. Meiss did not keep in touch with her shipmates and testified to having a very limited female community.[61] Meiss teetered on the margins of both operative definitions of whiteness and of womanhood.

Meiss's difficulty in marshalling the image of a respectable white woman may have contributed to the fact that her accused were found not guilty. The judge, who had earlier banned her husband from the courtroom for prompting her, instructed the jury to find the men not guilty because of contradictory evidence. Meiss was outraged, claiming that the defence lawyer 'was a d—nation liar,' and that she would 'like to get hold of him.'[62] This case certainly reveals some of the profound ways that white working-class women's behaviour and identity in British Columbia departed from formal colonial discourse. Esther Meiss or Mary Hodges or Ester Hurst was not the imperial subject that FMCES had intended her to be. She does not seemed to have worked as a domestic servant. Rather than reforming the disorderly, easy sociability of working-class white men in the colony, she seems to have participated in it, changing partners and attending dance halls, and, if witnesses against her are to be believed, taking cash and goods in exchange for sex. Instead of serving as a beacon for Britishness, she adopted a Jewish identity. In doing so, Meiss suggested the vulnerability of notions of whiteness and revealed how she had hoodwinked the do-gooders who subsidized her passage. She did not take up the role of the dutiful working-class housewife. Meiss avoided her shipmates and alienated her few female friends. She embezzled the housekeeping money, and complained bitterly and publicly when her husband failed to support her in a manner she deemed appropriate.

While a spectacular example, Meiss was not the only assisted emigrant who clearly defied the role accorded to her. Soon after the arrival of the *Robert Lowe*, a group was charged with thieving at the Immigration Barracks. In 1864 five of the *Robert Lowe*'s passengers – Charlotte Anne Eaton nee Bates, Bessie Lyons, Jane Smith, Ann Fish, and Jane Atkinson – were charged with having failed to pay the balance of their passages.[63]

These were not the only working-class white women who failed to be the 'mothers of the race' and instead flouted definitions of appropriate femininity. Fanny Clarke, described as 'a woman of gay character' in 1863, was famed both for prostitution and cross-dressing. Her disorderly behaviour came to the attention of the colonial government when her companion, Richard Gollenge, was dismissed from his post of gold commissioner for Sooke mines in 1864 on the grounds that he was 'leading an intemperate and disreputable life.'[64] Gollenge was a long-term colonist and another casualty of Governor Arthur Kennedy's attempt to reformulate sexual practice on Vancouver Island. At a bizarre, trial-like special meeting of the executive council, Kennedy made two charges: that Gollenge had been 'seen in a state of intoxification in open day' and 'associating and playing Cards with a Common Prostitute in a Public drinking tent.'[65] That prostitute was Fanny Clarke, and witnesses spoke of her notorious reputation. One testified that she was 'known I should imagine to the whole community as a Prostitute.' Worse, witnesses like publican Henry Kibblewhite testified that she cross-dressed:

Q. How was the woman dressed at that time?
A. She had on a pair of my trousers.
Q. Partly in Male attire?
A. Yes.
Q. Do you know anything of the Character of that woman by repute, or otherwise
A. I believe she is well known as a Common Prostitute, I do not think she makes any secret of it.

Christian Ochsner, a road contractor, supplied similar evidence, although emphasising Gollenge's and Clarke's gender-inappropriate behaviour vis-à-vis their horse:

Q. What kind of saddle had he upon that horse
A. A Lady's saddle, a side saddle
Q. Was there any body with him on that occasion
A. There was a female called Fanny Clarke walking behind
Q. How was she dressed on that occasion
A. In man's attire, In man's Clothing.
Q. Do you know what is the Character of this woman, Fanny Clarke
A. She bears a very bad Character
Q. She is by repute, a notorious Prostitute.
A. Yes.

Despite this evidence, it was Gollenge's drunkenness at the hearing that finally resulted in his dismissal.[66] These proceedings apparently had little reformatory effect on Clarke, who was charged a few months later with assaulting another woman.[67] Clarke's overt, and ongoing refusal to live as white ladies were supposed to shows again how working-class white women's behaviour could profoundly depart from their construction in colonial discourse.

Assumptions of white women's purity were also shaken by their participation in mixed-race relationships. Irish-born Margaret Robinson was married to one of Saltspring Island's prominent African-American settlers, William Robinson.[68] Margaret seems to have spent a good deal of energy defending herself and her children against unwanted sexual attention and rumour. In 1862 Methodist missionary Ebenezer Robson reported that '*Mrs Robinson* has been *chastising a neighbour by beating him about the head* with a club' because he 'had circulated some false reports concerning her and she resorted to this extreme mode of punishment in the absence of her liege lord who would doubtless have avenged her worry had he been at home.'[69] In 1864, when the Robinson's farmhand was charged with raping their daughters, the press took care to describe them as 'three mulatto girls' whose mother was 'a white woman.'[70] But two years later, when Margaret charged Henry Lester with sexually assaulting her, race was not raised as an issue. Saltspring's black settlers rallied around her, and only the accused challenged the veracity of her claim and nobody publicly doubted her right to make it.[71] While Margaret's implicit refusal to serve as boundary marker for racial purity seems to have put her respectable status into doubt, it was her own pride and the support of the Black community that ultimately protected her.

White women reinforced as well as challenged the connections between white womanhood and imperial respectability. Some white women seem to have relished, or at least enjoyed, the power they reaped from being icons of racial separation and hierarchy. 'Mary E.' a *Tynemouth* emigrant and Yale schoolteacher, wrote: 'I am quite surrounded by Chinese and Indians.' She also spoke of the racially liminal figures of backwoods miners, telling her family that 'They are the most uncivilized-looking beings when they first come down; you would be quite frightened to be accosted by one at Brighton.' In the end, Mary found the 'others' less threatening than anticipated and enjoyed the status this racial context afforded white women. 'There are very few white women here, so they are treated with politeness by all,' she explained, adding that this status guaranteed them an audience with the local luminaries, including the 'Governor, the Bishop, the Judge, and all the great folks.'[72]

Another white woman argued that colonial life offered opportunities for higher planes of female satisfaction, prefiguring the turn-of-the-century discourse around motherhood and imperialism analysed by Anna Davin.[73] 'Colonista,' the letter writer who claimed 'five years' residence on the Pacific coast of British North America,' contended that the absence of servants made for more satisfying gender and family relations. 'In the colonies women, like men, must work,' she wrote, turning the usual comment about the absence of servants on its head. As a partial result, 'the tie between mother and children is a very strong one in colonial life.' Colonista thought that colonial contexts nurtured more 'natural' gender arrangements. 'The wife may become truly the housewife; the husband may pursue any occupation without – as long as it is an honest and respectable one – losing estate.'[74] Her choice of 'Colonista' as a nom de plume suggests that this author was labouring to represent herself as colonialism both personified and feminized.

Another white woman saw gender as a barrier rather than an empowerment. Jane Fawcett, a Victoria housewife, complained bitterly about the presence of First Nations people 'permitted by our wretched imbecile government, to be *in* or about the city thieving, and drinking whiskey ... and public prostitution.' She also doubted the pedigree of the Douglas administration: 'A more ignorant self interested, crawling administration could not be anywhere ... that I think we might as well have no government as the present one; and the Governor with his *Squa*[w] *wife*, and half breed daughters, and those under him.' It was her gender, she told her sister, that kept her from putting things to right: 'If I were a man, I could not sit tamely by, and see what I do; for I feel strongly ... I want to see those abuses altered, and I should like this country better than I now do.'[75] Fawcett, in despairing that her gender limited the extent to which she could participate in the ongoing effort to assert white supremacy, suggests, like Colonista, yet another way that women were located, and could further locate themselves, within the colonial project.

Fawcett utilized the spectre of white-Aboriginal relationships to explain or justify her own racism and anger. Perhaps her wrath about white men's conjugal attachments to local women was widely shared. But not all white women took their roles as boundary markers so seriously or so literally. Certainly Susan Moir Allison seems to have harboured no particular resentment towards Suzanne, her husband's former partner, or to Suzanne's children. Their lives in the Okanagan were profoundly enmeshed. Yet Margaret Orsmby's edition of Susan's memoirs fails to explain that Suzanne was Mr Allison's former partner, suggesting that Susan Allison's perspective may have been buried alongside the story of her husband's multiple families.[76] Perhaps, though, Susan was not resentful because she did not need to be, so sure was she in her role as the white woman and legitimate wife. As in the southern households analysed by Nell Painter, a troubling brew of silence, racism, and female community marks the case of Susan and Suzanne and suggests how the politics of gender, race, and colonialism not only carved out roles for white and First Nations women, but shaped their relationship to each other.[77]

White women's special role in the colonial project could also lead to loneliness and isolation. The scarcity of other white women and the socially imposed but individually perpetuated barriers between white and First Nations women meant that establishing female bonds was difficult. Dressmaker Annie Deans wrote to her family that 'it is always my lament that if I had a female Friend here I would like [it] much better.'[78] A Cowichan settler remarked that 'his own wife came out from her friends in Glasgow, and feels painfully the seclusion in a forest, where it is impossible often for her to see another female,'[79] suggesting both the depths of racially exclusive definitions of gender and white female loneliness. For others, fear rather than loneliness was the keynote. When Stannard spent the night in New Westminster's Grand Hotel with her mistress, she was so nervous about staying where 'there were no females in the house except for ourselves' that a simple knock on their door made her 'suspect foul play.'[80] Louisa Townsend, a middle-class *Tynemouth* migrant, remembered being virtually cloistered when she first arrived on the mainland. 'I know there were a lot of soldiers and I was never allowed to go out on the street alone,' she recalled, speaking volumes to the centrality of fear to white women's experience in colonial British Columbia.[81] Whether the soldiers – read working-class men – were the source of her fear or symbols of a different threat remains unclear.

Class separated white women from each other as gender separated them from men and race divided them from First Nations women. For bourgeois white women, the absence of an adequate supply of domestic labour was the most disturbing aspect of white women's scarcity. Adelaide Ash spent a substantial amount of energy recording her servant's wages and comings and goings, and Moody was also preoccupied with her inability to manage and retain female household help in a colonial context. Such concerns coloured their social relations as well. When Moody told her sister that a dinner with '4 ladies & 1 gentlemen' was 'an event in the history of the place, where female[s] are so scarce,' she deployed a definition of 'female' which spoke as much about class and race as it did about gender.[82]

Yet ideals of racial separation, as the case of Susan Allison suggests, did not always define white women's lives in an uncomplicated way. Their lives, like men's, could be deeply intertwined with First Nations peoples, lifestyles, and customs. The ability of settler women to be simultaneously racist and culturally hybrid sometimes struck metropolitan observers as ironic. Scientist Robert Brown described visiting Isabella Robb at her Comox farm in the summer of 1864. Robb, the former matron of the *Tynemouth*, apparently prided herself on being the 'first white woman' in the settlement. Yet, to Brown's metropolitan eyes, Robb seemed more Aboriginal than white. She ate Native foods and mixed her English and Chinook with ease. 'The old lady,' Brown wrote, 'apologized to me for having nothing better to offer. "Mowich" (deer), she said, was scarce just now. Formerly there was "hyou" (plenty) but now the "Siwashes" (Indians) brought in little and wanted for that little *hyou chickaman* (plenty money).' Brown found the juxtaposition of Robb's racism and cultural and linguistic hybridity a peculiar one. 'Mrs Robb is an Englishwoman and of course with all a Britisher's contempt for savages, but like all others out here mixed in her conversation Indian Jargon.'[83]

Moral Regulation and White Women

White women's special relationship to the colonial project, however significant, was neither natural nor stable. The willingness of women like Robinson, Meiss, and Clarke to depart from the norms of respectable white womanhood suggests how white women, especially working-class ones, tested the limits of colonial discourse. The fragmented character of white womens' identities and the fraught nature of their relationship to each other, settler men, and First Nations women similarly unsettled imperial categories. To be sure, white women rarely overtly or systematically challenged the politics of colonialism or racial separation and hierarchy. Yet their individual divergences were enough of a problem that British Columbia developed a series of institutions designed to manage and regulate white women. Girls' schools, female charities, campaigns against 'immoral' wage work, and efforts to protect individual white women all suggest the deep ambivalence that lay behind the faith in white women's colonial prowess. White women were proclaimed a natural imperial force, yet careful regulation and specific intervention were required for them to be so.

Girls' educational facilities aimed to foster and shape white female morality. In 1859 the Sisters of St Ann opened a school in Victoria that quickly dominated the field of female middle-class education. Anglicans, disturbed that 'the Roman Catholic Sisters of Mercy are the only persons here engaged in the education of girls of the better classes' opened the Angela College a year later. Stressing 'English habits, and feelings, and refinement, and above all, the pure, and sober, and evangelical religion of England's church'[84] and representing itself as a paragon of imperial rectitude, this school implicitly attacked the sisters' association with the colony's mixed-blood bourgeois. Yet Catholics and Anglicans agreed that the appropriate object of female education should be to emphasize morality, religion, and domesticity. In 1865 Governor Kennedy greeted the moving and renaming of the Anglican school with nation-building glee. 'No race of useful people could descend from any but good and virtuous mothers,' he argued.[85] Roman Catholic leaders offered analogous remarks when the sisters opened a new building in 1871, commenting that the convent school would provide an education that would make a woman 'both a useful member of society by her learning and acquirements and a virtuous mother of family, a blessing in the household, a source of joy and happiness in domestic life.'[86] Debates around the necessity of separate schooling for poor girls, however, suggest that this component of colonial discourse, like so many others, was always refracted through the lens of class.[87]

Charities, like schools, worked to produce a specific definition of imperial womanhood. As in the Asian contexts studied by Ann Laura Stoler, charities were founded because white female poverty was seen as an overt insult to colonial prestige. In 1865 the *British Colonist* argued that 'above all the melancholy sights in a new country is a number of indigent women who cannot obtain employment.'[88] Female charities were created in an effort to shelter the settler community from such 'melancholy sights.' In 1859 'a number of the ladies of Victoria' formed 'a Society for relieving the sick and clothing the naked.'[89] In 1864 the Female Aid Association began to offer indoor and outdoor relief specifically to indigent white women, who were apparently thought

Creating imperial womanhood: St Ann's School, Victoria, 1871.

worthy of special philanthropy.[90] These philanthropies formed a nucleus of the group responsible for opening Victoria's Female Infirmary. The arrival of two terminally ill women on the *Robert Lowe* in a community where no facility would accept indigent women provided the necessary motivation to create a special institution. 'The efforts which had been made in England with some success, to lessen the disproportion between the sexes in this country, made it the more necessary that we should not leave those who might fall sick upon their arrival friendless and homeless,' Edward Cridge noted.[91] The Female Infirmary opened in November 1864, with a sick ward, a lying-in ward, and two private rooms. Managed by the usual cast of do-gooding wives of local politicians, clergy, and businessmen, the infirmary was supported through limited government support and fund-raising efforts like bazaars and benefit concerts. In 1868 the Female Infirmary amalgamated with the Royal Hospital, although 'the ladies' continued to pay for 'their' patients.[92]

Charities worked to produce a certain model of colonial womanhood in two separate, but related ways. By giving gender and race specific relief, the infirmary and the association ensured that white women had access to a minimum standard of living and would thus not humiliate the community with their inappropriate poverty. With placing socially marginal women in one central space, the infirmary also limited poor, sick women's contact with the larger society. In doing so, the infirmary and the aid association also shaped white middle-class womanhood by providing bourgeois women a legitimate and non-threatening public role in the colonial project.

Like poverty, certain wage work was thought to be degrading for white women and the community as a whole. A campaign demanding that Victoria saloons hiring women be denied licences raged throughout 1863 and 1864. Barroom work was thought to degrade individual women and, like female poverty, further embarrass the striving white community. An opponent of waitresses presented preventing women's work in bars as an act of empire analogous to the female immigration movement:

> Besides all this it is an absolute reproach to society here that so many girls should be induced by high wages to enter an employment which has every tendency to blast their reputation and render them outcasts from the world. There is an absolute and great disproportion between the sexes in this country. There is a want of good steady industrious girls to furnish

virtuous wives for our men and make them something else than the reckless restless mortals so numerous on this coast. To supply this want must be one of the objects of any measure for the encouragement of emigration, and anything that will interfere with this end should be tabooed.[93]

Despite these claims and the eighty-page petition supporting them, saloons hiring women were licensed.[94]

Female morality and respectability was a crucial yet contested element of white self-definition in British Columbia. As symbols of the separateness and superiority of the white race, white women needed to be kept at elevated standards. Sometimes, schooling young women, creating charitable groups designed to aid indigent white women, and labouring to keep white women from certain trades was sufficient. At other times, more spectacular intervention was required to prop up this important colonial index. The case of Victoria's Mills sisters suggests how far the colonial state and some members of the white community were willing to go to preserve the image of white women. While unmarried, the three Mills sisters were otherwise exemplars of imperial womanhood: pious, respectable, and holding up their end of the racial bargain. They attended church regularly, and two of them kept a private school while the other laboured as a dressmaker. Dr John Ash, their physician, described them as 'industrious worthy people of excellent character.'[95] Yet something went deeply wrong for the Mills sisters in the autumn of 1869. According to Ash, Margaret, who had been ill for sometime, became 'furiously maniacal' and 'ran screaming into the street in a state of nudity followed by her sister.' The two women, by now 'raving mad,' were taken to the Victoria police station where Jane recovered, but Margaret 'subsided into a state of dementia.' Given the impropriety of keeping white women in gaol, they were sent home, where they were nursed by their sister Catherine.[96]

The white community was deeply and publicly concerned about the Mills sisters from the onset of their overt deviance. The Millses were respectable white women and thus bell-wethers for the white community as a whole. It was, the press worried, 'the saddest that has ever come under our notice, as they are women of education and highly reputable character and supported themselves by teaching. They worshipped at St John's Church.' The residence of white women at the local gaol was thought especially worrisome. The Millses' church offered to have the women 'taken to a private residence,' and the *British Colonist* agreed that the gaol was an inappropriate place for them.[97] Errant First Nations women and white men could be sent to gaol, but respectable white women required a different treatment.

Community concern intensified when the informal home-care program collapsed. Margaret did not improve, and, when Ash was called to examine her, she 'had a paroxysm of manic screaming, tearing her clothes, and trying to get away from the house to the waterside (where she would probably have tried to drown herself).' Ash recommended that she be removed from the family home and that the colonial government maintain her at the nearest asylum, in Stockton, California. After a brief and unsuccessful search for relatives willing to support Margaret, the government agreed to pay her travelling costs and half of her maintenance fees.[98]

By any estimation, this was a generous offer in a colony with no public asylum and where hospitals and schools were supported only with great reluctance. But the prospect of respectable white women in gaol or screaming naked in the streets was enough to send the most tight-fisted state into generous action. Not only did they agree to Ash's initial proposal, but they proved remarkably willing to meet the Millses' needs as they defined them. The Millses, unwilling to entrust Margaret to strangers, rejected the original plan. 'They cannot be made to believe that the removal of their sister to a place where they could not visit her, and where she would be in the charge of strangers could be more beneficial to her than their own constant and devoted care,' wrote an irritated Ash. One had given up her job, the other proposed to sell her furniture and sewing machine, and they planned to support themselves by washing. In keeping with their generosity, the colonial government agreed when Ash suggested they support them directly, allocating 100 dollars, or a remarkable one-fifth of the annual colonial budget for charitable expenses, to the Millses' household.[99]

But generosity did not solve the problem. A few months later, the British Colonist reported that 'the hallucinations have returned,' and the two sisters were 'impressed with the one ruling idea that everybody with whom they came in contact is trying to poison them.' Worse, Catherine succumbed to the family malady, becoming 'violently insane' and accusing 'the wives of many respectable citizens with poisoning her.'[100] The final collapse of the Mills family proved troubling enough to the fragile identity of colonial Victoria to lead to institutional action. Local officials finally created a facility designed especially to cope with the Millses and women like them. In June of 1871 they proudly proclaimed that 'a temporary lunatic Asylum for Females has been fitted up in the Victoria Prison, under the charge of a Female Keeper.' Flora Ross, a mixed-blood woman, was hired as their keeper, a post she would maintain after a separate asylum was built.[101]

Catherine, Margaret, and Jane Mills tell us much about the history of white women in colonial British Columbia, about the power of colonial discourse and its profound limits. The white community's extensive, vigilant, and generous efforts to create a solution as respectable as the 'insane ladies' shows how white women served as a beacon for racial pride and suggests the lengths to which the beleaguered colonial community was willing to go to protect it. Yet the sad lives of the Millses also suggests the very real hollowness of the rhetoric that surrounded white women in colonial contexts. Despite images of merry backwoods heterosexuality, all three Mills women supported themselves with badly paid wage labour, apparently untouched by the famously favourable marriage market. Ironically, it was the Millses' independence and relative poverty that rendered them so needful of colonial protection and largesse. The Mills sisters, so much a part of colonial visions of white womanhood and so far from them, expose some of the profound tensions that surrounded white women in British Columbia.

The 'Unspeakable Benefit' Reconsidered

Despite the efforts to manage white women through schools, charities, and individual regulation, white women's behaviour departed significantly from representations of white women in imperial discourse. It is thus not surprising that local observers frequently expressed disappointment with white women's performance. Certainly some critics had always doubted whether assisted female immigration was a useful way of building the colony and constructed it as generative of more, rather than less, immorality. As early as 1859 the *Weekly Victoria Gazette* criticized a proposal of white female immigration, arguing that 'we know not whether to weep most at its ignorance, or rejoice at its innocence.' The only women the colony would attract, they thought, would be 'the outcast and degraded.'[102] The *Victoria Press* took umbrage at the calculation that underpinned female immigration. 'To bring down matrimony to a commercial speculation,' it wrote, 'is a scheme of philosophy that will not be long in destroying the "venerable" nature of the "institution," or sapping the foundation of a healthy society.'[103]

The experience of white female migration in the 1860s fuelled these doubts. Especially when discussing the *Tynemouth* and *Robert Lowe*, writers were profoundly dismayed with the immigrants' failure to live up to the standards white women were supposed to represent. The *British Columbian* commented that a number of women could 'fairly attribute their ruin' to the *Tynemouth*.[104] Some thought that the failure of these working-class women to meet the standards of colonial discourse could be blamed largely on the emigration agencies' selection process. Tal. O Eifion claimed that patron Angela Burdett Coutts lacked judgment in 'her consignment of girls for miners' wives.'[105] Others blamed the flawed character of immigration schemes, arguing that the women were 'treated on passage out with as much consideration as a drove of swine,' and hoped that future migrants would be 'religiously guarded from the officious "meddling and muddling" of the pseudo-philanthropic semi-religious immigration societies, and their committees, agents, or friends, who busied themselves in the dispatch of the emigrant steamships Robert Lowe and Tynemouth.'[106]

Some thought it was British Columbian social life, not the emigration process, that ruined the young white women. 'Of course in such a place as Victoria, crammed as it then was with perhaps the most dissipated and reckless set of men on earth, there was no lack of temptation to the new comers,' commented one critic.[107] What British Columbia contained in temptations it lacked in moral regulation. Explaining the immigrants' downfall, another wrote that 'the temptations of gold, rich trinkets and fine dresses ... is too great to be long resisted by those who have been brought up in penury and have no one man to constantly remind them how much more precious than gold and precious stones is a virtuous woman.'[108] Maria Rye would probably have agreed. In 1865, when visiting Australia, she explained to her colleague Barbara Leigh Bodichon that Britons underestimated the moral perils of colonies. Emigrants, she argued, needed to be firm, labour-loving women if they were to survive intact:

> I think it very hard for you who are at a distance from the colonies to understand them – they are so intensely good, & so intensely bad, according to the life made of them ... I still think to the full as strongly as when I left home that women – educated or not, may come here with the very greatest possible advantages to themselves – but I see even clearer than ever that they must be broken of a certain stamp. – women who dislike work, or who are not really steady in their principles are a thousand fold better off at home – there are scores of such women in Scotland, they are

not exactly idlers – not at all immoral – but they work because they *must* – & are virtuous because they are surrounded by scores of good homes & by inducements of strong every kind to go right – all this vanishes, or you waste all vanishes here – & the colonies [are] like the testing fire of the apostle.[109]

Even Rye, who was so key in promoting white women as able to save the colonies from themselves, privately worried that women were more often corrupted by them.

By the close of the colonial period, reformers' faith in the political usefulness of white female migration was profoundly shaken. Edmund Verney wrote to his father that the women were too obsessed with speedy marriages, easy labour, and high wages to be of much good. He preferred the young, guileless ones among the *Tynemouth's* women, who, it seems, had no personal agendas to conflict with his own. Verney deemed the entire affair 'anything but a cause for self-congratulation and pride.'[110] In 1872 Gilbert Sproat declared that his experience with three separate female immigration efforts had undermined his faith in the entire project. Sproat thought that the fundamental problem was that single female migration necessarily led to immorality. Women needed to be monitored by families to be anything other than a social menace. In general, Sproat thought, '*unmarried female* emigration does not lead to good results.' He continued that 'no right thinking observant person will advocate female immigration by sea voyage from Europe to British Columbia. It is unjust to the women, and upon the whole, is disadvantageous to the province.'[111]

By the early 1870s family migration was increasingly presented as the only way to solve the inevitable moral dilemmas presented by female immigration. 'The very delicate and difficult question of introducing single unmarried women into British Columbia might be partly solved by sending out a few, in [the] charge of the heads of families – the women being from the same district as the families, and thus having an addition[al] guard for their self-respect,' Sproat argued.[112] Assisted white female migration was problematic in large part because it suggested the possibility, and sometimes delivered the disturbing presence, of working-class female independence. Family migration, on the other hand, ensured that young women would not be allowed to run amok without adequate supervision. 'They would never leave the proper surveillance of their natural guardians,' wrote the *British Colonist* in 1869.[113] These arguments were premised on beliefs of male authority and on abiding assumptions about the nuclear family's status as the natural unit of social organization. Indeed, anything other than family groups, wrote one fan of family migration, produced an '*artificial assortment* of human beings.'[114] Just as it was difficult to square white women's lives with the grandiose promises of colonial discourse, it was difficult indeed to reconcile 'artificial assortments' with imperial visions of white womanhood.

In reconsidering the 'unspeakable benefit' of white women, commentators suggested some of the ways that white women's experience was shaped by, departed from, and challenged imperial discourse. In colonial British Columbia, white women's experience was defined by limited opportunities for labour and financial dependence. Rather than subverting prevailing gender divisions and distinctions, the colonial social context seems to have intensified them. That white women were routinely expected to serve as boundary markers between races and as symbols of imperial authority further entrenched these connections between white women, race, and respectability. While white women reaped power from these connections, they were also isolated by them. Perhaps more significantly, white women, like their male counterparts, frequently failed to live up to this discourse, and in doing so, exposed some of the salient limits of colonial representations. Indeed, the tendency of white women to depart from definitions of colonial womanhood led to regulatory schemes dedicated to fostering normative standards of whiteness and femininity. Even with such efforts, commentators were usually disappointed with the performance of white women who, despite promises, did not succeed in creating an orderly white settler society. White women were hardly an 'unspeakable benefit' to British Columbia's colonial project but neither were they wholly outside of it.

Conclusion:
Gender, Race, and Our Years on the
Edge of Empire

Our years on the edge of empire were dominated by a protracted and many-pronged effort to reconstruct British Columbia as a white society. This effort was premised on powerful and overlapping critiques of both First Nations and settler society. Dispossession and settlement were not discrete processes: they were mutually dependent and deeply intertwined. Marginalizing First Nations and fostering white society were two sides of one colonial coin, and it is gender that makes their entwined character most clear. Examining the place of gender in British Columbia's colonial project has implications for how we understand British Columbia's past and its present. For historians, these years on the edge of empire suggest the significance of imperialism to British Columbia history and the importance of gender to this and other colonial projects. For British Columbians, especially white ones, the connections between gender, race, and colonial society raised between 1849 and 1871 suggest the necessity of rethinking our fraught relationship to race and place.

British Columbia's problems were the empire's problems. The social history of mid-nineteenth-century British Columbia cannot be adequately understood unless we approach it as a chapter in the international history of imperialism. Mid-nineteenth-century settlers spoke of themselves, their neighbours, and their place using the language of imperialism: they were a civilized and white people surrounded by savage Indians in an empty and undeveloped place that could be transformed into an exemplary British colony. As a diverse body of work usually lumped together under the awkward rubric of 'post-structural' or 'post-modern' theory reminds us, language counts. The language of colonial British Columbia suggests the centrality of imperialism to that society. There was nothing natural or destined about a patch of northwestern North America becoming an outpost of British empire: to the extent it became one demands and deserves our self-conscious explication. This task is eased considerably by the development of a rich literature on colonial and postcolonial societies that suggests the important connections between local colonial projects and empire writ large.

While British Columbia is imperial history, it is hardly an example of imperialism's unmitigated success. The many and varied efforts to transform British Columbia from a First Nations territory to a white settler colony do not suggest imperial triumph as much as they hint at imperial vulnerability. Much of this vulnerability stemmed from the active resistance of British Columbia's large First Nations population. Colonial weakness also was generated by the conflicts encoded in imperialism's very structure. Empires were designed and promulgated in the name of high-minded ideals and responsibilities and in the interests of power and money. Yet they were practically enforced by large bodies of men whose commitment to colonialism's putative aims was always different and sometimes weak. Throughout the imperial world, officials debated how unruly lots of unattached soldiers, miners, and other working-class men could be transformed into suitable representatives of their race, fit to rule over their racial inferiors. In French Indochina and the Dutch Indies, as Ann Laura Stoler has demonstrated, poor white migration was restricted and *petit blancs* regulated,[1] while in British India, an elaborate system of regulated prostitution was inaugurated around military cantonments.[2] Reformers proffered different solutions in British Columbia. There, they tackled the sharpest symbols of colonial difference by working to regulate the rough homosocial culture that flourished in the colony's backwoods, transforming the many conjugal relationships forged between First Nations women and settler men, tinkering with land and immigration policies, and, ultimately, importing white women.

However various and constant, these efforts did not succeed in transforming British Columbia into the orderly white-settler colony that so dominated settler dreams. As Tina Loo has wisely commented, historians of Aboriginal-white relations have 'been forced to grapple with two countervailing pressures: the need, on the one hand, to acknowledge Aboriginal resistance and agency, and the need, on the other, to recognize their subjugation.'[3] Colonialism was both fragile and formidable in mid-nineteenth-century British Columbia. To be sure, imperialism was triumphant insofar as the years between 1849 and 1871 marked the onset of sustained European occupation, a political, economic, and cultural arrangement that has subsequently been persistently challenged but never defeated. However successful the colonial state was in conclusively asserting its authority, it fundamentally failed to recast the society it governed in its own image. First Nations resistance and persistence thwarted visions of a European-dominated agricultural society, as did the unwillingness of settlers to live up to the narrow roles accorded them in colonial discourse. Aboriginal people remained the majority of the population until the final years of the nineteenth century, and the small colonial settlements continued to depart from the norms and values of mainstream Anglo-American society.

Recognizing the significance of colonialism to British Columbia history necessitates rethinking First Nations history and its relation to Canadian history as a whole. Canadian history as it has generally been articulated in the late twentieth century tends to neutralize colonialism by describing it as 'settlement' and subtly but pervasively implying that Aboriginal people ceased to be significant historical players sometime around 1812 in central Canada and 1886 in Western Canada. It is as if the ultimate success of the colonial project in Canada blinds us to its own history. First Nations stories are instead relegated to what we might call 'genre-Aboriginal history.' At best this scholarship offers sensitive cultural studies, while at worst it suspends the First Nations in an anthropological moment that, as Anne McClintock argues, situates non-Western people irrevocably outside of history.[4] A perhaps uniquely North American variation that persists in Canadian history textbooks is to associate First Nations people with the land, to insert them in discussions of landscape and geography, and in doing so, substitute the archeological moment for the anthropological one.

The frameworks through which historians have analysed First Nations people and their relationship to Canadian society need to be revised if we are to adequately comprehend societies like mid-nineteenth-century British Columbia. Its social history cannot be adequately accessed unless First Nations demographic dominance, social centrality, and political agency are recognized. To suggest that Aboriginal history is social history is not to deny either the cultural specificity of First Nations experience or Western historical methodology. There are profound limits on the extent to which a methodology premised on written records can capture the history of oral cultures. Work produced, in Himani Bannerji's words, 'solely within the parameter of neglect of the question of location and the colonized's history, language, and culture' is necessarily partial and profoundly flawed.[5] Non-Aboriginal historians like myself need not only to borrow the ethnohistorical methodologies being developed by scholars like Georges Sioui, but to recognize the limits as well as the benefits of research that is simultaneously cross-cultural and historical.[6] Doing so does not invalidate historical scholarship on First Nations society as much as it complicates it.

It is not First Nations history alone that deserves our critical rethinking. Analysing British Columbia history as colonial history also prompts a recognition and exploration of the history of whiteness. White people, like peoples of colour, were racialized, and the historical processes by which whiteness was constituted and empowered can and must be excavated. Yet, as Catherine Hall notes, because whiteness is a signifier of dominance and 'the dominant rarely reflect on their dominance in the ways that the subjected reflect on their subjection,'[7] it has rarely been the subject of serious investigation. The history of colonial British Columbia stands as a sharp example of how whiteness was far from given or salient. Whiteness was constructed, problematic, and fragile, an identity that was simultaneously created and destabilized by the backwoods experience. In First Nations territories and among a plural settler community, people both learned to be white and had their whiteness threatened. Whiteness was at once powerful and precarious. Exploring its dual character puts a signifier of dominance under the analytic lens usually reserved for subjection.

Colonialism was never about race alone. Gender was key to colonialism in British Columbia just as it was to the imperial world. It figured prominently both in the critique of British Columbia society and in that society's attempted remaking. The very processes of cultural contact were themselves literally and highly gendered. First Nations and settler usually met not as ungendered subjects but as men and women. The colonial society they built fostered gendered identities and relations that departed meaningfully from the norms and mores of dominant Anglo-American culture. White male homosocial culture and heterosexual relationships forged between First Nations women and settler men stand as special examples of the novelty of gender on this edge of empire. Gender was similarly prominent in the attempts to reconstruct British Columbia as an orderly white society. For many critics and reformers, homosocial culture and mixed-race relationships – and the notions of manliness and womanliness they contained – seemed special affronts to visions of imperial respectability. For them, the colony was not simply a poor fit with models of appropriate racial subjectivity and behaviour, but a place that fostered alternative and perhaps dangerous ways of being male, female, and sexual. Campaigns to bring metropolitan manliness to the backwoods, to reformulate or eradicate mixed-race relationships, and to create activist land and immigration policies were all attempts to alter gender. That these campaigns culminated in the importation of working-class women from Britain indicates the significance of white womanhood to the gendered history of colonial British Columbia.

But exploring the place of gender in British Columbia's colonial project means more than noting the existence or significance of women. It means, as historians of gender have now long attested, interrogating the significance of manhood as well as womanhood. Had masculinity been neither historical nor variable, the rich homosocial culture would never have developed in British Columbia's backwoods, nor would it have become the object of a spate of regulatory schemes. Nor, for that matter, would the fates of settler men connected to First Nations women have become the objects of such anxiety. Examining masculinity does not, however, necessarily mean a weakening of our commitment to critically analysing gendered power relations or relinquishing serious feminist scholarship for a hazy 'I've got gender, you've got gender' approach. Undertaking critical scholarship on masculinity, like whiteness, instead means exposing the deep connections between gender and race and power in a way that recognizes their historicity and interconnectedness.

In colonial British Columbia, gender derived its particular shape and significance not from its separateness but from its deep connections to race. As the growing international literature probing the entangled nature of gender, race, and imperialism suggests, it is as futile to speak of women or men as undifferentiated masses as it is to read contact and colonialism outside of the lens of gender. Colonial social organization and discourse ensured that what it meant to be a white woman or a First Nations woman was profoundly different. Gender was deeply racialized and indeed cannot be comprehended otherwise. In British Columbia, it was racialized in a way that often explicitly benefited white women, who were accorded a prestige and authority by virtue of their unique position within the colonial project. Recognizing the specificity of white womanhood, in British Columbia or elsewhere, is a small step in the larger effort to interrogate the salient limits on universalizing analyses of gender and patriarchy. False and ultimately dangerous notions of universal womanhood have informed Canadian gender history as much as they have underpinned other literatures. In response, we need what Ruth Frankenberg calls 'the reciprocal specification of *white* womanhood' as demanded by the rigorous examination by women of colour of the refraction of gender through race.[8]

To suggest that white women held a special if contested place in the construction of the local colonial project is not to blame the brutal enterprise of imperialism on a handful of relatively powerless settler women. A series of works have persuasively argued that, contrary to reputation, white women were not the 'ruin of empire,' destructive and petty agents bent on wrecking harmonious race relations in colonial contexts.[9] To suggest otherwise is to romanticize colonial experience before white women's arrival and to exaggerate white women's racism in the interest of absolving white men of their fundamental responsibility for imperialism. While these studies have been crucial in restoring women's place in colonial history, they have also, as both Margaret Jolly and Jane Haggis point out, minimized or indeed rendered invisible the politics of race and empire. 'In the ways in which white women have been brought to the fore of the historical and analytical stage,' writes Haggis, 'colonialism is no longer a problem of power, exploitation, and oppression, but rather of the gender identity of the rulers.'[10] Haggis's trenchant critique serves as an important caution for historians of white women and colonialism. While examining white women can problematize their privilege, it can also unwittingly reaffirm it by ignoring or minimizing white women's embeddedness in structures and practices of racial domination. Studies of white women in colonial contexts, indeed, can repeat some of the hoariest tropes of Western gendered wisdom by portraying white women as sensitive, kindly, benevolent, and suffering.

Without denying that white people's experience was profoundly gendered, historians need to recognize that white women were also racialized, and critically examine their relationships with people of colour and to the colonial projects. White women were not the 'ruin of empire,' but neither were they hapless, misunderstood, latent anti-racists. Rather, much like Marx's proverbial men, they made their own history, but not in circumstances of their own making. White women in colonial British Columbia were ordinary women imbued by others with a specific racial and social mission. Few explicitly challenged this mission, but few dutifully fulfilled it. Much like their male counterparts in the backwoods who tormented reformers by living a vision of white manhood that departed significantly from that promoted in mainstream nineteenth-century Anglo-American culture, white women in mid-nineteenth-century British Columbia frequently failed to live up to the roles colonial discourse assigned them. Their lives were dominated by work and dependence on men, and by a sometimes empowering and sometimes restricting place within colonial discourse that some embraced and others challenged. Acknowledging the combination of power and powerlessness that characterized their lives suggests some of the limits of the concept of 'agency' to describe the simultaneity of choices and constraints that characterizes so much of human history.

The issues of colonialism and the significance of gender to it did not conveniently disappear when British Columbia became a Canadian province in the summer of 1871. As much as British Columbia has persistently thwarted efforts to remake it in the name of Britannic order, settler British Columbia has persisted in asserting its own whiteness. In the mid-nineteenth century, claims to whiteness were articulated primarily against the First Nations majority. In the late-nineteenth and twentieth century, these claims to whiteness were increasingly voiced in response to the presence of East Asians and, to a lesser extent, South Asians. If Aboriginal presence suggested the frailty of British Columbia's colonial society, the plurality of the settler society seemed to imperil the effort to recast it in the name of Britishness and whiteness. British Columbia has struggled constantly against these perceived threats to prove to itself and others that it was, to borrow Patricia Roy's apt phrase, 'a white man's province.'[11]

The power, danger, and irony of these constant claims to whiteness lie in the fact that British Columbia was never 'a white man's province.' Its roots as a First Nations territory have never been successfully erased. From the plural colonial settlements of the 1860s to the land claims struggles of the 1990s, Aboriginal people have asserted their presence and territorial claims to the place we call British Columbia. The settler population has similarly belied aspirations to whiteness and, more especially, Britishness. British Columbian colonial settlements were never 'little Englands.' They were diverse, hybrid collections of humans drawn, in varying degrees, from East Asia, Europe, Australasia, South Asia, the Americas, and the African diaspora.

The extent to which British Columbia was ever a 'white man's province' was achieved only with the help of massive Aboriginal depopulation and the draconian immigration policies of the last decades of the nineteenth and the first half of the twentieth centuries. British Columbia made the transition from a struggling colony to a secure province in the fin de siècle, the same years that saw disease and dispossession bring First Nations population to an all time low. The two phenomena are not unrelated. Nor is the fact that the heyday of British Columbia's whiteness between 1911 and 1961 tidily coincided with the zenith of anti-Asian legislation. As Veronica Strong-Boag points out, the years when British Columbia most closely resembled a 'white man's province' were the same ones when the so-called Gentleman's Agreement of 1908 limited Japanese immigration, the 'continuous journey' regulation excluded immigrants from the Indian subcontinent, the Chinese Exclusion Act of 1923 severely restricted Chinese immigration, and Japanese Canadians were interred and later dispersed in the name of the Second World War.[12] British Columbia's whiteness, to the extent that it was ever achieved, was accomplished through human action and history rather than destiny.

In contemporary newspapers and conversations, white British Columbians often long for the days when our society was unquestionably British, when our tea and crumpets were not disrupted by Asian neighbours or First Nations demands for land and recognition. When we do so, we long for a fiction of our own invention. When we argue that special immigration laws, language policies, or building codes are required to protect the 'Canadian' character of our communities, we both construct Canada in overtly racialized terms and misunderstand our own history. From the Komagata Maru of 1914 to the 'illegal' Chinese migrants of 1999, it has been ordinary people who have borne the painful brunt of our failure to understand our own society. When we fear the renegotiation – however imperfect – of British Columbia's relationship with First Nations people contained in the process that has produced the recent Nisga'a treaty, we deny the devastation of colonialism and our own complicity in it.[13] The fiction of a white British Columbia persists not because it accurately describes our history, but because it implicitly serves white interests and salves white consciousness.

White British Columbians need to rethink our relationship to the society we call home. Doing so involves critically re-accessing our history. If we look seriously at that history, we will not find a 'white man's province,' but a society where colonialism was constantly challenged both by First Nations presence and settlers' divergence with imperial ideals. As much as reformers consistently argued that British Columbia's future was as a respectable white settler colony anchored in orderly gendered and racial identities, British Columbia asserted its own distinct social organization. Evaluating and valuing the history of gender and race on this edge of empire helps us rethink not only our past, but the vision of the future it silently but so surely props up.

Notes

Introduction: Analysing Gender and Race on the Edge of Empire

1 See, for seminal texts, Joan Wallach Scott, *Gender and the Politics of History* (New York: Columbia University Press, 1988); Edward Said, *Orientalism* (New York: Vintage, 1975); Michel Foucault, *The History of Sexuality*, vol. 1, *An Introduction*, Robert Hurley, trans. (New York: Vintage, 1979). On the problem with the 'post-colonial,' see Anne McClintock, 'The Angel of Progress: Pitfalls of the Term "Post-Colonialism,"' *Social Text* 31–2 (1990) 84–98.

2 For studies that treat whiteness as a race, see David Roediger, *The Wages of Whiteness: Race and the Making of the American Working Class* (London: Verso, 1991); Vron Ware, *Beyond the Pale: White Women, Racism, and History* (London: Verso, 1992).

3 *Aboriginal People and Politics: The Indian Land Question in British Columbia, 1849–1989* (Vancouver: UBC Press, 1990) xi.

4 Frankenberg writes: 'I am uncomfortable with the term "mixed" in relation to race, because it seems to found notions of racial identity on terms that are not only biological rather than social, political, or historical, but also *simplistically* biological. However, I am at a loss to think of an adequate alternative.' Ruth Frankenberg, *White Women, Race Matters: The Social Construction of Whiteness* (Minneapolis: University of Minnesota Press, 1993) 126.

5 Where to locate British Columbia is an old historiographic problem. See Allan Smith, 'The Writing of British Columbia History,' and Barry M. Gough, 'The Character of the British Columbia Frontier,' in W. Peter Ward and Robert A.J. McDonald, eds., *British Columbia: Historical Readings* (Vancouver: Douglas and McIntyre, 1981).

6 Cole Harris, *The Resettlement of British Columbia: Essays on Colonialism and Geographical Change* (Vancouver: UBC Press, 1997) xi.
7 George F.G. Stanley, *The Birth of Western Canada: A History of the Riel Rebellions* (Toronto: University of Toronto Press, 1960 [1936]).
8 Ann Laura Stoler and Frederick Cooper, 'Between Metropole and Colony: Rethinking a Research Agenda,' in Frederick Cooper and Ann Laura Stoler, eds., *Tensions of Empire: Colonial Cultures in a Bourgeois World* (Berkeley: University of California Press, 1997) 4–11.
9 Nicholas Thomas, *Colonialism's Culture: Anthropology, Travel, and Government* (Princeton: Princeton University Press, 1994) 104. Also see John and Jean Comaroff, *Ethnography and the Historical Imagination* (Boulder, CO: Westview Press, 1992).
10 Antoinette Burton, *Burdens of History: British Feminists, Indian Women, and Imperial Culture, 1865–1915* (Chapel Hill: University of North Carolina Press, 1994); Catherine Hall, *White, Male, and Middle Class: Explorations in Feminism and History* (London: Routledge, 1991); Anne McClintock, *Imperial Leather: Race, Gender, and Sexuality in the Colonial Conquest* (New York: Routledge, 1995); Mrinalini Sinha, *Colonial Masculinity: The 'Manly Englishman' and the 'Effeminate Bengali' in the Late Nineteenth Century* (Manchester: Manchester University Press, 1995); Ann Laura Stoler, *Race and the Education of Desire: Foucault's History of Sexuality and the Colonial Order of Things* (Durham: Duke University Press, 1995).
11 Ruth Pierson, 'Introduction,' in Ruth Roach Pierson and Nupur Chaudhuri, eds., *Nation, Empire, and Colony: Historicizing Gender and Race* (Bloomington and Indianapolis: University of Indiana Press, 1998) 2.
12 See, for Canadian examples, Joy Parr, *The Gender of Breadwinners: Men, Women, and Change in Two Industrial Towns, 1880–1950* (Toronto: University of Toronto Press, 1990); Mark Steven Rosenfeld, '"She Was a Hard Life": Work, Family, Community Politics, and Ideology in the Railway Ward of a Central Ontario Town, 1900–1960,' PhD Dissertation, York University, 1990; Steven Penfold, '"Have You No Manhood in You?": Gender and Class in the Cape Breton Coal Towns, 1920–1926,' *Acadiensis* 13:2 (Spring 1994) 21–44; Madge Pon: 'Like a Chinese Puzzle: The Construction of Chinese Masculinity in *Jack Canuck*,' in Joy Parr and Mark Rosenfeld, eds., *Gender and History in Canada* (Toronto: Copp Clark, 1996).
13 For general discussions see Joy Parr, 'Gender History and Historical Practice,' *Canadian Historical Review* 76:3 (Sept. 1995) 354–76; Gail Cuthbert Brandt: 'Postmodern Patchwork: Some Recent Trends in the Writing of Women's History in Canada,' *Canadian Historical Review* 72:4 (Dec. 1991) 441–70. For the debate, see Joan Sangster, 'Beyond Dichotomies: Re-

Assessing Gender History and Women's History in Canada,' *Left History*
3:1 (Spring/Summer 1995) 109–21 and responses by Karen Dubinsky and
Lynne Marks, Franca Iacovetta and Linda Kealey, Steven Penfold and
Sangster in *Left History* 3:2 and 4:1 (Fall 1995 and Spring 1996).

14 This is a point made in Kathryn McPherson, Cecilia Morgan, and Nancy
M. Forestell, 'Introduction: Conceptualizing Canada's Gendered Pasts,' in
Kathryn McPherson, Cecilia Morgan, and Nancy M. Forestell, eds.,
Gendered Pasts: Historical Essays in Femininity and Masculinity in Canada
(Toronto: Oxford University Press, 1999).

15 Hazel V. Carby, 'White Woman Listen! Black Feminism and the Boundaries
of Sisterhood,' in Centre for Contemporary Cultural Studies, ed., *The
Empire Strikes Back: Race and Racism in 70s Britain* (London: Huchinson,
1983) 232. Also see Himani Bannerji, 'But Who Speaks for Us? Experience
and Agency in Conventional Feminist Paradigms,' in *Thinking Through:
Essays on Feminist, Marxism, and Anti-Racism* (Toronto: Women's Press,
1995); Chandra Mohantry, 'Under Western Eyes: Feminist Scholarship and
Colonial Discourse,' *Feminist Review* 30 (Autumn 1988) 61–88.

16 See Bettina Bradbury, 'Women's History and Working-Class History,'
Labour / Le Travail 19 (Spring 1987) 23–43; Bettina Bradbury, 'Women and
the History of Their Work in Canada: Some Recent Books,' *Journal of
Canadian Studies* 28:3 (Fall 1993) 159–78; Craig Heron, 'Towards Synthesis
in Canadian Working-Class History: Refections on Bryan Palmer's Rethinking,' *Left History* 1:1 (Spring 1993) 109–21.

17 See Sarah Carter, *Capturing Women: The Manipulation of Cultural Imagery in
Canada's Prairie West* (Montreal and Kingston: McGill-Queen's University
Press, 1997); Ruth Roach Pierson, 'Experience, Difference, Dominance and
Voice in the Writing of Canadian Women's History,' in Karen Offen, Ruth
Roach Pierson, and Jane Rendall, eds., *Writing Women's History: Interna-
tional Perspectives* (Bloomington: Indiana University Press, 1991); Ruth
Roach Pierson, 'Colonization and Canadian Women's History,' *Journal of
Women's History* 4:2 (Fall 1992) 134–56.

18 Tina Loo, *Making Law, Order and Authority in British Columbia, 1821–1871*
(Toronto: University of Toronto Press, 1994); Elizabeth Vibert, *Traders' Tales:
Narratives of Cultural Encounters in the Columbia Plateau, 1807–1846* (Nor-
man and London: University of Oklahoma Press, 1997); Harris, *The Reset-
tlement of British Columbia*; Kay Anderson, *Vancouver's Chinatown: Racial
Discourse in Canada, 1875–1980* (Montreal and Kingston: McGill-Queen's
University Press, 1991); Christopher Bracken, *The Potlatch Papers: A Colonial
Case History* (Chicago: University of Chicago Press, 1997).

19 See Jackie Lay, 'To Columbia on the Tynemouth: The Emigration of Single

Women and Girls in 1862,' in Barbara Latham and Cathy Kess, eds., *In Her Own Right: Selected Essays on Women's History in B.C.* (Vancouver: Camosun College, 1980); Jacqueline Gresko, '"Roughing it in the Bush" in British Columbia: Mary Moody's Pioneer Life in New Westminster 1859–1863,' in Barbara Latham and Roberta Pazdro, eds., *Not Just Pin Money: Selected Essays on the History of Women's Work in British Columbia* (Victoria: Camosun College, 1984); Sylvia Van Kirk, 'A Vital Presence: Women in the Cariboo Gold Rush, 1862–1875,' in Gillian Creese and Veronica Strong-Boag, eds., *British Columbia Reconsidered: Essays on Women* (Vancouver: Press Gang, 1992). Also see special issue of *BC Studies*, 105/106 (Spring–Summer 1995).

20 Carol Cooper: 'Native Women of the Northern Pacific Coast: An Historical Perspective, 1830–1900,' *Journal of Canadian Studies* 27:4 (Winter 1992–3) 44–75; Jo-Anne Fiske, 'Colonization and the Decline of Women's Status: The Tsimshian Case,' *Feminist Studies* 17:3 (Fall 1991) 509–36; Margaret Whitehead, '"A Useful Christian Woman": First Nations Women and Protestant Missionary Work in British Columbia," *Atlantis* 18:1–2 (1994) 142–66; Jean Barman, 'Taming Aboriginal Sexuality: Gender, Power, and Race in British Columbia, 1850–1900,' *BC Studies* 115/116 (Autumn/Winter 1997–8) 237–66; Michael Harkin, 'Engendering Discipline: Discourse and Counterdiscourse in the Methodist–Heiltsuk Dialogue,' *Ethnohistory* 43:4 (Fall 1996) 642–61.

21 See Nellie de Bertrand Lugrin, *The Pioneer Women of Vancouver Island* (Victoria: Canadian Women's Press Club of Victoria, 1924); Elizabeth Forbes, *Wild Roses at Their Feet: Pioneer Women of Vancouver Island* (Vancouver: British Columbia Centennial '71 Committee, 1971); Marnie Anderson, *Women of the West Coast: Then and Now* (Sidney, BC: Sand Dollar Press, 1993).

22 See Robin Fisher, 'Contact and Trade, 1774–1849,' in Hugh J.M Johnson, ed., *The Pacific Province* (Vancouver: Douglas and McIntyre: 1996).

23 Cole Harris, 'Towards a Geography of White Power in the Cordilleran Fur Trade,' *Canadian Geographer* 39:2 (1995) 132.

24 Tennant, *Aboriginal Peoples and Politics*, 3. For a discussion of the earlier estimate, see Wilson Duff, *The Indian History of British Columbia*, vol. 1, *The Impact of the White Man* (Victoria: Province of British Columbia, 1969) 38.

25 Jean Barman, *The West beyond the West: A History of British Columbia* (Toronto: University of Toronto Press: 1991) 38.

26 Tennant, *Aboriginal Peoples and Politics*, 6–9; Fisher, 'Contact and Trade,' 48–9.

27 Jack Little, 'The Foundations of Government,' in Johnson, ed., *Pacific*

Province, 68; James E. Hendrickson, 'The Constitutional Development of Colonial Vancouver Island and British Columbia,' in Ward and McDonald, eds., *British Columbia: Historical Readings*, 246.

28 Richard Mackie, 'The Colonization of Vancouver Island, 1849–1858,' *BC Studies* 96 (Winter 1992–3) 40.

29 Alfred Waddington, *The Fraser Mines Vindicated, or, the History of Four Months* (Victoria: De Cosmos, 1858) 16.

30 Little, 'The Foundations of Government,' in Johnson, ed., *Pacific Province*, 73–4.

31 In W. Kaye Lamb, ed., 'The Census of Vancouver Island, 1855,' *British Columbia Historical Quarterly* 4:1 (1940) 52.

32 The 'settled' population also included urban Aboriginal people. See Edward Mallandaine: *First Victoria Directory: Third [Fourth] Issue, and British Columbia Guide* (Victoria: Mallandaine, 1871) 94–5.

33 Sharon Meen, 'Colonial Society and Economy,' in Johnson, ed., *The Pacific Province*, 113. Also see Duff, *The Indian History*, 42.

34 Barman, *The West beyond the West*, 129. Also see Robert Galois and Cole Harris, 'Recalibrating Society: The Population Geography of British Columbia in 1881,' *Canadian Geographer* 38:1 (1994) 37–53.

35 'Letter From the Mouth of the Quesnelle,' *British Colonist*, 9 Nov. 1865.

36 Daiva Stasiulis and Nira Yuval-Davis, 'Introduction: Beyond Dichotomies – Gender, Race, Ethnicity and Class in Settler Societies,' in Daiva Stasiulis and Nira Yuval-Davis, eds., *Unsettling Settler Societies: Articulations of Gender, Race, Ethnicity and Class* (London: Sage, 1995) 21.

37 See Paul A. Phillips, 'Confederation and the Economy of British Columbia,' in W. George Shelton, ed., *British Columbia and Confederation* (Victoria: University of Victoria: 1967) 57.

38 Meen, 'Colonial Society and Economy,' 111.

39 See Mackie, 'The Colonization of Vancouver Island'; Sylvia Van Kirk, 'Tracing the Fortunes of Five Founding Families of Victoria,' *BC Studies*, 115/116 (Autumn/Winter 1997–8) 148–79.

40 Their critique of the HBC 'family compact,' was not new. See Loo, *Making Law, Order and Authority*, chapter 2.

41 See Lamb, ed., 'The Census of Vancouver Island, 1855,' 54–5. On the taking of this census, see James Douglas to John Russel, 21 Aug. 1855, Colonial Office, Vancouver Island Original Correspondence, CO 305/6, University of British Columbia Library (hereafter UBCL) Reel R288: 4.

42 See 'British Columbia – Blue Books of Statistics &c 1870,' 135–6. See Mallandaine, *First Victoria Directory*, 95 for what seems to be a breakdown of these figures.

43 'Later from Cariboo,' *British Columbian*, 6 Jan. 1864.
44 Great Britain, Colonial Office, 'British Columbia – Blue Books of Statistics, 1861–1870,' BCA, CO 64/1, Reel 626A.
45 James Robb to Colonial Secretary, 2 March 1865, 'Colonial Correspondence,' BCA, GR 1372, Reel B-1361.
46 Lux, '"We're All Off in the Spring to Cariboo,"' *British Columbian*, 14 Nov. 1861.

1 'Poor Creatures Are We without Our Wives': White Men and Homosocial Culture

1 Charles Hayward, 'Diary 1862,' British Columbia Archives (hereafter BCA), Reel A-741.
2 Leonore Davidoff and Catherine Hall, *Family Fortunes: Men and Women of the English Middle Class, 1780–1850* (Chicago: University of Chicago Press: 1987); Anthony E. Rotundo, 'Body and Soul: Changing Ideals of American Middle-Class Manhood,' *Journal of Social History* 16:4 (1983) 23–38; Wally Seccombe, 'Patriarchy Stabilized: The Construction of the Male Breadwinner Wage Norm in Nineteenth-Century Britain,' *Social History* 2:1 (Jan. 1986) 53–76.
3 Robert J.C. Young, *Colonial Desire: Hybridity in Theory, Culture and Race* (London: Routledge, 1995) chapter 4; Graham Dawson, *Soldier Heroes: British Adventure, Empire, and the Imagining of Masculinities* (London: Routledge, 1994); Mrinalini Sinha, *Colonial Masculinity: The 'Manly Englishman' and the 'Effeminate Bengali' in the Late Nineteenth Century* (Manchester: Manchester University Press, 1995).
4 Mary Poovey, *Uneven Developments: The Ideological Work of Gender in Mid-Victorian England* (Chicago: University of Chicago Press: 1988).
5 John Emmerson, *Voyages, Travels, and Adventures by John Emmerson of Wolsingham* (Durham, England: Wm. Ainsley, 1865) 150; Anonymous, *The Handbook of British Columbia and Emigrant's Guide to the Gold Fields* (London: W. Oliver [1862]) 70.
6 Capt. C.E. Barrett-Lennard, *Travels in British Columbia: With the Narrative of a Yacht Voyage Round Vancouver's Island* (London: Hurst and Blackett, 1862) 170.
7 Vancouver Island, Police and Prisons Department, Esquimalt, 'Charge Book 1862–1866,' BCA, GR 0428.
8 Beta Mikron [William Coutts Keppel, Earl of Albermarle], 'British Columbia and Vancouver's Island,' *Fraser's Magazine* 63 [1858] 499.
9 Phillip Nind to Colonial Secretary, in James Douglas to Duke of Newcastle,

2 May 1861, Great Britain, Colonial Office, British Columbia Original Correspondence (hereafter CO), National Archives of Canada (hereafter NAC), MG 11, CO 60/10, Reel B-84.

10 Captain P. Hankin, 'Memoirs' (Transcript), BCA, Add Mss E/B/H19A, 51.

11 Jock Phillips, *A Man's Country? The Image of the Pakeha Male: A History* (Auckland: Penguin, 1987) 27.

12 'A Glimpse of Cariboo,' *British Colonist*, 24 Aug. 1866.

13 'Diary of R.H. Alexander Commencing Tuesday, April 29th, 1862' (Transcript), City of Vancouver Archives (hereafter CVA) Add Mss 246, File 4, 50.

14 Edmund Hope Verney to Harry Verney, 16/01/1862, in Allan Pritchard, ed., *Vancouver Island Letters of Edmund Hope Verney, 1862–1865* (Vancouver: UBC Press, 1996) 70.

15 J.R. Wright to Amos Wright, 23 Sept. 1866, 'Correspondence of Jessie Hassard Wright,' BCA, Add Mss 1976.

16 Rev. Ebenezer Robson, 'Notes from the Diary of Rev. Ebenezer Robson, D.D., Pioneer Wesleyan Missionary at Fort Hope, B.C., from Mar. 12 to May 13 1860' (Transcript), BCA, Add Mss H/D/R57/.2A, 2.

17 John Keast Lord, *At Home in the Wilderness: What to Do There and How to Do It* (London: Robert Hardiwcke, 1876).

18 E.E. Delavault and Isabel McInnes, ed. and trans., 'Letter from Charles Major, dated Fort Hope, Sept. 20, 1859,' in 'Two Narratives of the Fraser River Gold Rush,' in *British Columbia Historical Quarterly* (hereafter *BCHQ*) 1 (July 1941) 230.

19 Eric Duncan, *From Shetland to Vancouver Island: Recollections of Seventy-Five Years* (Edinburgh: Oliver and Boyd, 1937) 138–9.

20 Mirabile Dictu, 'Bush Life,' *British Colonist*, 27 Mar. 1865.

21 Dorothy Blakey Smith, ed., 'Henry Guillod's Journal of a Trip to Cariboo, 1862,' *BCHQ* 19 (July–Oct. 1955) 206.

22 Vera Angier, 'Are Men the Best Cooks?' *The Beaver* 290 (Autumn 1959) 52–3.

23 Blair, 'Diary,' 126.

24 Emmerson, *Voyages, Travels, and Adventures*, 39.

25 William G. Cox to Colonial Secretary, 9 April 1864, in Frederick Seymour to Duke of Newcastle 10 June 1864, NAC, MG 11, CO 60/18, Reel B-911.

26 R.C. Lundin Brown, *Klatsassan, And Other Reminiscences of Missionary Life In British Columbia* (London: Society for Promoting Christian Knowledge, 1873) 185.

27 R.J. Dundas, in J.J. Halcombe, *The Emigrant and the Heathen, or, Sketches of Missionary Life* (London: Society for Promoting Christian Knowledge [1870?]) 215.

28 Rev. William Burton Crickmer to Anonymous, 1 July 1860, 'Letters' (Transcript from original held at BCA), Anglican Church of Canada, Archives of the Diocese of New Westminster / Ecclesiastical Province of British Columbia, Vancouver School of Theology, University of British Columbia (hereafter ADNW / EPBC), PSA 50, File 3, 9.

29 'The Miners Ten Commandments,' *Cariboo Sentinel*, 8 Sept. 1866. This originated in California in 1853.

30 Lord, *At Home in the Wilderness*, 1.

31 R.H. Pidcock, 'Adventures in Vancouver Island 1862' (Transcript), BCA, Add Mss 728, vol. 4a, 10.

32 Emmerson, *Voyages, Travels, and Adventures*, 80.

33 Hayward, 'Diary,' np.

34 In Richard Arthur Preston, ed., *For Friends at Home: A Scottish Emigrant's Letters from Canada, California, and the Cariboo, 1844–1864* (Montreal and Kingston: McGill-Queen's University Press, 1979) 302.

35 See Emmerson, *Voyages, Travels, and Adventures*, 64.

36 Hayward, 'Diary,' n.p.

37 Andrew J. Rotter, '"Matilda for Gods Sake Write": Women and Families on the Argonaut Mind,' *California History* 63:2 (Summer 1979) 128–41.

38 George Hills, 'Journal 1836–1861' (Transcript), ADNM / EPBC, MS 65a, PSA 57, 411.

39 'The Cariboo Hospital,' *Cariboo Sentinel*, 21 May 1866.

40 Dundas in Halcombe, *The Emigrant and the Heathen*, 205.

41 William Mark, *Cariboo: A True and Correct Narrative to the Cariboo Gold Diggings, British Columbia* (Stockton: W.M. Wright, 1863) 29; Emmerson, *Voyages, Travels, and Adventures*, 56.

42 Robert Stevenson, 'Diary' and 'Miscellaneous Materials relating to,' BCA, Add Mss 315.

43 Louis LeBourdais, 'Billy Barker of Barkerville,' *BCHQ* 1:1 (1937) 167.

44 Nobody, 'Letter from Comox – Progress of the Settlement,' *British Colonist*, 4 Oct. 1867.

45 D.W. Higgins, *The Mystic Spring and Other Tales of Western Life* (Toronto: William Briggs, 1904) 56.

46 R. Byron Johnson, *Very Far West Indeed: A Few Rough Experiences on the North-West Pacific Coast* (n.p: 1985 [London: Sampson Low, Marston, Low & Searle, 1872]) 14.

47 Edgar Fawcett, *Some Reminiscences of Old Victoria* (Toronto: William Biggs, 1912) 20–1.

48 Dorothy Blakey Smith ed., *Lady Franklin Visits the Pacific Northwest: Being Extracts from the Letters of Miss Sophia Craycroft, Sir John Franklin's Niece,*

Feb. to April 1861 and April to July 1870 (Victoria: Provincial Archives of British Columbia Memoir No. XI, 1979) 71.

49 A Returned Digger, *The Newly Discovered Gold Fields of British Columbia*, 8th ed. (London: Darton and Hodge, 1862) 8.

50 Richard Charles Mayne, *Four Years in British Columbia and Vancouver Island* (London: John Murray, 1862; reprint, Toronto: S.R. Publishers, 1969) 350.

51 E. Anthony Rotundo, 'Romantic Friendship: Male Intimacy and Middle-Class Youth in the Northern United States, 1800–1900,' *Journal of Social History* 23:1 (Fall 1989) 1; Steven Maynard, 'Rough Work and Rugged Men: The Social Construction of Masculinity in Working-Class History,' *Labour / Le Travail* 23 (Spring 1989) 159–69; Carroll Smith-Rosenberg, 'The New Woman as Androgyne: Social Disorder and Gender Crisis, 1870–1939,' in *Disorderly Conduct: Visions of Gender in Victorian America* (New York: Oxford University Press, 1985).

52 'Legislative Council Proceedings,' *British Colonist*, 20 Mar. 1867.

53 Ann B. Scott to Edward Cridge, 1 June 1871, 'Edward Cridge, Correspondence Inward,' BCA, Add Mss 320, Box 1, File 4.

54 See correspondent re Hannah Jarman to Edward Cardwell, 28 July 1865, NAC, MG 11, CO 305/27, Reel B-249.

55 'Registration of Births, Deaths, and Marriages,' *British Colonist*, 16 Jan. 1863.

56 'Divorces,' *Cariboo Sentinel*, 25 Feb. 1871.

57 C. Sharp, 'A Glimpse of Cariboo,' *British Colonist*, 24 Aug. 1866.

58 'Letter from Williams Creek,' *British Colonist*, 25 June 1863.

59 See Jeffrey Weeks, 'Discourse, Desire and Sexual Deviance: Some Problems in a History of Homosexuality,' in *Against Nature: Essays on History, Sexuality and Identity* (London: Rivers Oram, 1991).

60 Watchman, '"Twaddling Sensations of Anonymous Writers,"' *British Colonist*, 2 Mar. 1866.

61 Higgins, *The Mystic Spring*, 35–6. Also see D.W. Higgins, *The Passing of a Race and More Tales of Western Life* (Toronto: William Briggs, 1905), esp. 'The Pork Pie Hat.'

62 A.F. Pemberton to Acting Colonial Secretary, 25 Feb. 1865, 'Colonial Correspondence,' BCA, GR 1372, Reel B-1394.

63 See Higgins, *The Passing of a Race*, 116; Edward Mallandaine, *First Victoria Directory; Comprising General Directory* (Victoria: Mallandaine, 1860) 26; 'Distinguished Arrival,' *Weekly Victoria Gazette*, 1 June 1859.

64 'John Butts Again,' *Vancouver Times*, 30 Mar. 1861; 'Police Court,' *Vancouver Times*, 17 Jan. 1865; 'Lodgings for the Remainder of the Season,' *Vancouver Times*, 4 Feb. 1865; 'Butts Again in Trouble' *Victoria Press*, 9 Apr. 1861;

'Street Cleaning,' *Victoria Press*, 9 Oct. 1861; 'Improving,' *Victoria Press*, 19 Oct. 1861; 'John Butts Once More,' *British Colonist*, 8 Apr. 1861; '"Necessity the Mother of Invention,"' *Victoria Press*, 3 June 1862; 'John Butts,' *Victoria Press*, 22 Aug. 1862.

65 'Turkey Stealing,' *Victoria Press*, 5 July 1861; Charles Bayley, 'Early life on Vancouver Island' (1878?) (Transcript), BCA, E/B/B34.2, 18.

66 'Lecture,' *Victoria Press*, 2 Apr. 1862; John Butts, 'Mr. Butts at the Temperance Meeting,' *Victoria Press*, 1 Oct. 1862; 'The Municipal Elections – Nomination Day,' *Vancouver Times*, 9 Nov. 1864. For complaints about treatment of Butts, see John Butts, 'Our Municipal Council,' *Victoria Press*, 14 Sept. 1862.

67 'Assault Case,' *Victoria Press*, 14 Apr. 1862.

68 'Sodomy,' *British Colonist*, 31 Jan. 1860; 'Police Court,' *British Colonist*, 2 Feb. 1860.

69 'Trial of John Butts,' *British Colonist*, 18 Feb. 1860.

70 See gaol records included in Aug. F. Pemberton to William A.G. Young, 7 Feb. 1860 and Aug. F. Pemberton to William A.G. Young, 13 Feb. 1860, BCA, 'Colonial Correspondence,' GR 1372, Reel B-1356.

71 Deposition of William Williams, 30 Jan. 1860, 'Minutes of Evidence, Police Court,' *R* v *John Butts*, 31 Jan. 1860, in British Columbia, Attorney General, 'Documents 1857–1966' (hereafter 'Attorney General Documents') BCA, GR 419, Box 1, File 1860/23.

72 Evidence of Thomas Cooper, 1 Feb. 1860; Evidence of Andrew Coyle, 2 Feb. 1860, 'Attorney General Documents,' BCA, GR 419, Box 1, File 1860/23.

73 Deposition of William M Dunham, 31 Jan. 1860, 'Attorney General Documents,' BCA, GR 419, Box 1, File 1860/23. On sex between men and working-class boys, see Steven Maynard, "Horrible Temptations": Sex, Men, and Working-Class Male Youth in Urban Ontario, 1890–1935,' *Canadian Historical Review* 78 (June 1997) 191–235.

74 Deposition of Francis Jackson, 31 Jan. 1860; 'Attorney General Documents, BCA, GR 419, Box 1, File 1860/23.

75 Dunham, 'Attorney General Documents,' BCA, GR 419, Box 1, File 1860/23.

76 'Trial of John Butts,' *British Colonist*, 18 Feb. 1860.

77 'Trial of John Butts,' *British Colonist*, 18 Feb. 1860; Untitled, *British Colonist*, 18 Feb. 1860.

78 Testimony of John Butts, 9 Feb. 1860, BCA, GR 419, Box 1, File 1860/23. The press reported that Butts said 'The whole charge is a conspiracy to get my house and lot from me.' See 'Trial of John Butts,' *British Colonist*, 18 Feb. 1860.

79 'Laying Low,' *British Colonist*, 18 Feb. 1860; 'Incorrigible,' *Victoria Press*, 4 June 1862; 'Police Court,' *Victoria Press*, 5 June 1862; 'In Again,' *Victoria Press*, 28 Oct. 1861; 'Not Incorrigible,' *Victoria Press*, 23 July 1862; 'Police Court,' *Victoria Press*, 19 Aug. 1862.

80 Untitled, *Vancouver Times*, 30 July 1865; 'Rouge and Vagabond,' *Vancouver Times*, 31 July 1865; 'John Butts,' *Vancouver Times*, 16 Aug. 1865; 'John Butts,' *British Colonist*, 14 Sept. 1866.

81 'Gone from Our Gaze,' *Cariboo Sentinel*, 10 Apr. 1866.

82 See Joseph Needham to Colonial Secretary, 1 Mar. 1866, 'Colonial Correspondence,' BCA, GR 1372, Reel B-1350; *R v Matthew Rasid*, 'Attorney General Documents,' BCA, GR 419, Box 5, File 1866/11; 'Assizes,' *British Colonist*, 22 Mar. 1865.

83 *R v Kingswell*, 'Attorney General Documents,' BCA, GR 419, Box 9, File 1870/24. This case is included in the '1870' file and case name, but the court documents included in this file are dated 1873.

84 Tina Loo, *Making Law, Order and Authority in British Columbia, 1821–1871* (Toronto: University of Toronto Press, 1993) esp. Chapters 3 and 6.

85 Ronald Hyam, *Empire and Sexuality: The British Experience* (Manchester: Manchester University Press, 1990) 212.

86 Robert J.C. Young, *Colonial Desire: Hybridity in Theory, Culture and Race* (London: Routledge, 1995) 25–6.

87 Julie Cruikshank, 'Images of Society in Klondikegold Rush Narratives: Skookum Jim and the discovery of Gold,' *Ethnohistory* 39:1 (Winter 1992) 20–41.

88 Tal. O Eifion, 'Our Moral, Social, and Political Condition,' *Cariboo Sentinel*, 28 Feb. 1867.

89 Paul Phillips, 'The Underground Economy: The Mining Frontier to 1920,' in Jean Barman and Robert A.J. McDonald, eds., *Readings in the History of British Columbia* (Richmond, BC: Open Learning Agency, 1989) 149.

90 Arthur N. Birch, Untitled, *British Columbia Government Gazette*, 5 Nov. 1864, NAC, MG 11, CO 63/1, Reel B-1488.

91 Major, 'Letter,' 231.

92 Hayward, 'Diary,' np.

93 Gail Bederman, *Manliness and Civilization: A Cultural History of Gender and Race in the United States, 1880–1917* (Chicago: University of Chicago Press, 1995).

94 George M. Grant, *Ocean to Ocean: Sandford Fleming's Expedition through Canada in 1872* (Toronto: James Cambell, 1873) 267.

95 James Douglas to John Packington, 11 Nov. 1852, University of British Columbia Library (hereafter UBCL), CO 305/3, Reel R288:1.

96 Robert Melrose, 'Diary, Aug. 1852–July 1857' (photostat), BCA Add Mss, E/B/M49.1A, 18.

97 James E. Hendrickson, ed., *Journals of the Colonial Legislatures of the Colonies of Vancouver Island and British Columbia, 1851–1871*, vol. 1, *Journals of the Council, Executive Council, and Legislative Council of Vancouver Island, 1851–1866* (Victoria: Provincial Archives of British Columbia, 1980) 14–15.

98 'Debating Class,' *British Colonist*, 1 Dec. 1866.

99 'The License Question,' *Victoria Press*, 4 July 1862; Irene Genevieve Marie Zaffaroni, 'The Great Chain of Being: Racism and Imperialism in Colonial Victoria, 1858–1871,' MA Thesis, University of Victoria, 1987, 129–30.

100 Johnson, *Very Far West Indeed*, 142.

101 'Lighthearted Prisoners,' *Victoria Press*, 6 May 1861.

102 *Report of the Columbia Mission, 1860*, 67.

103 Viscount Milton and W.B. Cheadle, *The North-West Passage by Land: Being the Narrative of an Expedition from the Atlantic to the Pacific* (London: Cassell, Petter, and Galpin, 1865) 359.

104 Carl Friesach, 'Extracts from *Ein Ausflug nach Britisch-Columbien im Jahre 1858*,' in Delavault and McInnes, 'Two Narratives,' 221–31.

105 In Dorothy Blakey Smith, ed. *The Reminiscences of Doctor John Sebastian Helmcken* (Vancouver: University of British Columbia Press, 1975) 208.

106 Pro Bono Publico, 'The Dance House,' *British Colonist*, 23 Dec. 1861.

107 Ephraim Evans, 'Rev. Dr. Evans on the Dance Houses,' *British Colonist*, 25 Dec. 1861.

108 Bard of the Lowhee, 'A Reminiscence of Cariboo Life,' *Cariboo Sentinel*, 14 Nov. 1868.

109 'Gambling in British Columbia,' *Weekly Victoria Gazette*, 1 June 1859.

110 *Report of the Columbia Mission 1860*, 45; Higgins, *The Passing of a Race*, 257–8.

111 Gunther Peck, 'Manly Gambles: The Politics of Risk on the Comstock Lode,' *Journal of Social History* 26:4 (Summer 1993) 714.

112 'The Prize Fight,' *Cariboo Sentinel*, 25 Oct. 1866.

113 David Peterson del Mar, *What Trouble I Have Seen: A History of Violence against Wives* (Cambridge: Harvard University Press, 1996) 21–3.

114 Matthew B. Begbie, 'Journey into the Interior of British Columbia, Communicated by the Duke of Newcastle, read Dec. 12 1859,' (np: nd) 247.

115 In George F.G. Stanley, ed., *Mapping the Frontier: Charles Wilson's Diary of the Survey of the 49th Parallel, 1858–1862, while Secretary of the British Boundary Commissions* (Toronto: Macmillian, 1970) 24.

116 Barrett-Lennard, *Travels in British Columbia*, 170.

117 Untitled, *Cariboo Sentinel*, 15 Dec. 1866.

118 Quoted in Capt. Fenton Aylmer, ed., *A Cruise in the Pacific: From the Log of a Naval Officer*, vol. 2 (London: Hurst and Blackett, 1860) 89.
119 Major, 'Letter,' 231.
120 Guillod, 'Journal,' 200.
121 Anonymous, *The New Government Colony: British Columbia and Vancouver Island: A Complete Hand-Book* (London: William Penney, 1858) 3.

2 'The Prevailing Vice': Mixed-Race Relationships

1 R.C. Lundin Brown, *British Columbia. The Indians and Settlers at Lillooet. Appeal for Missionaries* (London: R. Clay: Sons, and Taylor, 1870) 6, 7.
2 'Census,' *British Colonist*, 10 June 1868.
3 Mary Louise Pratt, *Imperial Eyes: Travel Writing and Transculturation* (London: Routledge, 1992) 4.
4 Ranya Green, 'The Pocahontas Perplex: The Image of Indian Women in American Culture,' in Ellen Carol DuBois and Vicki L. Ruiz, eds., *Unequal Sisters: A Multi-Cultural Reader in U.S. Women's History* (New York: Routledge, 1990); David D. Smits, 'The "Squaw Drudge": A Prime Index of Savagism,' *Ethnohistory* 29:4 (1982) 281–306.
5 Sarah Carter, *Capturing Women: The Manipulation of Cultural Imagery in Canada's Prairie West* (Montreal and Kingston: McGill–Queen's University Press, 1997) Chapter 5.
6 Willard E. Ireland, ed., 'Gold-Rush Days in Victoria, 1858–1859,' by James Bell, *British Columbia Historical Quarterly* (hereafter *BCHQ*) 12 (July 1948) 237. Emphasis in original.
7 'Notes From the Northwest,' *British Colonist*, 30 Oct. 1863.
8 Dorothy Blakey Smith, ed., 'The Journal of Arthur Thomas Bushby, 1858–1859,' in *BCHQ* 21 (1957–8) 122.
9 See, for instance, Matthew Macfie, *Vancouver Island and British Columbia: Their History, Resources, and Prospects* (London: Longman, Green, Longman, Roberts, and Green, 1865; reprint, Toronto: Coles Canadiana, 1972) 441–2.
10 Sitkum Siwash (Half-Coastal Aboriginal), 'Lines to a Klootchman,' *Weekly Victoria Gazette*, 30 Apr. 1859. Translations mine.
11 Terry Goldie, *Fear and Temptation: The Image of the Indigene in Canadian, Australian, and New Zealand Literatures* (Montreal and Kingston: McGill-Queen's University Press, 1989) 64.
12 John Keast, Lord, *The Naturalist in Vancouver Island and British Columbia* (London: Richard Bentley, 1866) vol. 1, 233.

13 J.B. Good to Sir, 8 June 1861, Society for the Propagation of the Gospel in Foreign Parts, 'Letters Received Columbia 1861–1867' (Transcript), British Columbia Archives (hereafter BCA), Add Mss H/A/So2, vol. 2, 8.

14 'Hard Up for A Drink,' *British Colonist*, 3 July 1862. Translation mine.

15 'Halo Shame,' *British Colonist*, 18 July 1865. Translation mine.

16 'How To Get Rid of the Troublesome Question,' *British Colonist*, 29 July 1862.

17 Thomas Crosby, *Among the An-ko-me-nums of the Pacific Coast* (Toronto: William Briggs, 1907) 62.

18 John Domer, *New British Gold-Fields: A Guide to British Columbia and Vancouver Island* (London: William Henry Angel, 1858) 26.

19 Erica Smith, '"Gentlemen, This Is No Ordinary Trial": Sexual Narratives in the Trial of the Reverend Corbett, Red River, 1863,' in Jennifer S.H. Brown and Elizabeth Vibert, eds., *Reading beyond Words: Contexts for Native History* (Peterborough, ON: Broadview Press, 1996)

20 T.F. Elliot to Arthur Birch, 9 Nov. 1866, in Frederick Seymour to the Earl of Carnarvon, 11 Jan. 1867, Great Britain, Colonial Office, British Columbia Original Correspondence (hereafter CO) BCA, GR 1486, CO 60/27, Reel B-1439.

21 Joseph W. Trutch, 'Memo,' 13 Jan. 1870, in A. Musgrave to Earl of Granville, 29 Jan. 1870, BCA, GR 1486, CO 60/38, Reel B-1448.

22 Dr Edward B. Bogg, 'Journal of Her Majesty's Hired Surveying Vessel, Beaver, 1863,' Public Records Office (hereafter PRO), ADM 101/276, 16-16a.

23 J.J. Halcombe, *The Emigrant and the Heathen, or, Sketches of Missionary Life* (London: Society for Promoting Christian Knowledge [1870?]) 238.

24 'New Westminster Charivari,' *British Colonist*, 14 Feb. 1864.

25 'Arrest of Street Walkers,' *British Colonist*, 8 May 1860.

26 Phillip Hankin, 'Memoirs' (Transcript), BCA, Add Mss E/B/H19A, 54. Translation mine.

27 See Frederick Seymour to Edward Cardwell, 1 May 1865, BCA, GR 1486, CO 60/21, Reel B-1435.

28 Hankin, 'Memoirs,' 54.

29 Carroll Smith-Rosenberg, 'Captured Subjects / Savage Others: Violently Engendering the New American,' *Gender and History* 5:2 (Summer 1993) 178.

30 Janice Acoose/Misko-Kìsikàwihkwè (Red Sky Woman): *Iskwewak – Kah' Ki Yaw Ni Wahkomakanak: Neither Indian Princesses Nor Easy Squaws* (Toronto: Women's Press, 1995) 85.

31 Sylvia Van Kirk, *'Many Tender Ties': Women in Fur Trade Society in Western*

Canada, 1670–1870 (Winnipeg: Watson and Dwyer, 1980); Jennifer S.H. Brown, *Strangers in Blood: Fur Trade Company Families in Indian Country* (Vancouver: University of British Columbia Press, 1980).

32 George Hills, 'Journal 1836–1861' (Transcript), Archives of the Diocese of New Westminster/Ecclesiastical Province of British Columbia (hereafter ADNW/EPBC) MS 65a, PSA 57, 370.

33 John Emmerson, *Voyages, Travels, and Adventures by John Emmerson of Wolsingham* (Durham: Wm. Ainsley, 1865) 37.

34 George M. Grant, *Ocean to Ocean: Sandford Fleming's Expedition through Canada in 1872* (Toronto: James Cambell, 1873) 273.

35 Ebenezer Robson, 'Diary,' BCA, Reel 17A, np. Emphasis original.

36 Vancouver Island, Police and Prisons Department, 'Esquimalt Charge Book 1862–1866,' BCA, GR 0428.

37 Crosby, *Among the An-ko-me-nums*, 180.

38 George Hills, 'Journal 1 Jan-10 June 1863' (Transcript), ADNW/EPBC, 29.

39 Brown, *British Columbia*, 7.

40 J.S. Matthews, 'Memo of conversation with Mrs Madeline Williams, aged Indian woman, also known as Gassy Jack's wife, living with her grand-daughter, Nita Williams, in a small cottage at the west end of the Indian Reserve, North Vancouver, 13 June 1940,' 'Indian Wives of White Men,' City of Vancouver Archives (hereafter CVA), Add Mss 54, vol. 13, File 06612.

41 'Register of Baptisms and Marriages, 1860–1881, St Paul's Nanaimo,' ADBCA, Text 30, Box 8; 'Parochial Register of Baptisms and Marriages for district of St. John's Victoria 1860–1871,' ADBCA, Text 202, Box 6; 'Holy Trinity Cathedral Marriage Register,' CVA, Add Mss 603, vol. 1, Reel m-21; 'Christ Church Hope Marriage Register 1862–1872,' ADNW/EPBC, RG4.0.34; 'St John the Divine Yale Marriage Register,' ADNW/EPBC.

42 George Hills, 'Hills Journal 1866' (Transcript), ADNW/EPBC, 65.

43 'Memorandum of conversation of Aug. Jack Khahtsahlano, who called at the City Archives,' 31 Oct. 1938, 'Indian Wives of White Men,' CVA, Add Mss 54, vol. 13, File 06612. Mrs Walker would be the daughter of the white bridegroom, Joe Silvey, aka 'Portuguese Joe.' His bride was a high-born Squamish woman, Khaltinat.

44 Mayne, *Four Years in British Columbia and Vancouver Island*, 248.

45 'Diary of R.H. Alexander Commencing Tuesday, Apr. 29th, 1862' (Transcript) CVA, Add Mss 246, File 48, 8.

46 N.P., 'Nanaimo,' *Victoria Press*, 27 June 1861.

47 'Memo of conversation (over the phone) with Miss Muriel Crakanthorp,' in Matthews, 'Indian Wives of White Men,' CVA, Add Mss 54, vol. 13, File

06612, 2; Jean Barman, 'Lost Okanagan: In Search of the First Settler Families,' *Okanagan History* (1996) 9–20.

48 J.S. Matthews, 'Memo of Conversation with Mrs James Walker, 721 Cambie Street ... [who] kindly called at the City Archives, 27 May 1940'; 'Memorandum of conversation of Aug. Jack Khahtsahlano, who called at the City Archives,' 31 Oct. 1838, in Matthews, 'Indian Wives of White Men,' CVA, Add Mss 54, vol. 13, File 06612, 2.

49 *Third Report of the Columbia Mission with List of Contributions, 1861* (London: Rivingtons [1862]) 26; Robin Hood, 'From Nanaimo,' *Victoria Press,* 28 June 1861.

50 Pratt, *Imperial Eyes,* 97.

51 'A Disorderly Neighbourhood,' *British Colonist,* 14 Oct. 1861.

52 J.C.B. Cave to Captain Franklyn, 5 Dec. 1864, in W.H. Franklyn to Colonial Secretary, 5 Dec. 1864, BCA, 'Colonial Correspondence,' GR 1372, Reel B-1329.

53 Anne McClintock, *Imperial Leather: Race, Gender and Sexuality in the Colonial Contest* (New York: Routledge, 1995) 30.

54 W.H. Franklyn to Henry Wakeford, 13 July 1864, 'Colonial Correspondence,' BCA, GR 1372, Reel B-1329.

55 'Extract of letter from Mr Robert Brown, Commander of Exploring Expedition 1864, dated 1st June 1865,' in Arthur Kennedy to Edward Cardwell, 3 Sept. 1866, Great Britain, Colonial Office, Vancouver Island Original Correspondence (hereafter CO), National Archives of Canada (hereafter NAC), MG 11, CO 305/29, Reel B-250.

56 *Report of the Columbia Mission, With List of Contributions, 1860* (London: Rivingtons, [1861]) 66.

57 'Alleged Rape,' *British Colonist,* 28 Oct. 1862.

58 Chartres Brew to Acting Colonial Secretary, 9 June 1862, 'Colonial Correspondence,' BCA, GR 1372, Reel B-1311.

59 'Assaulting a Squaw,' *British Colonist,* 25 Feb. 1862; 'Assault on a Squaw,' *British Colonist,* 13 Feb. 1862; 'Breaking a Squaw's Arm,' *British Colonist,* 13 Feb. 1862; 'Assault,' *Victoria Press,* 17 Feb. 1862; 'Assault Case,' *Victoria Press,* 24 Feb. 1862; 'Assaulting a Squaw,' *Victoria Press,* 24 Mar. 1862; 'Richard Hovey,' *Victoria Press,* 4 Apr. 1862.

60 Matthews, 'Memorandum of conversation of Aug. Jack Khahtsahlano,' 31 Oct. 1938, in 'Indian Wives of White Men,' CVA, 2.

61 Mosquito, 'Mary Come Home,' *Cariboo Sentinel,* 13 Feb. 1869. Translation mine.

62 Karen Dubinsky, *Improper Advances: Rape and Heterosexual Conflict in Ontario, 1880–1929* (Chicago: University of Chicago Press, 1993) 78–9.

63 Crosby, *Among,* 60.

64 Charles Lillard, ed., Gilbert M Sproat, *The Nootka: Scenes and Studies of Savage Life* (1868; reprint, Victoria: Sono Nis, 1987) 67.

65 Wilson Duff, *The Indian History of British Columbia*: vol. 1, *The Impact of the White Man* (1969; reprint, Victoria: Province of British Columbia Ministry of Tourism and Ministry Responsible for Culture, 1992) 102.

66 Hills, 'Journal 1836–1861,' 509–10; 'A Social Grievance,' *Vancouver Times*, 4 Apr. 1866.

67 Phillip Hankin to Arthur Kennedy, 8 Feb. 1866, NAC, MG 11, CO 305/28, Reel B-249.

68 'The Indian Mortality,' *Victoria Press*, 17 June 1862.

69 Untitled, *Nanaimo Gazette*, 21 Apr. 1866.

70 'An Attempt to Prove the Necessity for a Stipendiary – the COST of the Attempt,' *Nanaimo Gazette*, 19 May 1866.

71 B.D., 'Letter from Cariboo,' *British Colonist*, 27 Mar. 1868.

72 F.N., 'The Maid of Lillooet,' *Victoria Press*, 20 Jan. 1862.

73 Matthew Begbie, in James Douglas to Duke of Newcastle, 24 Aug. 1860, NAC, MG 11, CO 60/8, Reel B-83.

74 Episcopalian, 'The Negro Question – Sewing Circles and Churches,' *British Colonist*, 31 Sept. 1861.

75 M.W.G. [Mifflin Winstar Gibbs] alias Blackstone, 'An Answer to "An Earnest Appeal,"' *Weekly Victoria Gazette*, 25 Aug. 1858.

76 'Extract from Lieutenant Wilkes Narrative of the United States Exploring Expedition'; in 'Testimony in Favour of the Hudson's Bay Company,' 1848, Great Britain, Colonial Office, Vancouver Island Original Correspondence, University of British Columbia Library, CO 305/1, Reel R288:1.

77 See, e.g., Edmund Hope Verney to Harry Verney, 15 May 1862; Edmund Hope Verney to Harry Verney, 16 Aug. 1862, in Allan Pritchard, ed., *Vancouver Island Letters of Edmund Hope Verney, 1862–1865* (Vancouver: University of British Columbia Press, 1996) 74–7, 84.

78 Lux, 'Magisterial Morality: A Voice from the Mountains,' *British Columbian*, 14 Nov. 1861.

79 A.F. Pemberton to Colonial Secretary, 2 Mar. 1870, BCA, 'Colonial Correspondence,' GR 1372, Reel B-1357.

80 I.D.C., '"A Man's a Man for a' That,"' *British Columbian*, 4 June 1862.

81 Kinahan Cornwallis, *The New El Durado; or, British Columbia* (London: Thomas Cautley Newby, 1858) 135.

82 See Emmerson, *Travels, Voyages, and Adventures*, 48–9.

83 Walter Colquhoun Grant to Brodie, 8 Aug. 1851, in James E. Hendrickson ed., 'Two Letters from Walter Colquhoun Grant,' *BC Studies* 26 (Jan.–Apr. 1973) 13.

84 *Annual Report of the Columbia Mission: for the Year 1867*, 72.

85 'Letter From Victoria – No. IV., '*Cariboo Sentinel*, 18 Sept. 1866.

86 'Profits of Agriculture,' *Cariboo Sentinel*, 24 July 1869.

87 'Immigration,' *Mainland Guardian*, 9 Feb. 1871.

88 Brown, 'Journal,' 122. Translations his.

89 'The Indian Reserve Question,' *British Columbian*, 13 Nov. 1867.

90 'A Reminiscence of 1850,' in Dorothy Blakey Smith, ed., *The Reminiscences of Doctor John Sebastian Helmcken* (Vancouver: University of British Columbia Press, 1975) 326.

91 'The Indian Reserve Question,' *British Columbian*, 13 Nov. 1867; Settler, 'Our Indian Liquor Traffic Act,' *Nanaimo Gazette*, 18 Sept. 1865; 'The Ravine,' *Victoria Press*, 29 Sept. 1862.

92 A.B., 'The Indians' *British Colonist*, 7 Sept. 1868.

93 *Tenth Annual Report of the Columbia Mission, for the Year 1868* (London: Rivingtons, 1969) 89.

94 In *Annual Report of the Columbia Mission 1860*, 51. Emphasis added.

95 I.D.C., '"A Man's a Man for a' That,"' *British Columbian*, 4 June 1862.

96 Brown, *Klatsassan*, 14.

97 'Our Relations with the Indians,' *British Columbian*, 10 June 1863.

98 'The Civilized Song of the Solomons,' *Victoria Press*, 9 Mar. 1862.

99 Bogg, 'Journal of Her Majesty's Hired Surveying Vessel, Beaver, 1863,' PRO, ADM 101/276, 16. Emphasis in original.

100 C.S., 'Vice at Nanaimo,' *Victoria Press*, 24 July 1861.

101 Robert J.C. Young, *Colonial Desire: Hybridity in Theory, Culture, and Race* (London: Routledge, 1995) 9.

102 'Miscegenation,' *Victoria Daily Chronicle*, 20 Mar. 1864.

103 *A Manual of Ethnological Inquiry Being a Series of Questions Concerning the Human Race, Prepared by a Sub-Committee of the British Association for the Advancement of Science ... Adapted for the Use of Travellers and Others, in Studying the Varieties of Man* (London: Taylor and Francis, 1852) in ADNW/EPBC, PSA 41, File 3, 'Documents.'

104 Homi Bhabha, 'Of Mimicry and Man: The Ambivalence of Colonial Discourse,' *Oct.* 28 (Spring 1984) 125–34.

105 Mayne, *Four Years*, 248.

106 In Robie L. Reid, ed., C.C. Gardiner, 'To The Fraser River Mines in 1858,' *British Columbia Historical Quarterly*, 1:1 (Oct. 1937) 248.

107 Henry Pellew Crease to William Duncan, 9 Nov. 1867, 'Colonial Correspondence,' BCA, GR 1372, Reel B-1326, File 498/19.

108 Bogg, 'Journal of Her Majesty's Hired Surveying Vessel, Beaver, 1863,' PRO, ADM 101/276, 16.

109 *Lecture Delivered by the Hon. Malcolm Cameron to the Young Men's Mutual Improvement Association* (Quebec: G.E. Desbartes, 1865) 21.
110 Mayne, *Four Years*, 277.
111 Surgeon P. Cormie, 'Journal of Her Majesty's Sloop: Sparrowhawk, 1869,' PRO, ADM/101/278, 24.
112 Cormie, 'Journal of Her Majesty's Sloop: Sparrowhawk, 1869,' PRO, ADM/101/278, 21–2. Emphasis in original.
113 Macfie, 379, 381.
114 See Matthew Macfie, *The Impending Contact of the Aryan & Turanian Races, With Special Reference to Recent Chinese Migrations* (London: Sunday Lecture Society, 1878) 17.
115 Hills, 'Journal 1862,' 29.
116 'The Revolt and its Lessons,' *British Colonist*, 3 Dec. 1869.
117 B.W. Pearse, 'Memo on the Letter of the Bishop of Columbia to the Right Honourable Earl of Kimberley,' nd, in British Columbia, Attorney General, 'Documents,' BCA, GR 419, Box 10, 'Indian Improvement – aid to missionary societies,' File 1871/23, 11–12.

3 Bringing Order to the Backwoods: Regulating British Columbia's Homosocial Culture

1 'Reading Room,' *British Colonist*, 10 Oct. 1859.
2 Jan Noel, *Canada Dry: Temperance Crusades before Confederation* (Toronto: University of Toronto Press, 1995) 12.
3 Untitled, *British Colonist*, 22 July 1859; Ebenezer Robson, 'Notes from the Diary of Rev. Ebenezer Robson, D.D., Pioneer Wesleyan Missionary at Fort Hope, B.C., from Mar. 12 to May 13 1860' (Transcript), British Columbia Archives (hereafter BCA), Add Mss H/D/R57/.2A, 19, 20.
4 Untitled, *British Colonist*, 22 July 1859.
5 'A Dashaway Society,' *British Colonist*, 26 Mar. 1861.
6 Untitled, *Weekly Victoria Gazette*, 3 Feb. 1860; *Constitution and By-Laws of the Dashaway Association of Victoria, V.I.* (Victoria: Colonist, [1860 or 1861?]) 2–3.
7 'Gymnastics,' *British Colonist*, 4 Feb. 1860; 'Gymnastic Exhibition,' *Victoria Press*, 15 Dec. 1861.
8 George Hills, 'Hills Journal 1861' (Transcript), Archives of the Diocese of New Westminster, Ecclesiastical Province of British Columbia (hereafter ADNW/EPBC) 46.
9 'Temperance Lecture,' *Nanaimo Gazette*, 19 May 1866.

10 Cornelius Bryant, 'Diary – Part II' (Transcript), Central Archives of the United Church of Canada (hereafter CAUCC), Victoria University, 86.047C/TR, File 2, 71, 76–7.
11 'Temperance Meeting at Victoria,' *British Columbian*, 18 Oct. 1862; 'Temperance Meeting' *Victoria Press*, 14 Oct. 1862; 'Lecture,' *British Columbian*, 17 Jan. 1863; Ebenezer Robson, 'Diary,' BCA, Reel 17A, np.
12 'Good Templars Soiree,' *Victoria Daily Chronicle*, 22 Oct. 1864.
13 'Good Templars Ball,' *British Colonist*, 20 Dec. 1870.
14 See, for instance, 'Independent Order of Good Templars, ' *British Colonist*, 8 Aug. 1863; 'Nanaimo Good Templars,' *British Colonist*, 18 Feb. 1871.
15 'The Good Templars,' *Victoria Daily Chronicle*, 24 Apr. 1864.
16 Edward Mallandaine, *First Victoria Directory; Comprising a General Directory* ... (Victoria: Edw. Mallandaine & Co, 1860) 55, 25, 26.
17 Robson, 'Diary,' np.
18 Lynne Marks, *Revivals and Roller Rinks: Religion, Leisure, and Identity in Late-Nineteenth-Century Small-Town Ontario* (Toronto: University of Toronto Press, 1996) chapter 4.
19 'Young Men's Christian Association,' *British Colonist*, 15 Sept. 1859.
20 'Intellectual Improvement,' *Victoria Press*, 24 Sept. 1861.
21 George Hills, 'Journal 1836–1861' (Transcript), ADNW/EPBC, MS 65a, PSA 57, 326–7.
22 'Mechanics Institute,' *British Colonist*, 5 Jan. 1865.
23 'Young Men's Christian Association,' *British Columbian*, 26 Oct. 1864; 'Municipal Council,' *British Columbian*, 22 Oct. 1864.
24 'The Mechanics Institute,' *Vancouver Times*, 13 Sept. 1865.
25 'The Mechanics Literary Institute,' *Vancouver Times*, 14 May 1865.
26 'The Mechanics Institute,' *Vancouver Times*, 11 Jan. 1865.
27 'Mechanics Literary Institute,' *British Colonist*, 25 Dec. 1865.
28 'A Reading Room,' 24 Sept. 1864; Robson, 'Diary,' np; 'Our Literary Institute,' *Nanaimo Gazette*, 27 Nov. 1865; Burrard Inlet Mechanic's Institute, 'Minute Book' (Transcript), BCA, Add Mss E/C/B94.
29 'Visitors at the Mechanics Institute,' *British Colonist*, 17 Dec. 1864.
30 Edmund Hope Verney to Harry Verney, 11 Dec. 1864, in Allan Pritchard, ed., *Vancouver Island Letters of Edmund Hope Verney, 1862–1865* (Vancouver: University of British Columbia Press, 1996) 236; 'Debating Society,' *Vancouver Times*, 16 Mar. 1865; 'Elocution Class,' *British Colonist*, 24 Apr. 1865.
31 'The Librarian's Lament,' *Nanaimo Gazette*, 13 Nov. 1865.
32 'Opening of the Central School,' *British Colonist*, 2 Aug. 1865.
33 'Mechanics's Literary Institute,' *British Colonist*, 6 Aug. 1871.

34 'The Public Library and Reading Room,' *British Columbian*, 17 July 1865; 'Public Library,' *British Columbian*, 1 July 1868.

35 'Every Day Life in Cariboo,' *British Colonist*, 12 May 1864.

36 'Institute,' *Cariboo Sentinel*, 16 July 1868; 'Literary Institute,' *Cariboo Sentinel*, 30 Oct. 1868.

37 'Chronicles of the Cariboo,' *Cariboo Sentinel*, 24 May 1866.

38 'Our New Candidate,' *Cariboo Sentinel*, 20 Sept. 1866.

39 'Cariboo Literature,' *Cariboo Sentinel*, 17 Apr. 1869; James Anderson, *Sawney's Letters and Cariboo Rhymes* (Barkerville, BC: *Cariboo Sentinel*, 1868; reprint, Toronto: Bibliographic Society of Canada, 1950).

40 'Extracts From Sawney's Third Letter,' *Cariboo Sentinel*, 2 July 1868.

41 'Goodbye to Sawney,' *Cariboo Sentinel*, 25 Nov. 1871.

42 'Institute and Reading Room,' *British Colonist*, 16 Nov. 1864. Emphasis in original.

43 'Mechanics Literary Institute,' *British Colonist*, 16 Dec. 1870.

44 'Every Day Life in Cariboo,' *British Colonist*, 12 May 1864.

45 'The Lecture To-Night,' *British Colonist*, 10 Jan. 1865; 'Mechanics Institute Conversazione,' *Vancouver Times*, 16 Dec. 1865.

46 'Lecture,' *British Colonist*, 4 Dec. 1866; 'The Mechanics Institute,' *British Colonist*, 13 Dec. 1865.

47 'Letter from Cariboo,' *British Columbian*, 4 Apr. 1865.

48 'The Mechanics Institute,' *Vancouver Times*, 11 Jan. 1865.

49 'The Mechanics Institute,' *Vancouver Times*, 11 Jan. 1865.

50 C.S. Nicol to Henry Wakeford, 19 Aug. 1864, 'Colonial Correspondence,' BCA, GR 1372, Reel B-1350.

51 Robert A.J. McDonald, 'Lumber Society on the Industrial Frontier: Burrard Inlet, 1863–1886,' *Labour / Le Travail*, 33 (Spring 1994) 89.

52 Burrard Inlet Mechanic's Institute, 'Minute Book,' 7, 10, 14–15.

53 Edmund Hope Verney to Harry Verney, 29 Nov. 1864, in Pritchard, ed., *Vancouver Island Letters*, 232.

54 Edward Mallandaine, *First Victoria Directory, Second Issue, and British Columbia Guide* (Victoria: Higgins and Long, 1868) 23, 24, 38, The class profile was similar in 1869. See Edward Mallandaine, *First Victoria Directory, Third Issue, and British Columbia Guide ...* (Victoria: E. Mallandaine, 1869) 16, 26, 27, 38.

55 'Public Library and Reading Room,' *British Columbian*, 21 Dec. 1864.

56 See, for instance, W.K. Bull to Colonial Secretary, 11 Feb. 1868, 'Colonial Correspondence,' BCA, GR 1372, Reel B-1312.

57 Valerie Burton, 'The Myth of Bachelor Jack: Masculinity, Patriarchy, and

Seafaring Labour,' in Colin Howell and Richard J. Twomey, eds., *Jack Tar in History: Essays in the History of Maritime Life and Labour* (Fredericton: Acadiensis Press, 1991) 179.

58 Judith Fingard, *Jack in Port: Sailortowns of Eastern Canada* (Toronto: University of Toronto Press, 1983) 234.

59 'A Sailors' Home,' *British Colonist*, 5 Nov. 1867.

60 'A Sailor's Home,' *British Colonist*, 6 Mar. 1867.

61 'The Sailor's Home,' *British Colonist*, 3 Jan. 1868.

62 Neptune, 'Sailors' Home,' *British Colonist*, 12 Nov. 1867.

63 'The Sailor's Home,' *British Colonist*, 3 Jan. 1868; J. Nagle, 'Sailors' Home,' *British Colonist*, 4 Aug. 1868.

64 'Discourteous,' *British Colonist*, 20 Jan. 1869; J.N., 'A Sailor's Home,' *British Colonist*, 2 Sept. 1869.

65 Charles Dickens, 'Episcopacy in the Rough,' *All the Year Round*, 23 Feb. 1861, 471. Emphasis in original.

66 *Third Report of the Columbia Mission with List of Contributions, 1861* (London: Rivingtons [1862]) 49.

67 *Tenth Annual Report of the Columbia Mission, for the Year 1868* (London: Rivingtons, 1969) 25.

68 J.E., Untitled, *Cariboo Sentinel*, 11 June 1868.

69 Tal. O Eifion, 'Our Moral, Social, and Political Condition,' *Cariboo Sentinel*, 28 Feb. 1867.

70 *Fifth Annual Report of the Columbia Mission for the Year 1863* (London: Rivingtons, 1864) 7.

71 A.C. Garret, 'Sketches of a Missionary Tour to Cariboo,' 2 June 1865, ADNW/EPBC, M.S #3, 76. Emphasis in original.

72 Rev. C. Knipe, 'Mission to the Mines of Cariboo British Columbia – 1862,' in G. Columbia to Bullock, 4 Feb. 1863, in Society for the Propagation of the Gospel in Foreign Parts, 'Letters Received Columbia 1861–1867,' vol. 2 (Transcript), BCA, Add Mss H/A/So2, 81–94.

73 Clergy of the Diocese, 'Religious,' *Cariboo Sentinel*, 9 July 1868.

74 W. Smithe, 'Religious,' *Cariboo Sentinel*, 16 July 1868.

75 'Religious,' *Cariboo Sentinel*, 23 July 1868.

76 *Eleventh Annual Report of the Columbia Mission for the Year 1869* (London: Rivingtons, 1870) 53.

77 *Eleventh Annual Report of the Columbia Mission*, 53.

78 'Cariboo Church Institute,' *Cariboo Sentinel*, 19 Dec. 1868; *Eleventh Annual Report of the Columbia Mission*, 57.

79 *Eleventh Annual Report of the Columbia Mission*, 55.

80 'Lecture on Manliness,' *Cariboo Sentinel,* 21 Aug. 1869; 'Lecture and Divine Service at Van Winkle,' *Cariboo Sentinel,* 11 Mar. 1871.
81 'Ecclesiastical – A Church to Let,' *Cariboo Sentinel,* 28 Oct. 1871.
82 Ebenezer Robson, 'How Methodism Came to British Columbia' (Transcript), ca. 1902, CAUCC, 86.226C, 22.
83 'British Columbia Mission,' *British Colonist,* 11 Sept. 1861; 'The British Columbia Missionary Meeting,' *British Colonist,* 31 Jan. 1861.
84 'The British Columbia Missionary Meeting,' *British Colonist,* 31 Jan. 1861.

4 Marriage, Morals, and Segregation: Regulating Mixed-Race Relationships

1 Matthew Macfie, 'A Laudable Marriage,' *British Colonist,* 19 May 1861; Alex. C. Garret, 'The "Laudable Marriage,"' *British Colonist,* 20 May 1861; Matthew Macfie, 'The "Laudable Marriage" Again,' *British Colonist,* 23 May 1861.
2 Tina Loo, *Making Law, Order, and Authority in British Columbia, 1821–1871* (Toronto: University of Toronto Press, 1994) 4.
3 James E. Hendrickson, ed., *Journals of the Colonial Legislatures of the Colonies of Vancouver Island and British Columbia 1851–1871,* vol. 1, *Journals of the Council, Executive Council, and Legislative Council of Vancouver Island, 1851–1866* (Victoria: Provincial Archives of British Columbia, 1980) 25–6, 39–40; Matthew Macfie, *Vancouver Island and British Columbia: Their History, Resources, and Prospects* (London: Longman, Green, Longman, Roberts, and Green, 1865) 402.
4 'Couldn't Get Spliced,' *British Columbian,* 5 Nov. 1962
5 'A Marriage Law Wanted,' *British Columbian,* 11 Feb. 1863.
6 James Douglas to Sir Edward Bulwer Lytton, 3 May 1859, Great Britain, Colonial Office, Original Vancouver Island Correspondence, (hereafter CO), National Archives of Canada (hereafter NAC), MG 11, CO 305/10, Reel B-239; Matthew B. Begbie to Governor, 7 Mar. 1859, 'Colonial Correspondence,' British Columbia Archives (hereafter BCA), GR 1372, Reel B-1307; Arthur Kennedy to Edward Cardwell, 25 May 1865, NAC, MG 11, CO 305/25, Reel B-248.
7 R.C.L. Brown to W.A.G. Young, 16 Feb. 1863, 'Colonial Correspondence,' BCA, GR 1372, Reel B-1311.
8 John R. Gillis, *For Better, For Worse: British Marriages, 1600 to the Present* (New York: Oxford University Press, 1985) 231.
9 Bishop of Columbia to H.P. Crease, 2 May 1862, Text 57, Box 6, File I, 'Bishop of Columbia, Correspondence Outwards 1860–1884,' Anglican

Church of Canada, Anglican Diocese of British Columbia Archives (hereafter ACC/ADBC), 55–6.

10 'British Columbia, No. 21, An Ordinance Respecting Marriage in British Columbia,' *British Columbia Government Gazette*, 15 July 1865, NAC, MG 11, CO 63/2, Reel B-1489; Frederick Seymour to Duke of Buckingham and Chandos, 16 Sept. 1867, BCA, GR 1486, CO 60/29, Reel B-1440.

11 'House of Assembly,' *British Colonist*, 26 Apr. 1865.

12 'Our Colonial Statistics,' *Victoria Press*, 16 Dec. 1861.

13 Benedict Anderson, *Imagined Communities: Reflections on the Origin and Spread of Nationalism*, rev. ed. (London: Verso, 1991) 164.

14 Henry Pellew Crease to Colonial Secretary, 1 June 1865, 'Colonial Correspondence,' BCA, GR 1372, Reel B-1303.

15 Frederick Seymour to Duke of Buckingham and Chandos, 11 Aug. 1868, BCA, GR 1486, CO 60/33, Reel B-1444.

16 Robert Hillman to Edward Cardwell, 4 Oct. 1865, BCA, GR 1486, CO 60/23, Reel B-1437.

17 Henry P. Pellew Crease to Birch, nd, in Arthur Birch to Edward Cardwell, 28 Apr. 1866, BCA, GR 1486, CO 60/24, Reel B-1437.

18 Robert Hillman to Earl of Carnarvon, 27 Aug. 1866, BCA, GR 1486, CO 60/26, Reel B-1439.

19 Matthew B. Begbie, 'Memorandum for the Secretary of State for the Provinces'; 'Sketch of a Bill Providing for Indian Concubines, and Destitute Half-Breed Children of Persons Dying Intestate and Leaving Property in the Province,' in *Report of the Superintendent of Indian Affairs for British Columbia for 1872 & 1873* (Ottawa: I.B. Taylor, 1873) 34–7.

20 Matthew Macfie, 'A Laudable Marriage,' *British Colonist*, 19 May 1861.

21 'How to Get Rid of the Troublesome Question,' *British Colonist*, 29 May 1862.

22 George Hills, 'Journal 1836–1861' (Transcript), MS 65a, PSA 57, Archives of the Diocese of New Westminster/Ecclesiastical Province of British Columbia (hereafter ADNW/EPBC), 369–70.

23 Ebenezer Robson, 'Notes from the Diary of Rev. Ebenezer Robson, D.D., Pioneer Wesleyan Missionary at Fort Hope, B.C., from Mar. 12 to May 13 1860' (Transcript), BCA, Add MssH/D/R57/.2, np.

24 R.C. Lundin Brown, *Klatsassan, and Other Reminiscences of Missionary Life in British Columbia* (London: Society for Promoting Christian Knowledge, 1873) 151–3. Translation mine.

25 *Annual Report of the Columbia Mission for the Year 1864* (London: Rivingtons, 1865) 32.

26 *Annual Report of the Columbia Mission 1866* (London: Rivingtons, 1867) 19.

27 British Columbia, *Report of the Hon. H.L. Langevin, C.B., Minister of Public Works* (Ottawa: I.B. Taylor, 1872) 29.

28 *Report of the Columbia Mission, With List of Contributions, 1860* (London: Rivingtons, [1861]) 94–5

29 'Another Letter From Bishop Hills,' *British Colonist*, 14 Mar. 1861.

30 *Ninth Annual Report of the Columbia Mission, for the Year 1867* (London: Rivingtons, 1868) 18.

31 Myra Rutherdale, 'Revisiting Colonization through Gender: Anglican Missionary Women in the Pacific Northwest and the Arctic, 1860–1945,' *BC Studies* 104 (1994–5) 21.

32 Untitled, *Cariboo Sentinel*, 2 Dec. 1871.

33 Hills, 'Journal 1861,' 73.

34 Matthew Macfie, 'A Laudable Marriage,' *British Colonist*, 19 May 1861.

35 Alex C. Garret, 'The "Laudable Marriage,"' *British Colonist*, 20 May 1861.

36 Bishop Hills to Rev. C. Knipe, 6 Mar. 1861, 'Bishop of Columbia, Correspondence Outwards 1860–1884,' ADN/EPBC, Text 57, Box 6, File I, 33–45.

37 Hills, 'Journal 1863,' 37.

38 Hills to Knipe, 6 Mar. 1861.

39 William Duncan to Frederick Seymour, 18 Sept. 1867, BCA, 'Colonial Correspondence,' GR 1372, Reel B-1326.

40 Hills, 'Journal 1866,' 29.

41 *Annual Report of the Columbia Mission 1867*, 24–5.

42 John Mee to Edward Cridge, 22 Jan. 1868, BCA, 'Edward Cridge, Correspondence Inward, 1860–1868,' Add Mss 320, Box I, File 4.

43 Lux, 'Magisterial Morality: A Voice from the Mountains,' *British Columbian*, 14 Nov. 1861. Emphasis in original.

44 Philip Hankin to Acting Colonial Secretary, 1 Apr. 1865, BCA, 'Colonial Correspondence,' GR 1372, Reel B-1357; Philip Hankin to Acting Colonial Secretary, 16 May 1865, BCA, 'Colonial Correspondence,' GR 1372 Reel B-1357.

45 John W. Lyndon, ed., *Queen Charlotte Islands: A Narrative of Discovery and Adventure in the North Pacific*, by Frances Poole, C.E. (London: Hurst and Blackett, 1872; reprint, Vancouver: Douglas and McIntyre, 1972) 245–7, 255.

46 Robin Hood, 'From Nanaimo,' *Victoria Press*, 28 June 1861.

47 Thomas Crosby, *Among the An-ko-me-nums of the Pacific Coast* (Toronto: William Briggs, 1907) 60.

48 'A Disorderly Neighbourhood,' *British Colonist*, 14 Oct. 1861.

49 George Hills, 'Journal 1 Jan.–21 July 1862' (Transcript), ADNW/EPBC, 11.

50 Crosby, *Among*, 63.

51 See 'Squaw Barbarieed,' *Victoria Press*, 13 June 1861; Chief of Police to
    W.A.G. Young, 9 Aug. 1859, 'Colonial Correspondence,' BCA, GR 1372,
    Reel B-1356, File 1382.
52 Testimony of George Catman and Francis Gonieau, in *R v Na-Hor*, British
    Columbia, Attorney General, 'Documents 1857–1966,' BCA, GR 419, Box 1,
    File 1860/19. Translation mine.
53 'The Squaw Dance House,' *British Colonist*, 17 Dec. 1863; Censor, Untitled,
    British Columbian, 27 Feb. 1862. Emphasis in original.
54 'Dance House,' *British Colonist*, 28 Nov. 1862.
55 'The Dance House,' *British Colonist*, 12 Dec. 1861; Hills, 'Journal 1861,' 167.
56 'The Dance House,' *British Colonist*, 29 Dec. 1861.
57 Michael Harkin, 'Contested Bodies: Affliction and Power in Heiltsuk
    Culture and History,' *American Ethnologist* 21:3 (1994) 587.
58 Steven Acheson, 'Culture Contact, Demography and Health among the
    Aboriginal Peoples of British Columbia,' in Peter H. Stephenson, Susan J.
    Elliott, Leslie T. Foster, and Jill Harris, eds., *A Persistent Spirit: Towards
    Understanding Aboriginal Health in British Columbia* (Victoria: University
    of Victoria, 1995) 12; Wilson Duff, *The Indian History of British Columbia*,
    vol. 1, *The Impact of the White Man* (Victoria: Royal British Columbia Mu-
    seum, 1869) 42–3. On earlier epidemics, see Steven Boyd, 'Smallpox in
    the Pacific Northwest: The First Epidemics,' *BC Studies* 101 (1994) 5–40;
    Steven Boyd, 'Commentary on Early Contact-Era Smallpox in the Pacific
    Northwest,' *Ethnohistory* 43:2 (Spring 1996) 307–29; Cole Harris, 'Voices
    of Smallpox around the Strait of Georgia,' in *The Resettlement of British
    Columbia: Essays on Colonialism and Geographic Change* (Vancouver:
    UBC Press, 1997)
59 'The Small-Pox among the Indians,' *Victoria Press*, 27 Apr. 1862; Augustus
    F. Pemberton, to W.A.G. Young, 24 June 1862, 'Colonial Correspondence,'
    BCA, GR 1372, Reel B-1356.
60 Frank Mort, *Dangerous Sexualities: Medico-Moral Politics in England since
    1830* (New York and London: Routledge and Kegan Paul, 1987) 213.
61 Jean and John Comaroff, 'Medicine, Colonialism, and the Black Body,' in
    Ethnography and the Historical Imagination (Boulder, CO: Westview Press,
    1992) 215–16.
62 'The Indian Question Again,' *British Columbian*, 19 Dec. 1861.
63 John Rammage to Governor Douglas, 8 Apr. 1862, BCA, 'Colonial Corre-
    spondence,' GR 1372, Reel 1347; 'The Executive Demented,' *British
    Columbian*, 21 May 1862.
64 'Report of the Board of Health,' *British Columbian*, 11 Nov. 1868.
65 'Lillooet,' *British Columbian*, 25 Feb. 1863.

66 James Douglas to John Russel, 21 Aug. 1855, UBCL, CO 305/6, Reel R288: 4.

67 Edward Cridge et al. to James Douglas, 6 Mar. 1856, enclosed in James Douglas to George Grey, 7 Mar. 1856, UBCL, CO 305/7, Reel R288: 3; William Duncan to Unknown, 22 June 1860, 'Colonial Correspondence,' BCA, GR 1372, Reel B-1326.

68 'Report of the Grand Jury,' *Victoria Gazette*, 15 Jan. 1859; William Leigh, Foreman, 'Report,' David Cameron to James Douglas, 14 Apr. 1860, BCA, 'Colonial Correspondence,' GR 1372, Reel B-1313.

69 'Squaws Arrested,' *Victoria Gazette*, 9 May 1860.

70 See, for instance, 'Arrest of Street Walkers,' *British Colonist*, 8 May 1860.

71 'Police Court,' *British Colonist*, 13 Mar. 1862.

72 'A Much Needed Regulation,' *British Colonist*, 20 Apr. 1861.

73 'Indians,' *Victoria Press*, 18 Aug. 1861.

74 'Indian Convictions,' *Victoria Press*, 5 Sept. 1861; Alex. C. Garret, 'Indian Police,' *Victoria Press*, 5 Sept. 1861.

75 Ephraim Evans, 'Rev. Dr Evans on the Dance Houses,' *British Colonist*, 25 Dec. 1861.

76 'The Small-Pox Among the Indians,' *British Colonist*, 28 Apr. 1862.

77 See M.B., 'From Nanaimo,' *Victoria Press*, 18 July 1862.

78 'Inconsistency,' *Victoria Press*, 19 May 1862.

79 'Removal of the Indians,' *Victoria Press*, 28 Apr. 1862.

80 'The Small-Pox and the Indians,' *Victoria Press*, 1 May 1862.

81 Crosby, *Among*, 170–1.

82 'Smallpox – Its Dissemination,' *British Columbian*, 28 Nov. 1868.

83 'Compulsory Departure of the Indians,' *Victoria Press*, 27 May 1862.

84 'The Indian Mortality,' *Victoria Press*, 17 June 1862

85 Hills, 'Hills Journal 1 Jan.–10 June 1863,' 12.

86 M.B., 'From Nanaimo,' *Victoria Press*, 18 July 1862; A.C. Elliot to W.A.G. Young, 3 Feb. 1863, BCA, 'Colonial Correspondence,' GR 1372, Reel B-1327.

87 Alex. C. Garret, 'Indian Police,' *Victoria Press*, 5 Sept. 1861.

88 Augustus F. Pemberton to W.A.G. Young, 12 Sept. 1861, BCA, 'Colonial Correspondence,' GR 1372, Reel B-1356.

89 'Migration of the Indians,' *Victoria Press*, 11 May 1862.

90 'The Small-Pox and the Indians,' *Victoria Press*, 1 May 1862.

91 See Ann Laura Stoler and Frederick Cooper, 'Between Metropole and Colony: Rethinking a Research Agenda,' in Frederick Cooper and Ann Laura Stoler, eds., *Tensions of Empire: Colonial Cultures in a Bourgeois World* (Berkeley: University of California Press, 1997).

92 'How to Get Rid of the Troublesome Question,' *British Colonist*, 29 May 1862.

93 'Compulsory Departure of the Indians,' *Victoria Press*, 28 May 1862.

94 'Prostitution Recognized by Government,' *British Colonist*, 2 June 1862.

95 'Small Pox,' *Victoria Press*, 6 June 1862; 'Small Pox,' *Victoria Press*, 17 June 1862.

96 City of Victoria, 'Meeting of the Town Council held this 22nd day of Dec. 1862,' 'Council Minutes,' vol. O, 25 Aug. 1862 to 11 July 1871, City of Victoria Archives (hereafter CVicA) City Record Series 1, 79.

97 'City Council,' *British Colonist*, 23 Dec. 1862; 'Meeting of the Town Council held this 5th day of Jan. 1863,' City of Victoria, 'Council Minutes,' CVicA, 82–5.

98 Philip Hankin to Colonial Secretary, 25 Aug. 1865 and note en verso from William A.G. Young, 15 Sept. 1865, BCA, 'Colonial Correspondence,' GR 1372, Reel B-1357.

99 A.F. Pemberton to Acting Colonial Secretary, 27 July 1869, BCA, 'Colonial Correspondence,' GR 1372, Reel B-1357; A.F. Pemberton to Colonial Secretary, 2 Mar. 1870, BCA, 'Colonial Correspondence,' GR 1372, Reel B-1357.

100 Paul Tennant, *Aboriginal Peoples and Politics: The Indian Land Question in British Columbia, 1849–1989* (Vancouver: UBC Press, 1990) 35.

101 See James E. Hendrickson, ed., *Journals of the Colonial Legislatures of the Colonies of Vancouver Island and British Columbia 1851–1871*, vol. 2, *Journals of the House of Assembly, Vancouver Island, 1856–1863* (Victoria: Provincial Archives of British Columbia, 1980) 72.

102 James Douglas to Duke of Newcastle, 8 Aug. 1860, NAC, MG 11, CO 305/14, Reel B-241.

103 Arthur Kennedy to Edward Cardwell, 1 Oct. 1864, CO 305/23, NAC, MG 11, Reel B-246.

104 'The Governor's Address to the Indians, Victoria Aug. 22nd, 1864,' in Arthur Kennedy to Edward Cardwell, 23 Aug. 1864, CO 305/23, NAC, MG 11, Reel B-246.

105 See *R v Sting and Solbergh*, British Columbia, Attorney General, 'Documents 1857–1966,' BCA, GR 419, Box 3, File 1864/10; 'Squaw Dance House,' *British Colonist*, 9 Dec. 1864.

106 Nicholas Thomas, *Colonialism's Culture: Anthropology, Travel, and Government* (Princeton, NJ: Princeton University Press, 1994) 116.

107 Hendrickson, ed., *Journals*, vol. 1, 84–5; Aug. F. Pemberton to W.A.G. Young, 24 June 1862, BCA, 'Colonial Correspondence,' GR 1372, Reel B-1356.

108 'Corporation By Laws, City Clerks Office 1862–1888,' CVicA, City Record Series 1, 7–11.

109 A.F. Pemberton to Colonial Secretary, 2 Feb. 1869, BCA, 'Colonial Correspondence,' GR 1372, Reel B-1357.

110 Hendrickson, ed., vol. 4, 112; W. Leigh to W.A.G. Young, 16 Jan. 1869, BCA, 'Colonial Correspondence,' GR 1372, Reel B-1348.

111 'Municipal By-Law, to Regulate the Sanitary Condition of the City and Port of Victoria, B.C.' *British Columbia Government Gazette*, 10 July 1869, NAC, MG 11, CO 63/4, Reel B-1490; 'Health By-Law, to Regulate the Sanitary Condition of the City and Port of New Westminster, British Columbia,' *British Columbia Government Gazette*, 16 July 1870, NAC, MG 11, CO 63/4, Reel B-1490.

112 Public Health, 'The Health Bill,' *British Colonist*, 29 Jan. 1869; Untitled, *British Colonist*, 27 Jan. 1869.

113 'Legislative Council,' 27 Jan. 1869; Frederick Seymour to Earl of Granville, 10 Mar. 1869, BCA, GR 1486, CO 60/35, Reel B-1445.

114 Ann L. Stoler, 'Making Empire Respectable: The Politics of Race and Sexual Morality in 20th-Century Colonial Cultures,' *American Ethnologist* 16:3 (1989) 635.

5 Land and Immigration, Gender and Race: Bringing White People to British Columbia

1 James Douglas to the Duke of Newcastle, 18 Oct. 1859, Great Britain, Col-onial Office, British Columbia Correspondence (hereafter CO 60) National Archives of Canada (hereafter NAC), MG 11, CO 60/5, Reel B-81.

2 'The Aborigines and the Soil,' *British Columbian*, 2 Dec. 1865.

3 Edward Gibbon Wakefield, 'A View of the Art of Colonization: With Present Reference to the British Empire: In Letters Between a Statesman and a Colonist,' in M.F. Lloyd Pritchard, ed., *The Collected Works of Edward Gibbon Wakefield* (1849; reprint, London: Collins, 1968) 972.

4 [Hudson's Bay Company], *Colonization of Vancouver Island* (London: Horace and Son, 1849) 4.

5 Richard Mackie, 'The Colonization of Vancouver Island, 1849–1858,' *BC Studies* 96 (Winter 1992–3) 9.

6 Richard Blanshard to Earl Grey, 3 Feb. 1851, Great Britain, Colonial Office, Vancouver Island Correspondence (hereafter CO 305), University of British Columbia Library [hereafter UBCL], CO 305/3, Reel R288:1.

7 David Demeritt, 'Visions of Agriculture in British Columbia,' *BC Studies* 108 (1995–6) 40.
8 'Our Future Destinies,' *British Colonist*, 16 Feb. 1861.
9 'Self-Supporting – Self-Dependent,' *British Colonist*, 17 Oct. 1859.
10 'Inducements to Emigrants,' *Vancouver Times*, 20 Apr. 1866.
11 Note en verso H.M. (Herman Merivale), James Douglas to the Duke of Newcastle, 18 Oct., NAC, MG 11, CO 60/5, Reel B-81.
12 A. Coville to John Packington, 1 Dec. 1852, UBCL, CO 305/3, Reel R288:1.
13 James Douglas to Duke of Newcastle, 12 Jan. 1860, NAC, MG 11, CO 60/6, Reel B-82.
14 'The Land Ordinance, 1870, in Force,' *British Colonist*, 21 Oct. 1870.
15 James Douglas to Duke of Newcastle, 24 July 1860, NAC, MG 11, CO 60/8, Reel B-83.
16 T.W.C. Murdoch to Frederic Rogers, 20 Nov. 1860, NAC, MG 11, CO 60/9, Reel B-84; James Douglas to Duke of Newcastle, 23 June 1861, NAC, MG 11, CO 60/10, Reel B-84.
17 T.W.F. Murdoch to Frederick Seymour, 31 Oct. 1868; Duke of Buckingham and Chandos to Frederick Seymour, 21 Dec. 1868, draft reply, in CO 60/34, British Columbia Archives (hereafter BCA), GR 1486, Reel B-1445.
18 Frederic Rogers to Herman Merivale, 6 Jan. 1860, NAC, MG 11, CO 305/15, Reel B-241.
19 'Foreigners,' *British Colonist*, 22 Feb. 1861.
20 Fred H. Hitchins, *The Colonial Land and Emigration Commission* (Philadelphia: University of Pennsylvania Press, 1931) 234.
21 Chief Commissioner of Lands and Works to James Douglas, 13 Aug. 1859, 'Colonial Correspondence,' BCA, GR 1372, Reel B-1337.
22 'The New Land Proclamation for Vancouver Island,' *British Colonist*, 8 Mar. 1861; A.J. Langley, *A Glance at British Columbia and Vancouver's Island in 1861* (London: Robert Hardwick, 1862) 7.
23 'A Homestead Law,' *Vancouver Times*, 3 Dec. 1864.
24 See 'No.16, An Ordinance to assimilate the Law exempting the Homestead and other Property from forced Seizure and Sale in certain cases in all parts of the Colony of British Columbia,' *British Columbia Government Gazette*, 30 Mar. 1867, NAC, MG 11, CO 63/3, Reel B-1490.
25 Henry P.P. Crease to Frederick Seymour, 21 June 1867, in Frederick Seymour to Duke of Buckingham and Chandos, 5 Sept. 1867, BCA, GR 1486, CO 60/29, Reel B-1440. Emphasis in original.
26 Bettina Bradbury, 'From Civil Death to Separate Property: Changes in the Legal Rights of Married Women in Nineteenth-Century New Zealand,' *New Zealand Journal of History* 29:1 (Apr. 1995) 40–66.

27 Mrs Sarah Brown to J.W. Trutch, Chief Commissioner of Lands and Works, 28 May 1868, 'Colonial Correspondence,' BCA, GR 1372, Reel B-1912; Joseph Trutch, to Mrs Sarah Brown, 30 June 1868, 'Colonial Correspondence,' BCA, GR 1372, Reel B-1912; Phoebe Campbell to Anonymous, 23 Oct. 1868, BCA, GR 1372, Reel B-1312; Mrs Sarah Brown to Chief Commissioner of Lands and Works, 3 Mar. 1869, 'Colonial Correspondence,' BCA, GR 1372, Reel B-1312.

28 Paul Tennant, *Aboriginal Peoples and Politics: The Indian Land Question in British Columbia, 1849–1989* (Vancouver: UBC Press, 1990) 34–8.

29 Henry P. Pellew Crease to Frederick Seymour, 2 Nov. 1867, in Frederick Seymour to Duke of Buckingham and Chandos, 22 Nov. 1867, CO 60/29, BCA, Reel B-1441.

30 Joseph W. Trutch to Frederick Seymour, 19 Nov. 1967, in Frederick Seymour to Duke of Buckingham and Chandos, 22 Nov. 1867, CO 60/29, BCA, GR 1486, Reel B-1441.

31 Sister Mary Providence to Joseph Trutch, 19 Jan. 1870, 'Colonial Correspondence,' BCA, GR 1372, Reel B-1364; Joseph Trutch to Sister Mary Providence, 25 Jan. 1870, 'Colonial Correspondence', BCA, GR 1372, Reel B-1364.

32 T.W.F. Murdoch to Frederick Seymour, 31 Oct. 1868, CO 60/34, BCA, GR 1486, Reel B-1445.

33 Henry Crease to Arthur Birch, 21 Apr. 1866, in Arthur Birch to Edward Cardwell, 21 Apr. 1866, CO 60/24, BCA, GR 1486, Reel B-1437.

34 R.W. Sandwell, 'Peasants on the Coast? A Problematique of Rural British Columbia,' in Donald H. Akenson, ed., *Canadian Papers in Rural History* 10 (Gananoque, ON: Langdale, 1996) 293.

35 E. Graham Alston, *A Handbook to British Columbia and Vancouver Island* (London: F. Algar, 1870) 15.

36 'Our Great Want,' *British Columbian*, 9 Jan. 1869.

37 'Emigration,' *Cariboo Sentinel*, 18 June 1868.

38 'Assisted Immigration,' *British Colonist*, 11 Dec. 1866.

39 Donald Harman Akenson, *The Irish in Ontario: A Study in Rural History* (Montreal and Kingston: McGill–Queen's University Press, 1984) 55.

40 Daiva Stasiulis and Nira Yuval-Davis, 'Introduction: Beyond Dichotomies – Gender, Race, Ethnicity and Class in Settler Societies,' in Daiva Stasiulis and Nira Yuval-Davis, ed., *Unsettling Settler Societies: Articulations of Gender, Race, Ethnicity and Class* (London: Sage, 1995) 7.

41 See Irene Genevieve Marie Zaffaroni, 'The Great Chain of Being: Racism and Imperialism in Colonial Victoria 1858–1871,' MA Thesis, University of Victoria, 1987, chapter 4.

42 'Address of the Grand Jury at Cayoosh to Governor Douglas,' in James Douglas to Duke of Newcastle, 9 Oct. 1860, CO 60/8, NAC, MG 11, Reel B-83.

43 'Our Chinese Population,' *Cariboo Sentinel*, 16 May 1867.

44 A. Coville to John Packington, 24 Nov. 1852, UBCL, CO 305/3, Reel R288:1.

45 George P. Martin to Charles Frederick, 15 Oct. 1854, enclosed in [name illegible] to Herman Merivale, 27 Jan. 1855, UBCL, CO 305/6, Reel R288:4.

46 James Douglas to John Russel, 21 Aug. 1855, UBCL, CO 305/6, Reel R288:4.

47 James E. Hendrickson, ed., *Journals of the Colonial Legislatures of the Colonies of Vancouver Island and British Columbia 1851–1871*, vol. 2, *Journals of the House of Assembly, Vancouver Island, 1856–1863* (Victoria: Provincial Archives of British Columbia, 1980) 285–6, 336–8, 442.

48 'Comparative Statement of the Estimated Expenditure of British Columbia for the Year 1865, and the Actual Expenditure of the Year ...' *British Columbia Government Gazette*, 10 Nov. 1866, NAC, MG 11, CO 63/3, Reel B-1489; James E. Hendrickson, ed., *Journals of the Colonial Legislatures of the Colonies of Vancouver Island and British Columbia 1851–1871*, vol. 4, *Journals of the Executive Council, 1864–1871, and of the Legislative Council, 1864–1866, of British Columbia* (Victoria: Provincial Archives of British Columbia, 1980) 227–9, 263–4, 270.

49 Arthur Birch to Earl of Carnarvon, 31 Oct. 1866, CO 60/25, BCA, GR 1486, Reel B-1438.

50 Hendrickson, ed., vol. 4, 93–6.

51 Hendrickson, ed., vol 4, 177.

52 'Emigration,' *British Columbian*, 15 June 1864.

53 'Immigration,' *British Colonist*, 9 Nov. 1869.

54 ''Tis Strange, 'Tis a Pity,' *British Columbian*, 22 May 1869.

55 'What Shall We Do with Them?' *British Columbian*, 4 June 1869.

56 Jack Little, 'The Foundations of Government,' in Hugh J.M. Johnson, ed., *The Pacific Province* (Vancouver: Douglas and McIntyre, 1996) 75.

57 George Hills, 'Journal 1861' (Transcript), Archives of the Diocese of New Westminster/Ecclesiastical Province of British Columbia, Vancouver School of Theology, (hereafter ADNW/EPBC), 43.

58 T.W.C. Murdoch and Frederic Rogers to Herman Merivale, 28 Apr. 1859, NAC, MG 11, CO 60/5, Reel B-81; Great Britain, House of Commons, Parliamentary Papers, vol. 38, 1863, No. 430, 'Emigration: Number of Emigrants who left the United Kingdom for the *United States, British North America*, the several Colonies of *Australasia, South Africa*, and other Places

respectively; distinguishing, as far as practicable, the Native Country of the Emigrants, 1860–1863,' Reel 69.303, 7.

59 H.M. (Herman Merivale), 8 Apr., note en verso in T.W.C. Murdoch to Frederic Rogers, 31 Mar. 1862, CO 60/14, MG 11, NAC, Reel B-87.

60 'English Immigration,' *Victoria Press*, 14 May 1862.

61 T.F.E. (Thomas Frederick Elliot) to Edward Cardwell, 7 July 1865, draft reply en verso of Frederick Seymour to Edward Cardwell, 13 Mar. 1865, BCA, GR 1486, CO 60/20, Reel B-1435.

62 George Graham to W.A.G. Young, Colonial Secretary, 18 Oct. 1862, 'Colonial Correspondence,' BCA, GR 1372, Reel B-1332.

63 G.M. Sproat to Provincial Secretary, 29 Aug. 1872, in British Columbia, Attorney General, 'Documents,' GR 419, Box 10, 'Papers Related to Immigration, 1872,' File 1872/1.

64 Charles Dickens, 'Episcopacy in the Rough,' *All the Year Round*, 23 Feb. 1861, 470–4.

65 Edward W. Said, *Orientalism* (New York: Vintage, 1979).

66 Viscount Milton and W.B. Cheadle, *The North-West Passage by Land. Being the Narrative of an Expedition from the Atlantic to the Pacific* (London: Cassell, Petter, and Galpin, 1865).

67 'Vancouver Island Authors Abroad,' *British Colonist*, 30 Aug. 1865.

68 Gilbert Malcolm Sproat, *British Columbia: Information for Emigrants* (London: Agent General for the Province, 1873) 30.

69 A Returned Digger, *The Newly Discovered Gold Fields of British Columbia*, 8th ed. (London: Darton and Hodge, 1862) 8.

70 Alexander Rattray, *Vancouver Island and British Columbia: Where They Are; What They Are; And What They May Become* (London: Smith, Elder, 1862) 170.

71 J.D. Churchill and J. Cooper. *British Columbia and Vancouver Island Considered as a Field for Commercial Enterprise* (London: Rees and Collin, 1866) 4.

72 England, Emigration Commissioners, *Survey of the Districts of Nanaimo and Cowichan Valley* (London: Groombridge, 1859) 14.

73 A Successful Digger, *Guide Book for British Columbia* (London: Dean, 1862) 5.

74 *Handbook to Vancouver Island and British Columbia with Map* (London: F. Algar, 1862) 28.

75 'What They Think of Our Natives Abroad,' *British Colonist*, 15 June 1861.

76 'The Immigration Bubble,' *Victoria Press*, 27 July 1861. Emphasis in original.

77 'Legislative Council,' *British Colonist*, 4 Feb. 1869.

78 Helmcken, in Dorothy Blakey Smith, ed., *The Reminiscences of Doctor John*

Sebastian Helmcken (Vancouver: University of British Columbia Press, 1975) 116.

79 'Vancouver Island Immigration,' *Victoria Press*, 10 July 1862.

80 Frederick Seymour to Duke of Buckingham and Chandos, 24 Sept. 1867, BCA, GR 1486, CO 60/29, Reel B-1440.

81 'Our Great, Great Want,' *British Colonist*, 6 Oct. 1870.

6 'Fair Ones of a Purer Caste': Bringing White Women to British Columbia

1 One of the Disappointed, Untitled, *British Columbian*, 7 June 1862.

2 See Peggy Pascoe, *Relations of Rescue: The Search for Female Moral Authority in the American West, 1874–1939* (New York: Oxford University Press, 1990); Margaret Strobel, *European Women and the Second British Empire* (Bloomington and Indianapolis: Indiana University Press, 1991); Napur Chaudhuri and Margaret Strobel, eds., *Western Women and Imperialism: Complicity and Resistance* (Bloomington and Indianapolis: Indiana University Press, 1992)

3 James Douglas to the Duke of Newcastle, 18 Oct. 1859, Great Britain, Colonial Office, British Columbia Correspondence (hereafter CO 60), National Archives of Canada (hereafter NAC), MG 11, CO 60/5, Reel B-80.

4 A Successful Digger, *Guide Book for British Columbia* (London: Dean and Sons, 1862) 23.

5 R.C. Lundin Brown, *British Columbia: An Essay* (New Westminster: Royal Engineer Press, 1863) 53.

6 'Inducements for Families to Settle in Victoria,' *British Colonist*, 30 Nov. 1861. Emphasis in original.

7 Matthew Macfie, *Vancouver Island and British Columbia: Their History, Resources and Prospects* (London: Longman, Green, Longman, Roberts and Green, 1865; reprint, Toronto: Coles Canadiana, 1972) 497.

8 Charles Good to Lord Office of the Government, 21 Aug. 1869, CO 60/35, British Columbia Archives (hereafter BCA), GR 1486, Reel B-1446.

9 In Dorothy Blakey Smith, ed., *Lady Franklin Visits the Pacific Northwest: Being Extracts from the Letters of Miss Sophia Craycroft, Sir John Franklin's Niece, Feb. to Apr. 1861 and Apr. to July 1870* (Victoria: Provincial Archives of British Columbia Memoir No. 11, 1974) 65–6.

10 Vancouver City Archives, Photograph Out.P.826, N.382 #1; Photograph Out.P.826, N.382, #2.

11 Alexander Rattray, *Vancouver Island and British Columbia: Where They Are; What They Are; And What They May Become* (London: Smith, Elder, 1862) 175.

12 'Domestic Servants,' *British Colonist*, 12 Nov. 1871.

13 James Gammage to Sir, 3 May 1859, Society for the Propagation of the Gospel in Foreign Parts, 'Letters Received Columbia 1858–1861' (Transcript) BCA, Add Mss H/A/So2, vol. 1, 33.

14 Robert Brown, 'Diary,' BCA, Add Mss 794, Box 1, File 17, 101–2.

15 Judith Worsnop, 'A Re-evaluation of "The Problem of Surplus Women" in 19th-Century England: The Case of the 1851 Census,' *Women's Studies International Forum* 13:1/2 (1990) 21–31.

16 Jessie Boucherett: 'How to Provide for Superfluous Women,' in Josephine E. Butler, ed., *Women's Work and Woman's Culture* (London: Macmillian, 1869); W.R. Greg, 'Why Are Women Redundant?' *National Review* 28 (Apr. 1862) 431–60.

17 B., 'Immigration – Important Letter from South Wales – What We Ought to Do,' *British Colonist*, 2 July 1869.

18 'The Redundancy of Women,' *British Columbian*, 11 June 1869.

19 Fairfax Moresby to Sir, 7 July 1851, Great Britain, Colonial Office, Vancouver Island Correspondence (hereafter CO), University of British Columbia Library (hereafter UBCL), CO 305/3, Reel R288:1.

20 Richard Charles Mayne, *Four Years in British Columbia and Vancouver Island* (London: John Murray, 1862; reprint, Toronto: S.R. Publishers, 1969) 75.

21 Colonista, 'Marriage or Celibacy?' *British Colonist*, 2 Sept. 1868.

22 'Immigration,' *Mainland Guardian*, 9 Feb. 1871.

23 *Third Report of the Columbia Mission with List of Contributions, 1861* (London: Rivingtons [1862]) 51–2.

24 A Returned Digger. *The Newly Discovered Gold Fields of British Columbia*, 8th ed. (London: Darton and Hodge, 1862) 6.

25 [Hudson's Bay Company], *Colonization of Vancouver Island* (London: Horace, 1849) 4.

26 Andrew Muir, 'Private Diary, 9 Nov. 1848–5 Aug. 1850' (Transcript), BCA, Add Mss E/B/M91A; James Douglas to Joseph McKay, 27 Sept. 1853, James Douglas–Joseph William McKay, 'Nanaimo Correspondence, August 1852–September 1853' (Transcript), BCA Add Mss A/C/20.1/N15.

27 Cited in the Earl of Lytton, *The Life of Edward Bulwer, First Lord Lytton*, vol. 2 (London: Macmillan, 1913) 292.

28 'British Columbia – Its Attractions as a Field for Emigration,' *British Columbian*, 30 Dec. 1863; 'Naval and Military Intelligence,' *The Emigrant Soldier's Gazette and Cape Horn Chronicle*, 1 (6 Nov. 1858) in Charles Sinnett: ed., *The Emigrant Soldiers' Gazette, and Cape Horn Chronicle* (New Westminster: The 'British Columbian,' 1863).

29 *The Emigrant Soldiers' Gazette, and Cape Horn Chronicle*, 11 (29 Jan. 1859) in Sinnett: ed, *The Emigrant Soldiers' Gazette*.

30 Colonel Moody to James Douglas, 29 Mar. 1860, in James Douglas to the Duke of Newcastle, 12 May 1860, NAC, MG 11, CO 60/6, Reel B-82.
31 G.C. Lewis to James Douglas, 11 Aug. 1860, draft reply, in James Douglas to the Duke of Newcastle, 12 May 1860, NAC, MG 11, CO 60/9, Reel B-83.
32 G.C.L. (G.C. Lewis), in R. Moody to Under Secretary of State, 9 Apr. 1860, NAC, MG 11, CO 60/9, Reel B-84.
33 T.W.C. Murdoch to Frederic Rogers, 14 Nov. 1860, NAC, MG 11, CO 60/9, Reel B-84.
34 'Unfounded,' *British Colonist*, 23 May 1861.
35 'Arrival of the "Marcella,"' *British Colonist*, 21 May 1861.
36 Maria S. Rye, 'XXIX – The Colonies and their Requirements,' *The English Woman's Review* 8:4 (1 November 1861) 165–71. See Jane Rendall, 'Friendship and Politics: Barbara Leigh Smith Bodichon (1827–91) and Bessie Raynar Parkes (1829–1925),' in Susan Mendus and Jane Rendall, eds., *Sexuality and Subordination: Interdisciplinary Studies of Gender in the Nineteenth Century* (London: Routledge, 1989).
37 A. James Hammerton, *Emigrant Gentlewomen: Genteel Poverty and Female Emigration, 1830–1914* (London: Croom Helm, 1979) 117.
38 Rye, 'XXIX – The Colonies and their Requirements,' 165.
39 Antoinette Burton, *Burdens of History: British Feminists, Indian Women, and Imperial Culture, 1865–1915* (Chapel Hill: University of North Carolina Press, 1994) 2.
40 'Columbian Emigration Society,' *Victoria Press*, 8 June 1862.
41 See, e.g., 'The Columbia Mission,' *London Times*, 28 Feb. 1862; 'Columbian Emigration Society,' *British Columbian*, 21 June 1862.
42 Antoinette Burton, 'From Child Bride to "Hindoo Lady": Rukhmabai and the Debate on Sexual Respectability in Imperial Britain,' *American Historical Review*, 103:4 (Oct. 1998) 1123.
43 In 'The Columbia Mission,' *London Times*, 28 Feb. 1862.
44 *Annual Report of the Columbia Mission 1861*, 42–56;
45 *Annual Report of the Columbia Mission 1861*, 43.
46 'Stray Letters of Emigration,' *The English Woman's Journal* 9:50 (1 Apr. 1862) 109.
47 In *Annual Report of the Columbia Mission 1861*, 53–4.
48 'Female Middle Class Emigration Society Annual Report, 1861,' Fawcett Library, London Guildhall University (hereafter FL), 1/FME, Box 1, File 1, 7.
49 S.C., 'Emigration for Educated Women,' *The English Woman's Journal* 8:87 (1 Mar. 1861) 2.
50 'Female Middle Class Emigration Society Annual Report, 1861,' 4, 7–8.

51 Sarah Crease, in M.S.R. and B.R.P., 'Stray Letters on the Emigration Question,' *The English Woman's Journal* 8:45 (11 Jan. 1861) 241.

52 Maria S. Rye, 'Female Middle Class Emigration,' *The English Woman's Journal* 10:55 (1 Sept. 1862) 29.

53 Maria S. Rye to Bishop Hills, 16 May 1862, ADNW/EPBC, 'Bishop Hills Correspondence,' Box 8 of 8, File 4.

54 Madame L.S. Bodichon to Anonymous, ND [1862]; Madame L.S. Bodichon to Lord Shaftesbury, 26 July 1862, FL, Autograph Letter Collection.

55 Maria S. Rye to Bishop Hills, 16 May 1862, ADNW/EPBC, 'Bishop Hills Correspondence,' Box 8 of 8, File 4. Emphasis in original.

56 Maria S. Rye, 'Female Middle Class Emigration,' *London Times*, 28 July 1862.

57 'Female Emigration,' *London Times*, 3 Nov. 1862.

58 Maria S. Rye to Lord Ripon, 21 Mar. 1871, British Museum, Manuscript Collections, Ripon Papers, vol. 133, Add Mss 43,623, ff81. Also see Nupur Chaudhuri, '"Who Will Help the Girls? Maria Rye and Victorian Juvenile Emigration to Canada, 1869–1895,' in Rita S. Kranidis, ed., *Imperial Objects: Essays on Victorian Women's Emigration and the Unauthorized Imperial Experience* (New York: Twayne, 1998).

59 See Patricia Clark, *The Governesses: Letters from the Colonies, 1862–1882* (London: Hutchinson, 1985); Susan Jackel, ed., *A Flannel Shirt and Liberty: British Emigrant Gentlewomen in the Canadian West, 1880–1914* (Vancouver: University of British Columbia Press, 1982).

60 'Electors of Victoria Town,' *British Colonist*, 20 Dec. 1859.

61 'Vancouver Island House of Assembly,' *Victoria Press*, 9 Oct. 1861.

62 'Enducements [*sic*] to Families to Settle in Victoria,' *British Colonist*, 30 Nov. 1861; 'Mr. Selim Franklin's Address to the Victoria Town Electors,' *British Colonist*, 20 Dec. 1859.

63 H.P.W. to Sir, 30 Apr. 1862, Society for the Propagation of the Gospel in Foreign Parts, 'Letters Received Columbia 1861–1867' (Transcript), BCA, Add Mss H/A/So2, vol. 2, 49–50.

64 'Columbia Emigration Society,' *Victoria Press*, 8 June 1862.

65 Edmund Hope Verney to Harry Verney, 7 Aug. 1862; Edmund Hope Verney to Harry Verney, 16 Aug. 1862, in Pritchard, ed., *Vancouver Island Letters*, 78–80, 83.

66 C.E.C., 'XIV – Middle-Class Female Emigration Impartially Considered: The Emigration of Educated Women Examined from a Colonial Point of View. By a Lady Who Has Resided Eleven Years in One of the Australian Colonies,' *The English Woman's Journal* 10:68 (1 Oct. 1862) 83.

67 S.C., 'Emigration for Educated Women,' 8. Emphasis in original.

68 'Letter from London,' *Victoria Press*, 29 June 1862.
69 'Hope for Educated Women,' *British Colonist*, 1 July 1862.
70 See, for instance, 'Female Emigration,' *Victoria Press*, 23 July 1862; 'Tynemouth,' *British Colonist*, 1 August 1862; 'Hope for Bachelors,' *British Columbian*, 10 May 1862.
71 'Prospects Brightening,' *Victoria Press*, 6 Aug. 1862.
72 'The "Tynemouth's" Invoice of Young Ladies,' *British Colonist*, 11 Sept. 1862.
73 Charles E. Redfern, 'Reminiscences of a Long Sea Voyage in 1862' (Transcript), BCA, Add Mss E/E/R24, 1–2; 'Arrival of the Tynemouth,' *Victoria Press*, 18 Sept. 1862; 'Police Court – Yesterday,' *Victoria Press*, 21 Sept. 1862; 'Police Court,' *Victoria Press*, 24 Sept. 1862; 'Amateur Sailors,' *Victoria Press*, 21 Sept. 1862; 'Another Prosecution Under the Passenger Act,' *Victoria Press*, 15 Oct. 1862.
74 Frederick Whymper, *Travel and Adventure in the Territory of Alaska* (Ann Arbor, MI: University Microfilms, 1966 [London: John Murray, 1868]) 2.
75 George Hills, 'Journal 1 Jan.–10 June 1863,' (Transcript), ADNW/EPBC, 30.
76 John Emmerson, *Voyages, Travels, and Adventures by John Emmerson of Wolsingham* (Durham, England: Wm. Ainsley, 1865) 139.
77 Charles Hayward, 'Diary 1862,' BCA, Reel A-741, np.
78 'Mission Work in British Columbia, Chiefly from the Journals of Rev. R.J. Dundas,' in J.J. Halcombe, *The Emigrant and the Heathen, or, Sketches of Missionary Life* (London: Society for Promoting Christian Knowledge, [1870?]) 226–7.
79 'Wouldn't Let Them Aboard,' *British Colonist*, 19 Sept. 1862.
80 'Landed,' *Victoria Press*, 19 Sept. 1862
81 'The Female Immigrants,' *Victoria Press*, 21 Sept. 1862.
82 'The Tynemouth and Her Cargo,' *British Columbian*, 24 Sept. 1862.
83 'The "Tynemouth's" Females,' *British Colonist*, 20 Sept. 1862.
84 'The Female Immigrants,' *Victoria Press*, 22 Sept. 1862.
85 'Arrival of the "Tynemouth,"' *British Colonist*, 19 Sept. 1862.
86 'The Tynemouth and Her Cargo,' *British Columbian*, 24 Sept. 1862.
87 Richard Courtney to W.A.G Young, 30 July 1862, 'Colonial Correspondence,' BCA, GR 1372, Reel B-1320.
88 Edmund Hope Verney to Harry Verney, 20 Sept. 1862, in Pritchard, ed., *Vancouver Island Letters*, 89.
89 Gilbert Malcolm Sproat, Robert Burnaby, and W.M. Davie to Governor, 29 Sept. 1862, 'Colonial Correspondence,' BCA, GR 1372, Reel B-1366; Michel Foucault, *Discipline and Punish: The Birth of the Prison*, trans. Alan Sheridan (New York: Vintage, 1977).

90 Rev. Cridge to James Douglas, 14 July 1863, 'Colonial Correspondence,' BCA, GR 1372, Reel B-1322.
91 'The Immigration Committee,' *Victoria Press*, 22 Sept. 1862.
92 Edmund Hope Verney to Harry Verney, 20 Sept. 1862, in Pritchard, ed., *Vancouver Island Letters*, 90.
93 'Shocking Depravity,' *British Colonist*, 29 Sept. 1862.
94 'Impressive Sermon,' *British Colonist*, 22 Sept. 1862.
95 B.R.P., 'XXVIII.- The Last News of the Emigrants' *The English Woman's Journal* 11:63 (1 May 1863) 185; Cridge to Douglas, 14 July 1863; Hills, 'Journal 1 Jan. – 10 June 1863,' 5.
96 'Female Middle-Class Emigration Society,' *London Times*, 12 Sept. 1862; 'Arrival of the Robert Lowe,' *British Colonist*, 12 Jan. 1863.
97 'Emigration Direct,' *Victoria Press*, 18 Sept. 1862.
98 'Arrival of the Robert Lowe,' *British Colonist*, 12 Jan. 1863.
99 'Arrival of the Robert Lowe,' *British Colonist*, 12 Jan. 1863.
100 'The Robert Lowe,' *British Colonist*, 13 Jan. 1863.
101 Edmund Hope Verney to Harry Verney, 6 Jan. 1863, in Pritchard, *Vancouver Island Letters*, ed., 114.
102 Cridge to Douglas, 14 July 1863; 'The Female Infirmary,' *British Colonist*, 21 Nov. 1864.
103 'Immigration Mass Meeting,' *British Colonist*, 14 Mar. 1864.
104 'Legislative Council,' *British Columbian*, 25 Jan. 1865.
105 'Female Emigration,' *British Columbian*, 20 June 1868; Untitled, *British Colonist*, 28 Jan. 1869.
106 Frederick Seymour to Earl of Granville, 17 Mar. 1868, in CO 60/35, BCA, GR 1486, Reel B-1445.
107 See James E. Hendrickson, ed., *Journals of the Colonial Legislatures of the Colonies of Vancouver Island and British Columbia 1851–1871*, vol. 4, *Journals of the Legislative Council of British Columbia, 1866–1871* (Victoria: Provincial Archives of British Columbia, 1980) 212–3, 218.
108 'Speech of his Excellency the Governor, at the Proration of the Legislative Council,' *British Columbia Government Gazette*, 15 Mar. 1869, NAC, MG 11, CO 63/4, Reel B-1490.
109 Henry Mason to The Bishop, 9 July 1869, in 'Female Immigration Letter Book,' 6–9.
110 A Subscriber, 'The Female Immigration Scheme,' *British Colonist*, 15 May 1869; Family Man, 'Immigration,' *British Colonist*, 26 Apr. 1869.
111 Minutes for 20 Apr. 1869 and 20 May 1869, in Henry Mason to the Colonial Secretary, 18 Sept. 1869, 'Colonial Correspondence,' BCA, GR 1372, Reel B-1345; Henry Mason to The Bishop, 26 June 1869, Henry Mason to

The Bishop, 9 July 1869, Henry Mason to Officer Administering the Government, 18 June 1869, in 'Female Immigration Letter Book,' 6–9, 10, 11; George Hills, 'Hills Journal 1869' (Transcript), ADNW/EPBC, 6; 'Female Immigration,' *British Columbian*, 21 Apr. 1869.

112 Untitled, *British Colonist*, 4 Feb. 1869.
113 Untitled, *British Colonist*, 26 Mar. 1869.
114 Slum Gullion, 'Hurry Up with the Girls (Rhymes Suggested by the Female Immigration Movement),' *Cariboo Sentinel*, 1 Apr. 1869.
115 A. Musgrave to the Earl of Granville, 18 Oct. 1869, CO 60/36, BCA, GR 1486, Reel B-1446; Hills, 'Journal 1869,' 43–4.
116 'Female Immigration,' *British Colonist*, 17 Aug. 1869.
117 'Arrival of Female Immigrants,' and 'Arrival of the Alpha,' *British Colonist*, 15 June 1870.
118 Wm. Pearse, John Robson, W.J. MacDonald to Colonial Secretary, 12 July 1870, 'Colonial Correspondence,' BCA, GR 1372, Reel B-1314.
119 'Legislative Council,' *British Colonist*, 13 Mar. 1869.
120 Wm. Pearse to Colonial Secretary, 29 Dec. 1870, GR 1372, 'Colonial Correspondence,' BCA, Reel B-1341.
121 Rita S. Kranidis, 'Introduction: New Subjects, Familiar Grounds,' in Rita S. Kranidis, ed., *Imperial Objects*, 3.

7 'An Unspeakable Benefit?': White Women in Colonial Society

1 *Third Report of the Columbia Mission with List of Contributions, 1861* (London: Rivingtons [1862]) 43.
2 Harriet Bradley, *Men's Work, Women's Work: A Sociological History of the Sexual Division of Labour in Employment* (Minneapolis: University of Minnesota Press, 1989) Part A.
3 'Womens' Rights,' *British Colonist*, 27 Sept. 1871.
4 Elizabeth Fisher and Louisa Macdonald to Governor Seymour, 1 May 1869, British Columbia Archives (hereafter BCA), 'Colonial Correspondence,' GR 1372, Reel B-1328.
5 Robert Stevenson, 'Partial Diary 1863' (Transcript) BCA, Add Mss 315 pt.2, 6.; Letter from Cariboo,' *British Columbian*, 18 June 1864.
6 'Trades Licences Assessment Roll,' *British Columbia Government Gazette*, 16 Mar. 1867, National Archives of Canada (hereafter NAC), CO 63/3, MG 11, Reel B-1489.
7 Sylvia Van Kirk, 'A Vital Presence: Women in the Cariboo Gold Rush, 1862–1875,' in Gillian Creese and Veronica Strong-Boag, eds., *British Columbia Reconsidered: Essays on Women* (Vancouver: Press Gang, 1992) 22.

8 Margaret A. Ormsby, ed., *A Pioneer Gentlewoman in British Columbia: The Recollections of Susan Allison* (Vancouver: University of British Columbia, 1976) 16.
9 'Burning of Barkerville,' *Cariboo Sentinel*, 23 Sept. 1868.
10 'Queen's Birthday Ball,' *Cariboo Sentinel*, 7 May 1866.
11 Walter B. Cheadle, *Cheadle's Journal of Trip Across Canada 1862–1863* (Edmonton: Hurtig, 1971) 240.
12 'The Blackfoot Country,' *British Colonist*, 7 Feb. 1866.
13 'Terpsichorean' *Cariboo Sentinel*, 13 Nov. 1869; 'Opening Night,' *Cariboo Sentinel*, 20 May 1867.
14 Edward Mallandaine, *First Victoria Directory, Third [Fourth] Issue, And British Columbia Guide* (Victoria: E. Mallandaine, 1871) 76.
15 'Second Letter To My Freend [sic] Sawney,' *Cariboo Sentinel*, 23 July 1866.
16 C. Sharp, 'A Glimpse of Cariboo,' *British Colonist*, 24 Aug. 1866.
17 'Dancing in Cariboo,' *British Colonist*, 27 July 1865.
18 Mary A. Norman to Bishop Hills, 18 Feb. 1862, 'Bishop Hills Correspondence,' Box 8 of 8, File 4, Anglican Church of Canada, Archives of the Diocese of New Westminster / Ecclesiastical Province of British Columbia, Vancouver School of Theology (hereafter ADNW/EPBC).
19 See, e.g., W., 'Female Middle-Class Emigration to British Columbia,' *London Times*, 2 Aug. 1862.
20 James Douglas to the Duke of Newcastle, 14 June 1863, NAC, MG 11, Great Britain, Colonial Office, Original Correspondence, Vancouver Island (hereafter CO 305) CO 305/20, Reel B-244.
21 W. Driscoll Gosset, 'Female Emigration,' *London Times*, 6 Dec. 1862.
22 'Female Middle Class Emigration Society Annual Report, 1861' Fawcett Library (hereafter FL), 1/FME, Box 1, File 1, 7–14.
23 George Hills, 'Journal 1 Jan.–10 June 1863' (Transcript), ADNW/EPBC, 6–7.
24 Mary Moody to Mother, 20 May 1862, Mary Moody, 'Outward Correspondence' (Transcript), BCA, Add Mss 60, vols. 1 & 2, 92–3.
25 S.R. Crease, 'The Bride Ships,' 'Crease Family Papers,' BCA, Add Mss 55, vol. 13, File 3, 83–5.
26 Vancouver Island, Police and Prisons Department, Esquimalt, 'Charge Book 1862–1866,' BCA, GR 0428.
27 *The New Gold Fields of British Columbia and Vancouver's Island* (London: Plummer's Library, 1862) 15.
28 George Hills, 'Journal 1861' (Transcript), ADNW/EPBC, 132.
29 Edmund Hope Verney to Harry Verney, 6 Jan. 1863 and Edmund Hope Verney to Harry Verney, 20 Apr. 1863, in Allan Pritchard, ed., *Vancouver*

Island Letters of Edmund Hope Verney, 1862–1865 (Vancouver: UBC Press, 1996) 115, 131.

30 James Douglas to Duke of Newcastle, 25 Oct. 1861, NAC, MG 11, CO 305/17, Reel B-242.

31 Susan Abercrombie Holmes (née Nagle), 'Diaries 1865–1911,' vol. 1, BCA, Add Mss 2576, Reel A-1628, 10–11, emphasis in original; Susan Abercrombie Holmes (née Nagle), 'Diaries 1865–1911' (Transcript) vol. 2, BCA, Add Mss 2576, 84.

32 Christ Church Hope, 'Marriage Register 1862–1872,' ADNW/EPBC, RG4.0.34; St John the Divine Yale, 'Marriage Register 1861–1895,' ADNW/EPBC; St John's Victoria, 'Parochial Register of Baptisms and Marriages 1860–1871,' ADNW/EPBC, Text 202, Box 6; Holy Trinity Cathedral New Westminster, 'vol. 1, *Marriage Register*, City of Vancouver Archives, Add Mss 603, Reel m-21; St Paul's Nanaimo, 'Register of Baptisms and Marriages, 1860–1881,' Anglican Church of Canada, Diocesan Archives of British Columbia, Text 330, Box 8. Marriages between two partners not readily identified as non-white and with full ages given are included.

33 Trever Burnard, 'A Failed Settler Society: Marriage and Demographic Failure in Early Jamaica,' *Journal of Social History* 28:1 (Fall 1994) 74; Ellen Gee, 'Marriage in Nineteenth-Century Canada,' *Canadian Review of Sociology and Anthropology* 9:3 (Aug. 1982) 311–25.

34 David Peterson del Mar, *What Trouble I Have Seen: A History of Violence against Wives* (Cambridge: Harvard University Press, 1996) 16.

35 See 'Protection to the Ladies,' *British Colonist*, 25 May 1862.

36 See, e.g., Sophia McLean to Frederick Seymour, 1 June 1865, 'Colonial Correspondence,' BCA, GR 1372, Reel B-1344; 'A Just Call for Charity,' *British Colonist*, 6 May 1863; 'A Distressing Case,' *British Colonist*, 17 Mar. 1866; 'Subscriptions,' *British Colonist*, 11 Apr. 1866.

37 'Police Court,' *Vancouver Times*, 1 Feb. 1866; 'An Amazon,' *British Colonist*, 17 May 1866; 'Incurable,' *British Colonist*, 29 May 1866; 'Ann Porteous,' *British Colonist*, 30 May 1866.

38 Catherine Edwards to Joseph Trutch, 16 Sept. 1865, 'Colonial Correspondence,' BCA, GR 1372, Reel B-1326.

39 'Female Suffrage: The Spiciest Evening of the Series. Victoria a City of Woman-Whippers,' *British Colonist*, 26 Oct. 1871.

40 'The Coroner's Inquest,' *Vancouver Times*, 5 Dec. 1864; 'The Death of Joanna Maguire,' *Vancouver Times*, 7 Dec. 1864; 'The Late Johanna Maguire,' *Vancouver Times*, 10 Dec. 1864.

41 'Shameful,' *Victoria Press*, 20 Oct. 1861; 'The Assault upon the Ex-Wife,' *British Colonist*, 11 Mar. 1870.

42 'Wife Whipping,' *Victoria Press*, 13 Dec. 1861.

43 'A Woman Stabbed by a "Man,"' *British Colonist*, 11 Sept. 1862.

44 'Wife Beating,' *British Colonist*, 11 Sept. 1866.

45 Advertisement, 'To the Ladies of British Columbia,' *British Columbian*, 20 June 1866. Emphasis in original.

46 'The Governor's Lady,' *British Colonist*, 21 Mar. 1864; 'The Departure of Governor Kennedy,' *British Colonist*, 24 Oct. 1866.

47 'Appendix 2: *In the Early Fifties*,' Dorothy Blakey Smith, ed., *The Reminiscences of Doctor John Sebastian Helmcken* (Vancouver: University of British Columbia Press, 1975) 293.

48 *The Handbook of British Columbia and Emigrant's Guide to the Gold Fields* (London: W. Oliver, [1862]) 72.

49 'Letter from Lytton City,' *Victoria Daily Chronicle*, 12 Mar. 1864.

50 'Later from Fraser River,' *Weekly Victoria Gazette*, 30 July 1858.

51 'Letter from the Cariboo,' *British Colonist*, 18 Apr. 1865.

52 Here, McClintock refers to the feminization of colonized land. But her analysis can be also be applied, in an almost opposite way, to the construction of white women as symbols of imperial conquest. See Anne McClintock, *Imperial Leather: Race, Gender, and Sexual in the Colonial Conquest* (London: Routledge, 1996) 24–5.

53 Economy, 'Public Improvements,' *British Colonist*, 8 Jan. 1859.

54 'Inducements to Families to Settle in Victoria,' *Victoria Press*, 2 Dec. 1861; 'The Indian Question Again,' *British Columbian*, 3 May 1862.

55 Untitled, *British Colonist*, 29 May 1869; 'A Captive Girl among the Mitinahts: Thrilling Incidents,' *British Colonist*, 24 Feb. 1871, emphasis in original; 'The Captive Girl,' *British Colonist*, 1 Mar. 1871; 'Not Our Child,' *British Colonist*, 2 Mar. 1871.

56 'Police Court,' *Nanaimo Gazette*, 6 November 1865; Amirah Inglis, *The White Women's Protection Ordinance: Sexual Anxiety and Politics in Papua* (London: Sussex University Press, 1975).

57 M. Stannard, *Memoirs of a Professional Lady Nurse* (London: Simpkin, Marshall, 1873) 192.

58 Matthew Macfie, *Vancouver Island and British Columbia: Their History, Resources, and Prospects* (London: Longman, Green, Longman, Roberts, and Green, 1865) 379.

59 Testimony of John Crowley, *R v O'Connor*, British Columbia, Attorney General, 'Documents, 1857–1966' (hereafter 'Attorney General Documents') BCA, GR 419, Box 2, File 1862/10.

60 'Deposition of Esther Meiss, Police Court Testimony, Victoria VI, 31st May 1864,' *R v Schultz and Trickey*, 'Attorney General Documents,' BCA, GR 419,

Box 4, File 1864/38; 'Court of Assizes: Rape,' *Victoria Daily Chronicle*, 1 Aug. 1864.

61 Police Court Testimony, Victoria VI, 31st May 1864, *R* v *Schultz and Trickey*.

62 Police Court Testimony, Victoria VI, 31st May 1864, *R* v *Schultz and Trickey*; 'Profane, But Forcible,' *Victoria Daily Chronicle*, August 1864.

63 'The Alleged Larceny,' *British Colonist*, 6 Mar. 1863; 'Female Immigrants,' *Victoria Daily Chronicle*, 28 June 1864.

64 'Brutal Treatment of a Woman,' *British Colonist*, 31 Jan. 1863; Arthur Kennedy to Edward Cardwell, 30 Nov. 1864, NAC, MG 11, CO 305/23, Reel B-246.

65 Henry Wakeford to Richard Gollenge, 21 Jan. 1864, in Arthur Kennedy to Edward Cardwell, 30 Nov. 1864, NAC, MG 11, CO 305/23, Reel B-246.

66 'Vancouver's Island, Extract from Minutes of Executive Council, 29th Nov. 1864,' in Arthur Kennedy to Edward Cardwell, 30 Nov. 1864, NAC, MG 11, CO 305/23, Reel B-246.

67 'Police Court,' *Vancouver Times*, 22 Feb. 1865.

68 Crawford Killian, *Go Do Some Great Thing: The Black Pioneers of British Columbia* (Vancouver: Douglas and McIntyre, 1978) 102; Ruth Sandwell, personal communication, 23 Aug. 1997.

69 Ebenezer Robson, 'Diary,' BCA, Reel 17A, np. Emphasis in original.

70 'The Rape Case,' *Victoria Daily Chronicle*, 29 July 1864.

71 *R* v *Henry Lester*, 'Attorney General Documents,' BCA, GR 419, Box 6, File 1866/25.

72 Mary E. to Aunt, 6 Nov. 1862, in B.R.P., 'XXVIII. – The Last News of the Emigrants,' *The English Woman's Journal* 11:63 (1 May 1863) 185.

73 Anna Davin, 'Imperialism and Motherhood,' *History Workshop* 5 (Spring 1978) 9–66.

74 'Marriage or Celibacy?' *British Colonist*, 2 Sept. 1868.

75 Jane Fawcett to Emma, 24 June 1860, Jane Fawcett, 'Extracts from Letters and Diary' (Transcript) BCA, Add Mss 1963, 90–2. Emphasis in original.

76 Ormsby, ed., *A Pioneer Gentlewoman*; Jean Barman, 'Lost Okanagan: In Search of the First Settler Families,' *Okanagan History* 60 (1996) 14–15.

77 Nell Irving Painter, 'Three Southern Women and Freud: A Non-Exceptionalist Approach to Race, Class, and Gender in the Slave South,' in Ann-Louise Shapiro, ed., *Feminists Revision History* (New Brunswick, NJ: Rutgers University Press, 1994).

78 George An [sic] Deans to Brother and Sister, 13 Aug. 1856, Annie Deans, 'Outward Correspondence' (Transcript), BCA, Add Mss E/B/D343A.

79 'The Cowichan District,' *Vancouver Times*, 9 Sept. 1864.

80 Stannard, *Memoirs*, 161–3.

81 Mrs. Mallandaine (née Townsend), quoted in N. de Bertrand Lugrin, *The Pioneer Women of Vancouver Island 1843–1866* (Victoria: Women's Canadian Club, 1928) 150.

82 Adelaide Annie Amelia (De Veulle) Ash, 'Diary Aug. 28, 1871 to Mar. 21 1872' (Transcript) BCA, Add Mss E/C/As31A c.2, 1, 36–7, 45; Mary Moody to Em, 15 Mar. 1861, Mary Moody, 'Outward Correspondence,' Transcript, BCA, Add Mss 60, vols. 1 & 2, 56.

83 Richard Somerset Mackie, *The Wilderness Profound: Victorian Life on the Gulf of Georgia* (Victoria: Sono Nis, 1995) 65; Robert Brown, 'Journal of the Vancouver Island Exploring Expedition,' in John Hayman, ed., *Robert Brown and the Vancouver Island Exploring Expedition* (Vancouver: UBC Press, 1989) 111. Translations his.

84 'An Occasional Paper – Letters from the Bishop of Columbia to Commissary Garret, Pemsanoe,' *British Colonist*, 13 Oct. 1860; John Downwall, *A Sermon Preached in St James' Church Piccadilly at the Annual Service of the Columbia Mission* (London: Rivingtons, 1862) 8.

85 'Collegiate School for Girls,' *British Colonist*, 13 Oct. 1865.

86 'Laying the Corner-Stone of St Ann's Convent School,' *British Colonist*, 13 Sept. 1871.

87 See, e.g., 'Popular Education,' *British Columbian*, 16 Feb. 1867; 'Our School Matters,' *Nanaimo Gazette*, 20 Nov. 1865.

88 Ann Laura Stoler, 'Rethinking Colonial Categories: European Communities and the Boundaries of Rule,' *Comparative Studies in Society and History* 31:1 (Jan. 1989) 152; 'Mr Macfie on Immigration:' *British Colonist*, 28 Nov. 1865.

89 Philanthropist, 'Society for the Relief of the Poor,' *British Colonist*, 22 July 1859.

90 See *Female Aid Association: Report for the Year Ending Feb., 1864* (n.p., n.d. [1864]).

91 'The Hospital for Females,' *Vancouver Times*, 23 Nov. 1864.

92 Female Infirmary, 'Papers relating to Ladies Committee, 1863–1868,' BCA, N/A/F34.1; Cridge, 'Diary, 1868' (Transcript), BCA, Add Mss 320, Box 7, 48.

93 'The Police Magistrate and Concert Saloons,' *British Colonist*, 14 Aug. 1863; Advertisement, 'Notice to Whom It May Concern,' *Victoria Daily Chronicle*, 31 Mar. 1864.

94 'The Waitress Question,' *British Colonist*, 12 July 1864; A.F. Pemberton to Henry Wakeford, 12 July 1864, 'Colonial Correspondence,' BCA GR 1372, Reel B-1356.

95 Edward Mallandaine, *First Victoria Directory, Second Issue, and British Columbia Guide* (Victoria: Higgins and Long, 1868) 38; Dr Ash to Colonial Secretary, 19 May 1870, 'Colonial Correspondence,' BCA, GR 1372, Reel B-1301.

96 Dr Ash to Colonial Secretary, 19 May 1870.

97 One of the Subscribers, 'Lunacy at the Police Barracks,' *British Colonist*, 10 Dec. 1869; 'The Insane Ladies,' *British Colonist*, 9 Dec. 1869.

98 See notes enclosed in Dr Ash to Colonial Secretary, 19 May 1870.

99 Notes enclosed in Dr Ash to Colonial Secretary, 3 June 1870, 'Colonial Correspondence,' BCA, GR 1372, Reel B-1301.

100 'Melancholy Case of Lunacy,' *British Colonist*, 20 Oct. 1870.

101 Anthony Musgrave to the Earl of Kimberley, 21 June 1871, CO 60/44, BCA, GR 1486, Reel B-1452; Mary Ellen Kelm, 'Ross, Flora Amelia (Hubbs),' *Dictionary of Canadian Biography*, vol. 12 (Toronto: University of Toronto Press, 1990) 929–30.

102 Untitled, *Weekly Victoria Gazette*, 28 Dec. 1859.

103 'Inducements to Families to Settle in Victoria,' *Victoria Press*, 2 Dec. 1861.

104 'Female Emigration,' *British Columbian*, 3 Feb. 1863.

105 Tal. O Eifion, 'A Missionary for Cariboo,' *Cariboo Sentinel*, 15 July 1867.

106 C.J.H., 'The "Female Immigration" Suits in the Summary Court,' *Victoria Daily Chronicle*, 29 June 1864.

107 Fenton Aylmer, ed., *A Cruise in the Pacific: From the Log of a Naval Officer*, vol. 2 (London: Hurst and Blackett, 1860) 295–6.

108 Monitor, 'The Vote of $3,000 in Aid of Immigration,' *Victoria Daily Chronicle*, 1 Mar. 1864.

109 Maria Rye to Madame L.S. Bodichon, 20 Sept. 1865, Autograph Letter Collection, FL.

110 Edmund Hope Verney to Harry Verney, 20 Sept. 1862, Edmund Hope Verney to Harry Verney, 14 Sept. 1862, Edmund Hope Verney to Harry Verney, 22 Sept. 1862, in Pritchard, ed., *Vancouver Island Letters*, 88, 91–2.

111 Gilbert Sproat to Lieutenant Governor, 3 Nov. 1871, 'Memo re European Immigration into B.C.,' BCA, Add Mss 257, File 3. Emphasis in original.

112 G.M. Sproat, 'Memorandum of a few Suggestions for opening the business of emigration to British Colombia, referred to as Memo C, in a letter of G.M. Sproat to the Honourable the Provincial Secretary, dated 29th Aug. 1872,' 'Attorney General Documents,' GR 419, Box 10, File 1872/1, 4–5.

113 Untitled, *British Colonist*, 17 Apr. 1869.

114 Family Man, 'Immigration,' *British Colonist*, 26 Apr. 1869. Emphasis in original.

Conclusion: Gender, Race, and Our Years on the Edge of Empire

1 Ann Laura Stoler, 'Rethinking Colonial Categories: European Communities and the Boundaries of Rule,' *Comparative Studies in Society and History* 31 (Jan. 1989) 135–61, and 'Sexual Affronts and Racial Frontiers: European Identities and Cultural Politics of Exclusion in Colonial Southeast Asia,' *Comparative Studies in Society and History* 34 (July 1992): 514–51.
2 Mrinalini Sinha, 'Gender and Imperialism: Colonial Policy and the Ideology of Moral Imperialism in Late-Nineteenth-Century Bengal,' in Michael S. Kimmel, ed., *Changing Men: New Directions in Research on Men and Masculinity* (New York: Sage, 1987); Kenneth Ballhatchet, *Race, Sex, and Class under the Raj: Imperial Attitudes and Policies and Their Critics, 1783–1905* (London: Weidenfeld and Nicholson, 1980).
3 Tina Loo, Review of Cole Harris, *The Resettlement of British Columbia: Essays on Colonialism and Geographic Change, BC Studies* 117 (Spring 1998) 66.
4 Anne McClintock, *Imperial Leather: Race, Gender, and Sexuality in the Colonial Conquest* (New York: Routledge, 1995) 36–9.
5 Himani Bannerji, 'Politics and the Writing of History,' in Ruth Roach Pierson and Nupur Chaudhuri, eds., *Nation, Empire, Colony: Historicizing Gender and Race* (Indianapolis: University of Indiana Press, 1998) 290.
6 Georges E. Sioui, *For an Amerindian Auto-History: An Essay on the Foundations of a Social Ethic*, Sheila Fischman, trans. (Montreal: McGill-Queen's University Press, 1992).
7 Catherine Hall, *White Male and Middle Class: Explorations in Feminism and History* (London: Routledge, 1992) 21.
8 Ruth Frankenberg, *White Women, Race Matters: The Social Construction of Whiteness* (Minneapolis: University of Minnesota Press, 1993) 10.
9 Claudia Knapman, *White Women in Fiji, 1835–1930: The Ruin of Empire?* (Sydney: Allen and Unwin, 1986); Helen Callaway, *Gender, Culture, and Empire: European Women in Colonial Nigeria* (Urbana: University of Illinois Press, 1987); Beverly Gartrell, 'Colonial Wives: Villains or Victims?' in Hilary Callan and Shirley Ardner, eds., *The Incorporated Wife* (London: Croom Helm, 1984); Margaret Strobel, *European Women and the Second British Empire* (Bloomington: Indiana University Press, 1991). In Canada, see Barbara Eileen Kelcey, 'Jingo Bells, Jingo Belles, Dashing through the Snow: White Women and Empire on Canada's Arctic Frontier,' PhD Dissertation, University of Manitoba, 1994.
10 Jane Haggis, 'Gendering Colonialism or Colonising Gender? Recent Women's Studies Approaches to White Women and the History of British Colonialism,' *Women's Studies International Forum* 13:1/2 (1990) 105–15. Also see

Margaret Jolly, 'Colonizing Women: The Maternal Body and Empire,' in Sneja Gunew and Anna Yeatman, eds., *Feminism and the Politics of Difference* (Halifax: Fernwood Press, 1993).

11 Patricia E. Roy, *A White Man's Province: British Columbia Politicians and Chinese and Japanese Immigrants, 1858–1914* (Vancouver: UBC Press, 1989).

12 Veronica Strong-Boag, 'Society in the Twentieth-Century,' in Hugh Johnson, ed., *The Pacific Province: A History of British Columbia* (Vancouver: Douglas and McIntyre, 1996) 277.

13 See articles in 'The Nisga'a Treaty,' a special issue of *BC Studies*, 120 (Winter 1998–9).

References

Abbreviations

ACC/ADBCA Anglican Church of Canada, Anglican Diocese of British Columbia Archives, Victoria, British Columbia

ADNW/EPBC Anglican Church of Canada, Anglican Diocese of New Westminster and Ecclesiastical Province of British Columbia, Vancouver School of Theology, University of British Columbia, Vancouver British Columbia

BCA British Columbia Archives, Victoria, British Columbia

BCHQ British Columbia Historical Quarterly

BM British Museum, London, England

CAUCC Central Archives of the United Church of Canada, Victoria University, Toronto, Ontario

CVA City of Vancouver Archives, Vancouver, British Columbia

CVicA City of Victoria Archives, Victoria, British Columbia

FL Fawcett Library, London Guildhall University, London, England

NAC National Archives of Canada

PRO Public Records Office, Kew Gardens, England

UBCL University of British Columbia Library

Primary Sources

Archival Sources

Ash, Adelaide Annie Amelia (De Veulle), 'Diary August 28, 1871 to March 21 1872' (Transcript). BCA, Add Mss E/C/As31A c.2.
'Autograph Letter Collection,' FL.

Bayley, Charles. 'Early Life on Vancouver Island' (Transcript). BCA, Add Mss E/B/B34.2.

Blair, George. 'Diary Feb. 17, 1862–Dec. 29, 1863' (Transcript). BCA, Add Mss 186.

Bogg, Edward B. 'Journal of Her Majesty's Hired Surveying Vessel, Beaver, 1863.' PRO, ADM/101/276.

Brown, Robert. 'Robert Brown Collection.' BCA, Add Mss 794.

Burrard Inlet Mechanic's Institute. 'Minute Book, September 17 1868 to April 12, 1884' (Transcript). BCA, Add Mss E/C/B94.

British Columbia. *British Columbia Government Gazette.* NAC, MG 11, CO 63.

British Columbia, Attorney General. 'Documents, 1857–1966.' BCA, GR 419.

British Columbia and Vancouver Island. 'Colonial Correspondence.' BCA, GR 1372.

Bryant, Cornelius. 'Diary,' Parts I and II (Transcript). CAUCC, 86.047C/TR, File 1, 2.

City of Victoria. 'Council Minutes.' Vol. O, 25 August 1862 to 11 July 1871. CVicA, City Record Series 1.

City of Victoria. 'Corporation By Laws, City Clerks Office 1862–1888,' CVicA.

Cormie, P. 'Journal of Her Majesty's Sloop: Sparrowhawk, 1869.' PRO, ADM/101/278.

Crease, Henry. 'Henry Pelling Pellew Crease Collection.' BCA, Add Mss 54.

Crease, Sarah, and H.P.P Crease and Susan Crease. 'Crease Family Papers,' BCA, Add Mss 55.

Christ Church Cathedral. 'Proceedings of the Ladies' Committee re the Restoration of the Parish Church and Cathedral, 1869–71, 1876–85.' BCA, Add Mss 520, Box 1, Folder 7.

Christ Church Hope. 'Marriage Register 1862–1872.' ADNW/EPBC, RG4.0.34.

Crickmer, William Burton. 'Letters.' ADNW/EPBC, PSA 50, File 3.

Cridge, Edward. 'Edward Cridge Papers.' BCA, Add Mss 320.

Deans, Annie. 'Outward Correspondence' (Transcript). BCA, Add Mss E/B/D343A.

Douglas, James, 'Letters.' BCA, Reel 246A

– and Joseph William McKay, 'Nanaimo Correspondence, August 1852–September 1853' (Transcript). BCA, Add Mss A/C/20.1/N15

Fawcett, Jane. 'Extracts from Letters and Diary.' BCA, Add Mss 1963.

Female Infirmary. 'Papers Relating to Ladies Committee, 1863–1868.' BCA, Add Mss N/A/F34.1.

Female Middle Class Emigration Society. 'Annual Reports.' FL, 1/FME, Box 1, File 1.

– 'Correspondence.' FL, 1/FME, Box 1, File 2, 3.

Garret, A.C. 'Sketches of a Missionary Tour to Cariboo Victoria June 2 1865.' ADNW / EPBC, MS #3.
– 'Reminiscences' (Transcript). ADNW / EPBC, PSA 52, File 57.
Good, John Booth. 'The Utmost Bounds of the West: Pioneer jottings of forty years missionary reminiscences of the Out West Pacific Coast A.D. 1861 A.D. 1900.' ADNW / EPBC, PSA 52, File 9 (Transcript from original held at BCA).
Great Britain, Colonial Office. 'Blue Books of Statistics, British Columbia, 1861–1870.' BCA, CO 64 / 1, Reel 626A.
– 'Blue Books of Statistics, Vancouver Island, 1863–65.' BCA, CO 478 / 3, Reel 625A.
– 'Original Correspondence, British Columbia, 1858–1871.' BCA, CO 60, GR 1486 and NAC, MG 11, CO 60.
– 'Original Correspondence, Vancouver Island, 1846–1867.' NAC, MG 11, CO 305 and UBCL.
Hankin, P. 'Memoirs' (Transcript). BCA, Add Mss E / B / H19A.
Harris, Douglas. 'Martha (Douglas) Harris Collection.' BCA, Add Mss 2789.
Hayward, Charles. 'Diary 1862.' BCA, Reel A-741.
Hills, George. 'Journal 1836–1861' (Transcript). ADNW / EPBC, MS 65a, PSA 57.
– 'Journals,' 1861–1871 (Transcripts). ADNW / EPBC.
– 'Bishop Hills Collection.' Box 8, ADNW / EPBC.
– 'The British Columbia and Yukon Church Aid Society Collection, Series I: The Bishop George Hills Papers.' ADNW / EPBC, Box PSA 42.
– 'Bishop George Hills Correspondence In and Out.' ACC / ADBCA, Text 57.
Holmes, Susan Abercrombie (Nagle). 'Diaries 1865–1911' (Transcript). BCA, Add Mss 2576, Reel A-1628.
Holy Trinity Cathedral. 'Marriage Register.' CVA, Add Mss 603, Vol. 1, Reel 21.
King, William C. 'Trip to California' (Transcript). BCA, Add Mss 99.
Matthews, J.S. 'Brideships.' CVA, Add Mss 54, Vol. 13, File 07020.
– 'Indian Wives of White Men.' CVA, Add Mss 54. Vol. 13, File 06612.
Melrose, Robert Melrose. 'Diary, August 1852–July 1857' (photostat). BCA Add Mss, E / B / M49.1A, 18.
Moody, Mary. 'Outward Correspondence' (Transcript). BCA, Add Mss 60, Vol. 1, 2.
Muir, Andrew. 'Private Diary, 9 November 1848–5 August 1850' (Transcript). BCA, Add Mss E / B / M91A.
'The Nightingale Papers.' BM, Vol. 61, Add Mss 45, 799.
Pearse, Benjamin William. 'Early Settlement of Vancouver Island, 1900' (Transcript). BCA, Add Mss E / B / P31.

Pidcock, R.H. 'Adventures in Vancouver Island 1862' (Transcript). BCA, Add Mss 728, Vol. 4a.

Redfern, Charles E. 'Reminiscences of a Long Sea Voyage in 1862' (Transcript). BCA, Add Mss, E/E/R24.

'Ripon Papers.' BM, Vol. 133, Add Mss 43,623.

Robson, Ebenezer. 'Diary.' BCA, Reel 17A.

– 'How Methodism Came to British Columbia.' CAUCC, 86.226C.

– 'Notes from the Diary of Rev. Ebenezer Robson, D.D., Pioneer Wesleyan Missionary at Fort Hope, B.C., from March 12 to May 13 1860' (Transcript). BCA, Add Mss H/D/R57/R57.2A.

St John's Church, Victoria. 'Parochial Register of Baptisms and Marriages for district of St John's Victoria 1860–1871.' ACC/ADBCA, Text 202, Box 6.

St John the Divine Church, Yale. 'Marriage Register 1861–1895, St John the Divine, Yale,' ADNW/EPBC.

St Paul's Church, Nanaimo. 'Register of Baptisms and Marriages, 1860–1881, St Paul's Nanaimo.' ACC/ADBCA, Text 330, Box 8.

Society for the Propagation of the Gospel in Foreign Parts. 'Letters Received Columbia 1858–1874' (Transcript). BCA, Add Mss H/A/So2, Vol. 1–3.

Stevenson, Robert. 'Papers,' BCA, Add Mss 315.

Vancouver Island, Police and Prisons Department, Esquimalt. 'Charge Book 1862–1866.' BCA, GR 0428.

Wesleyan Methodist Church (Great Britain). 'Foreign Missions: America, The British Dominions in North America, 1851–1893.' CAUCC, Reel D 8.1–2.

Wright, Amos. 'Correspondence of Jessie Hassard Wright.' BCA, Add Mss 1976.

Published Primary Documents

Alston, Graham E. *A Handbook to British Columbia and Vancouver Island.* London: F. Algar, 1870.

Anderson, Alexander C. *Hand-Book and Map to the Gold Region of Frazer's and Thompson's Rivers.* San Francisco: J.J. Le Count, 1858.

Anderson, James. *Sawney's Letters and Cariboo Rhymes.* Barkerville, BC: *Cariboo Sentinel*, 1868. Reprint, Toronto: Bibliographic Society of Canada, 1950.

Aylmer, Fenton, ed. *A Cruise in the Pacific: From the Log of a Naval Officer*, vol. 2. London: Hurst and Blackett, 1860.

Barrett-Lennard, C.E. *Travels in British Columbia: With the Narrative of a Yacht Voyage Round Vancouver's Island.* London: Hurst and Blackett, 1862.

Begbie, Matthew B. *Journey into the Interior of British Columbia*, 'Communicated by the Duke of Newcastle, read December 12 1859.' n.p.

Boucherett, Jessie. 'How to Provide for Superfluous Women,' in Josephine E.
    Butler, ed., *Woman's Work and Woman's Culture*. London: Macmillan, 1869.
British Columbia. *Report of the Hon. H.L. Langevin, C.B., Minister of Public
    Works*. Ottawa: I.B. Taylor, 1872.
Brown, Robert. 'Mission Work in British Columbia.' *Mission Life* (1 Sept. 1870).
Brown, R.C. Lundin. *British Columbia: An Essay*. New Westminster: Royal
    Engineer Press, 1863.
– *British Columbia. The Indians and Settlers at Lillooet. Appeal for Missionaries*.
    London: R. Clay, Sons, and Taylor, 1870.
– *Klatsassan, and Other Reminiscences of Missionary Life in British Columbia*.
    London: Society for Promoting Christian Knowledge, 1873.
Cameron, Malcolm. *Lecture Delivered by the Hon. Malcolm Cameron to the Young
    Men's Mutual Improvement Association*. Quebec: G.E. Desbartes, 1865.
Canada. *Report of the Superintendent of Indian Affairs for British Columbia for
    1872 and 1873*. Ottawa: I.B. Taylor, 1873.
Champness, W. 'To Cariboo and Back: An Emigrant's Journey to the Gold
    Field of British Columbia.' *Leisure Hour* 696 (29 Apr. 1863) 208–60.
Cheadle, Walter B. *Cheadle's Journal of Trip across Canada 1862–1863*. Edmon-
    ton: Hurtig, 1971.
Churchill, J.D., and J. Cooper. *British Columbia and Vancouver Island Considered
    as a Field for Commercial Enterprise*. London: Rees and Collin, 1866.
Columbia Mission. *Annual Reports, 1860–1869*. London: Rivingtons, n.d.
    [1861–1870].
Cornwallis, Kinahan. *The New El Durado: or, British Columbia*. London: Thomas
    Cautley Newby, 1858. Reprint, New York, Arno Press, 1973.
Cridge, E., and R.J. Dundas. *To the Miners of British Columbia Resident for the
    Winter in Victoria*. [Victoria?]: n.p., n.d.
Crosby, Thomas. *Among the An-ko-me-nums of the Pacific Coast*. Toronto:
    William Briggs, 1907.
– *Up and Down the North Pacific Coast by Canoe and Mission Ship*. Toronto: The
    Missionary Society of the Methodist Church, 1914.
Dashaway Association. *Constitution and By-Laws of the Dashaway Association of
    Victoria: V.I.* Victoria: Colonist, [1860 or 1861?].
Delavault, E.E., and Isabel McInnes, ed. and trans. 'Extracts from *Ein Ausflug
    nach Britisch-Columbien im Jahre 1858*,' by Carl Friesach; and Charles Major,
    'Letter from Charles Major, Dated Fort Hope, September 20, 1859,' in 'Two
    Narratives of the Fraser River Gold Rush.' *BCHQ* 1 (July 1941) 221–31.
Dickens, Charles. 'Episcopacy in the Rough.' *All the Year Round* (23 Feb. 1861),
    470–4.

Domer, John. *New British Gold-Fields: A Guide to British Columbia and Vancouver Island*. London: William Henry Angel, 1858.

Downwall, John. *A Sermon Preached in St James' Church Piccadilly at the Annual Service of the Columbia Mission*. London: Rivingtons, 1862.

Duncan, Eric. *From Shetland to Vancouver Island: Recollections of Seventy-Five Years*. Edinburgh: Oliver and Boyd, 1937.

Duthie, Wallace D., ed., John Sheepshanks, *A Bishop in the Rough*. London: Smith, Elder, 1909.

Emmerson, John. *Voyages, Travels, and Adventures by John Emmerson of Wolsingham*. Durham, England: Wm. Ainsley, 1865.

England, Emigration Commissioners. *Colonization Circulars Nos. 18–31*. London: G.E. Eyre and W. Spottiswoode, 1858–72.

Fawcett, Edgar. *Some Reminiscences of Old Victoria*. Toronto: William Briggs, 1912.

Female Aid Association: Report for the Year Ending February, 1864. Victoria: n.p., [1864].

Female Infirmary for the Sick and Destitute of All Denominations. Victoria: n.p., [1866].

Female Infirmary for the Sick and Destitute of All Denominations. Victoria: n.p., [1867].

Forbes, Charles. *Prize Essay. Vancouver Island: Resources and Capabilities, as a Colony*. Victoria: Colonial Government, 1862.

Garret, John. *Columbia Mission: A Sermon Preached in St Stephen's, Westminster*. London: Rivingtons, 1869.

Grant, George M. *Ocean to Ocean: Sandford Fleming's Expedition through Canada in 1872*. Toronto: James Campbell and Son, 1873.

Greg, W.R. 'Why Are Women Redundant?' *National Review* 28 (Apr. 1862) 431–60.

Halcombe, J.J. *The Emigrant and the Heathen, or, Sketches of Missionary Life*. London: Society for Promoting Christian Knowledge, n.d. [1870?].

– *Stranger than Fiction*. London: Society for Promoting Christian Knowledge, 1872.

The Handbook of British Columbia and Emigrant's Guide to the Gold Fields. London: W. Oliver, [1862].

Handbook to Vancouver Island and British Columbia with Map. London: F. Algar, 1862.

Harvey, Arthur. *A Statistical Account of British Columbia*. Ottawa: G.E. Desbartes, 1867.

Hayman, John, ed., *Robert Brown and the Vancouver Island Exploring Expedition*. Vancouver: UBC Press, 1989.

Hazlitt, William Carew. *British Columbia and Vancouver Island*. London: Routledge, 1858.

– *The Great Gold Fields of the Cariboo with an Authentic Description, Brought down to the Latest Period of British Columbia and Vancouver Island with an Accurate Map.* 1862. Reprint, Victoria: Klanak Press, 1974.

Hendrickson, James E. 'Two Letters from Walter Colquhoun Grant.' *BC Studies* 26 (Jan.–Apr. 1973) 3–15.

Hendrickson, James E., ed. *Journals of the Colonial Legislatures of the Colonies of Vancouver Island and British Columbia 1851–1871*, vol. 1, *Journals of the Council, Executive Council, and Legislative Council of Vancouver Island, 1851–1866.* Victoria: Provincial Archives of British Columbia, 1980.

– *Journals of the Colonial Legislatures of the Colonies of Vancouver Island and British Columbia 1851–1871*, vol. 2, *Journals of the House of Assembly, Vancouver Island, 1856–1863.* Victoria: Provincial Archives of British Columbia, 1980.

– *Journals of the Colonial Legislatures of the Colonies of Vancouver Island and British Columbia 1851–1871*, vol. 3: *Journals of the House of Assembly, Vancouver Island, 1863–1866.* Victoria: Provincial Archives of British Columbia, 1980.

– *Journals of the Colonial Legislatures of the Colonies of Vancouver Island and British Columbia 1851–1871*, vol. 4, *Journals of the Executive Council, 1864–1871, and of the Legislative Council, 1864–1866, of British Columbia.* Victoria: Provincial Archives of British Columbia, 1980.

– *Journals of the Colonial Legislatures of the Colonies of Vancouver Island and British Columbia 1851–1871*, vol. 5, *Journals of the Legislative Council of British Columbia, 1866–1871.* Victoria: Provincial Archives of British Columbia, 1980.

Higgins, D.W. *The Mystic Spring and Other Tales of Western Life.* Toronto: William Briggs, 1904.

– *The Passing of a Race and More Tales of Western Life.* Toronto: William Briggs, 1905.

[Hudson's Bay Company]. *Colonization of Vancouver Island.* London: Horace and Son, 1849.

Ireland, Willard E., ed. 'Gold-Rush Days in Victoria: 1858–1859,' by James Bell. *BCHQ*, 12 (July 1948) 231–46.

– 'First Impressions: Letter of Colonel Richard Clement Moody, R.E., To Arthur Blackwood, February 1, 1859.' *BCHQ* 15 (Jan.–Apr. 1951) 85–107.

Johnson, R. Byron. *Very Far West Indeed: A Few Rough Experiences on the North-West Pacific Coast*, 3rd ed. London: Sampson Low, Marston, Low and Searle, 1872.

Langley, A.J. *A Glance at British Columbia and Vancouver's Island in 1861.* London: Robert Hardwick, 1862.

Leduc, Joanne, ed. Thomas McMicking, *Overland from Canada to British Columbia.* Vancouver: University of British Columbia Press, 1981.

Lillard, Charles, ed. William Henry Collison. *In the Wake of the War Canoe*. Victoria: Sono Nis, 1981.

Lillard, Charles, ed. *The Nootka: Scenes and Studies of Savage Life*, by Gilbert M. Sproat. 1868. Reprint Victoria: Sono Nis, 1987.

[Lord, John Keast] J.K.L. '"How We Went to Fort Rupert," and Made a Strange Purchase.' *Once a Week*, 24 June 1865, 19–22.

Lord, John Keast. *At Home in the Wilderness: What to Do There and How to Do It*. London: Robert Hardiwcke, 1876.

– *The Naturalist in Vancouver Island and British Columbia*. 2 vol. London: Richard Bentley, 1866.

Lyndon, John W. ed., *Queen Charlotte Islands: A Narrative of Discovery and Adventure in the North Pacific*, by Frances Poole, C.E. London: Hurst and Blackett, 1872. Reprint, Vancouver: Douglas and McIntyre, 1972.

Macdonald, William John. *A Pioneer 1851*. Victoria: Author, [1914?].

Macfie, Matthew. *The Impending Contact of the Aryan and Turanian Races, with Special Reference to Recent Chinese Migrations*. London: Sunday Lecture Society, 1878.

– *Vancouver Island and British Columbia: Their History, Resources, and Prospects*. London: Longman, Green, Longman, Roberts, and Green, 1865.

Mallandaine, Edward. *First Victoria Directory; Comprising a General Directory ...* Victoria: E. Mallandaine, 1860.

– *First Victoria Directory, Second Issue, and British Columbia Guide*. Victoria: Higgins and Long, 1868.

– *First Victoria Directory, Third Issue, and British Columbia Guide* Victoria: Mallandaine, 1869.

– *First Victoria Directory, Third [Fourth] Issue, and British Columbia Guide*. Victoria: Mallandaine, 1871.

Mark, William. *Cariboo: A True and Correct Narrative to the Cariboo Gold Diggings, British Columbia*. Stockton: W.M. Wright, 1863.

Mayne, Richard Charles. *Four Years in British Columbia and Vancouver Island*. London: John Murray, 1862. Reprint, Toronto: S.R. Publishers, 1969.

Mikron, Beta [William Coutts Keppel, Earl of Albermarle]. 'British Columbia and Vancouver's Island.' *Fraser's Magazine* 58 (1858) 493–504.

Milton, Viscount, and W.B. Cheadle. *The North-West Passage by Land. Being the Narrative of an Expedition from the Atlantic to the Pacific*. London: Cassell, Petter, and Galpin, 1865.

Moore, James. 'The Discovery of Hill's Bar in 1858.' *BCHQ* 4 (July 1939) 215–20.

The New Gold Fields of British Columbia and Vancouver's Island. London: Plummer's Library, 1862.

The New Government Colony: British Columbia and Vancouver Island: A Complete Hand-Book. London: William Penney, 1858.

Nunis, Doyce B., ed. *The Golden Frontier: The Recollections of Herman Francis Reinhart, 1851–1869.* Austin: University of Texas Press, 1962.

Ormsby, Margaret, ed. *A Pioneer Gentlewoman in British Columbia: The Recollections of Susan Allison.* Vancouver: University of British Columbia Press, 1976.

'Our North Pacific Colonies.' *The Westminster Review* 170 (Oct. 1866) 199–206.

Pemberton, J. Despard. *Facts and Figures Relating to Vancouver Island and British Columbia Showing What to Expect and How to Get There.* London: Longman, Green, Longman, and Roberts, 1860.

Preston, Richard Arthur, ed. *For Friends at Home: A Scottish Emigrant's Letters from Canada, California, and the Cariboo, 1844–1864,* by James Thomas. Montreal and London: McGill-Queen's University Press, 1974.

Pritchard, Allan, ed. *Vancouver Island Letters of Edmund Hope Verney, 1862–1865.* Vancouver: UBC Press, 1996.

Rattray, Alexander. *Vancouver Island and British Columbia: Where They Are; What They Are; And What They May Become.* London: Smith, Elder, 1862.

Rawlings, Thomas. *Emigration, with Special Reference to Minnesota, U.S., and British Columbia.* London: Clayton, 1864.

Reid, Robie L., ed. 'To the Fraser River Mines in 1858,' by C.C. Gardiner. *BCHQ,* 1 (Oct. 1937) 243–53.

A Returned Digger. *The Newly Discovered Gold Fields of British Columbia.* 8th ed. London: Darton and Hodge, 1862.

Shadd, Mary A. *A Plea for Emigration; or, Notes of Canada West, In its Moral, Social, and Political Aspect with Suggestions Respecting Mexico, West Indies, and Vancouver's Island, for the Information of Colored Emigrants.* Detroit: George W. Pattison, 1852.

Sinnett, Charles, ed. *The Emigrant Soldiers' Gazette, and Cape Horn Chronicle.* New Westminster: The 'British Columbian,' 1863.

Skewton, Lavinina [pseud.]. *The 'Occasional Paper': One Letter from the Honorable Lady Lavinina Skewton, London: to the Bishop of Columbia.* Victoria: British Colonist, 1860.

Smith, Dorothy Blakey, ed. 'Henry Guillod's Journal of a Trip to Cariboo, 1862.' *BCHQ* 19 (July–Oct. 1955) 187–232.

– 'The Journal of Arthur Thomas Bushby, 1858–1859.' *BCHQ* 21 (1957–8) 83–198.

– *Lady Franklin Visits the Pacific Northwest: Being Extracts from the Letters of Miss Sophia Cracroft, Sir John Franklin's Niece, February to April 1861 and April to July 1870,* Memoir No.11. Victoria: Provincial Archives of British Columbia, 1974.

- *The Reminiscences of Doctor John Sebastian Helmcken*. Vancouver: University of British Columbia Press, 1975.
Snow, W. Parker. *British Columbia, Emigration, and Our Colonies Considered Practically, Socially, and Politically*. London: Piper, Stephenson, and Spence, 1858.
Society for the Propagation of Gospel in Foreign Parts. *Work in the Colonies: Some Account of the Missionary Operations of the Church of England in Connexion with the Society for the Propagation of the Gospel in Foreign Parts*. London: Griffith and Farran, 1865.
Sproat, Gilbert Malcolm. *British Columbia: Information for Emigrants*. London: Agent General for the Province, 1873.
- 'Career of a Scotch Boy Who Became Hon. John Tod: An Unfashionable True Story' and Madge Wolfenden, 'Appendix: Notes on the Tod Family.' *BCHQ* 18 (July–Oct. 1954) 133–238.
Stanley, George F.G., ed. *Mapping the Frontier: Charles Wilson's Diary of the Survey of the 49th Parallel, 1858–1862, While Secretary of the British Boundary Commissions*. Toronto: Macmillan, 1970.
Stannard, M. *Memoirs of a Professional Lady Nurse*. London: Simpkin, Marshall, 1873.
Stewart, William J. 'British Columbia.' n.p.: [1862?].
A Successful Digger. *Guide Book for British Columbia*. London: Dean and Sons, 1862.
Waddington, Alfred. *The Fraser Mines Vindicated, or, the History of Four Months*. Victoria: De Cosmos, 1858.
Wakefield, Edward Gibbon. 'A View of the Art of Colonization: With Present Reference to the British Empire.' In M.F. Lloyd Pritchard, ed., *The Collected Works of Edward Gibbon Wakefield*. London: Collins, 1868.
Walkem, Wymond W. *Stories of Early British Columbia*. Vancouver: News Advertiser, 1914.
Whymper, Frederick. *Travel and Adventure in the Territory of Alaska*. London: John Murray, 1868. Reprint, Ann Arbor: University Microfilms, 1966.
Williams, John G. *The Adventures of a Seventeen-Year-Old Lad and the Fortunes He Might Have Won*. Boston: Collins Press, 1894.

Newspapers (titles vary slightly)

British Colonist (Victoria), 1858–71.
British Columbian (New Westminster), 1861–69.
Cariboo Sentinel (Barkerville), 1865–71.
The English Woman's Journal (London), 1858–64.

The Englishwoman's Review (London), 1866–71.
London Times (London), 1858–71.
Mainland Guardian, (New Westminster), 1870–1.
Nanaimo Gazette (Nanaimo), 1865–7.
Northwest Collection Clipping File, Vancouver Public Library.
The Scorpion (New Westminster), 1864.
Vancouver Times (Vancouver) 1864–6.
Victoria Daily Chronicle (Victoria) 1864.
Victoria Press (Victoria), 1861–2.
Weekly Victoria Gazette (Victoria) 1858–60.

Secondary Sources

Acoose, Janice / Misko-Kìsikàwihkwè (Red Sky Woman). *Iskwewak – Kah' Ki Yaw Ni Wahkomakanak: Neither Indian Princesses Nor Easy Squaws.* Toronto: Women's Press, 1995.
Acheson, Steven. 'Culture Contact, Demography, and Health among the Aboriginal Peoples of British Columbia.' In Peter H. Stephenson et al., eds., *A Persistent Spirit: Towards Understanding Aboriginal Health in British Columbia.* Victoria: University of Victoria, 1995.
Akrigg, G.P.V., and Helen B. Akrigg. *British Columbia, 1847–1871.* Vancouver: Discovery Press, 1977.
Anderson, Benedict. *Imagined Communities: Reflections on the Origin and Spread of Nationalism.* Rev. ed. London: Verso, 1991.
Anderson, Karen. *Chain Her by One Foot: The Subjugation of Native Women in Seventeenth-Century New France.* London: Routledge, 1991.
Anderson, Kay. *Vancouver's Chinatown: Racial Discourse in Canada, 1875–1980.* Montreal and Kingston: McGill-Queen's University Press, 1991.
Anderson, Marnie. *Women of the West Coast: Then and Now.* Sidney, BC: Sand Dollar Press, 1993.
Backhouse, Constance. *Petticoats and Prejudice: Women and Law in Nineteenth-Century Canada.* Toronto: Osgoode Society, 1991.
Ballhatchet, Kenneth. *Race, Sex and Class under the Raj: Imperial Attitudes and Policies and Their Critics, 1783–1905.* London: Weidenfeld and Nicolson, 1980.
Bancroft, Hubert Howe. *History of British Columbia, 1792–1887,* vol. 32 in *The Works of Hubert Howe Bancroft.* San Francisco: History Company, 1887.
Bannerji, Himani. 'Politics and the Writing of History.' In Ruth Roach Pierson and Nupur Chauduri, eds., *Nation, Empire, Colony: Historicizing Gender and Race.* Indianapolis: University of Indiana Press, 1998.

– *Thinking Through: Essays on Feminism, Marxism, and Anti-Racism.* Toronto: The Women's Press, 1995.

Barber, Marilyn. 'The Gentlewomen of Queen Mary's Coronation Hostel.' In Barbara K. Latham and Roberta J. Pazdro, eds., *Not Just Pin Money: Selected Essays on the History of Women's Work in British Columbia.* Victoria: Camosun College, 1984.

Barman, Jean. 'Invisible Women: Aboriginal Mothers and Mixed-Race Daughters in Rural Pioneer British Columbia.' In Ruth Sandwell, ed., *Beyond the City Limits: Rural History in British Columbia.* Vancouver: UBC Press, 1999.

– 'Lost Okanagan: In Search of the First Settler Families,' *Okanagan History* (1996) 9–20.

– 'New Land, New Lives: Hawaiian Settlement in British Columbia.' In *Hawaiian Journal of History* 29 (1995) 1–32.

– 'Taming Aboriginal Sexuality: Gender, Power, and Race in British Columbia, 1850–1900,' *BC Studies* 115/116 (Autumn/Winter 1997/98) 237–66.

– *The West beyond the West: A History of British Columbia.* Toronto: University of Toronto Press, 1991.

Bederman, Gail. *Manliness and Civilization: A Cultural History of Gender and Race in the United States, 1880–1917.* Chicago: University of Chicago Press, 1995.

Belshaw, John Douglas. 'The British Collier in British Columbia: Another Archetype Reconsidered.' *Labour / Le Travail* 34 (Fall 1994) 11–36.

Berger, Carl. *The Sense of Power: Studies in the Ideas of Canadian Imperialism, 1867–1914.* Toronto: University of Toronto Press, 1970.

Berger, Mark T. 'Imperialism and Sexual Exploitation: A Response to Ronald Hyam's "Empire and Sexual Opportunity."' *Journal of Imperial and Commonwealth History* 17:1 (1988) 83–9.

Bhabha, Homi. 'Of Mimicry and Man: The Ambivalence of Colonial Discourse.' *October* 28 (Spring 1984) 125–34.

Bolt, Clarence. *Thomas Crosby and the Tsimshian: Small Shoes for Feet Too Large.* Vancouver: UBC Press, 1992.

Bourgeault, Ron. 'Race, Class and Gender: Colonial Domination of Indian Women.' *Socialist Studies: A Canadian Annual* 5 (1989) 87–115.

Bracken, Christopher. *The Potlatch Papers: A Colonial Case History.* Chicago: University of Chicago Press, 1997.

Bradbury, Bettina. 'From Civil Death to Separate Property: Changes in the Legal Rights of Married Women in Nineteenth-Century New Zealand.' *New Zealand Journal of History* 29:1 (1995) 40–66.

– 'Women's History and Working-Class History.' *Labour / Le Travail* 19 (Spring 1987) 23–43.

Bradley, Harriet. *Men's Work, Women's Work: A Sociological History of the Sexual Division of Labour in Employment*. Minneapolis: University of Minnesota Press, 1989.

Brandt, Gail Cuthbert. 'Postmodern Patchwork: Some Recent Trend in the Writing of Women's History in Canada.' *Canadian Historical Review* 72:4 (December 1991) 441–70.

Brouwer, Ruth Compton. *New Women for God: Canadian Presbyterian Women and Indian Missions, 1876–1914*. Toronto: University of Toronto Press, 1990.

Brown, Jennifer S.H. *Strangers in Blood: Fur Trade Company Families in Indian Country*. Vancouver: University of British Columbia Press, 1980.

Buckley, Suzann. 'British Female Emigration and Imperial Development: Experiments in Canada, 1885–1931.' *Hecate* 3:2 (1977) 26–40.

Burnard, Trever. 'A Failed Settler Society: Marriage and Demographic Failure in Early Jamaica.' *Journal of Social History* 28:1 (1994) 63–82.

Burton, Antoinette. *Burdens of History: British Feminists, Indian Women, and Imperial Culture, 1865–1915*. Chapel Hill: University of North Carolina Press, 1994.

– 'From Child Bride to "Hindoo Lady": Rukhmabai and the Debate on Sexual Respectability in Imperial Britain.' *American Historical Review* 103:4 (1998) 1119–46.

– 'A "Pilgrim Reformer" at the Heart of the Empire: Behramji Malabari in Late-Victorian London,' *Gender and History*, 8: 2 (August 1996) 175–96.

Burton, Valerie. 'The Myth of Bachelor Jack: Masculinity, Patriarchy and Seafaring Labour.' In Colin Howell and Richard J. Twomey, eds., *Jack Tar in History: Essays in the History of Maritime Life and Labour*. Fredericton: Acadiensis Press, 1991.

Butler, Anne M. *Daughters of Joy, Sisters of Mercy: Prostitutes in the American West, 1865–90*. Urbana: University of Illinois Press, 1985.

Cail, Robert E. *Land, Man, and the Law: The Disposal of Crown Lands in British Columbia, 1871–1913*. Vancouver: University of British Columbia Press, 1974.

Callaway, Helen. *Gender, Culture, and Empire: European Women in Colonial Nigeria*. Urbana: University of Illinois Press, 1987.

Carby, Hazel V. 'White Woman Listen! Black Feminism and the Boundaries of Sisterhood.' In Centre for Contemporary Cultural Studies, ed., *The Empire Strikes Back: Race and Racism in 70s Britain*. London: Huchinson, 1983.

Carter, Sarah. *Capturing Women: The Manipulation of Cultural Imagery in Canada's Prairie West*. Montreal and Kingston: McGill-Queen's University Press, 1997.

Castañeda, Antonia I. 'Sexual Violence in the Politics and Policies of Conquest: Amerindian Women and the Spanish Conquest of Alta California.' In

Adela de la Torre and Beatríz M. Pasquera, eds., *Building with Our Hands: New Directions in Chicana Studies*. Berkeley: University of California Press, 1993.

– 'Women of Color and the Rewriting of Western History: The Discourse, Politics, and Decolonization of History.' *Pacific Historical Review* (1992) 501–33.

Chaudhuri, Nupur. '"Who Will Help the Girls?" Maria Rye and Victorian Juvenile Emigration to Canada, 1869–1895.' In Rita S. Kranidis, ed., *Imperial Objects: Essays on Victorian Women's Emigration and the Unauthorized Imperial Experience*. New York: Twayne, 1998.

Chaudhuri, Nupur, and Margaret Strobel, eds. *Western Women and Imperialism: Complicity and Resistance*. Bloomington: Indiana University Press, 1992.

Clark, Patricia. *The Governesses: Letters from the Colonies, 1862–1882*. London: Hutchinson, 1985.

Clark, S.D. 'Mining Society in British Columbia and the Yukon.' In Robert A.J. McDonald and W. Peter Ward, eds., *British Columbia: Historical Readings*. Vancouver: Douglas and MacIntyre, 1981.

Cohen, Marjorie Griffin. *Women's Work, Markets, and Economic Development in Nineteenth-Century Ontario*. Toronto: University of Toronto Press, 1988.

Comaroff, John, and Jean Comaroff. *Ethnography in the Historical Imagination*. Boulder, CO: Westview Press, 1992.

Connell, R.W. 'The Big-Picture: Masculinities in Recent World History.' *Theory and Society* 22 (1993) 597–623.

Constantine, Stephen. 'Introduction: Empire Migration and Imperial Harmony.' In Stephen Constantine ed., *Emigrants and Empire: British Settlement in the Dominions between the Wars*. Manchester: Manchester University Press, 1990.

Cooper, Carol. 'Native Women of the Northern Pacific Coast: An Historical Perspective, 1830–1900.' *Journal of Canadian Studies* 27:4 (1992–3) 44–75.

Cruikshank, Julie. 'Images of Society in Klondike Gold Rush Narratives: Skookum Jim and the Discovery of Gold.' *Ethnohistory* 39:1 (1992) 20–41.

Davidoff, Leonore, and Catherine Hall. *Family Fortunes: Men and Women of the English Middle Class, 1780–1850*. Chicago: University of Chicago Press, 1987.

Davin, Anna. 'Imperialism and Motherhood.' *History Workshop*, 5 (Spring 1978) 9–66.

Dawson, Graham. *Solider Heroes: British Adventure, Empire, and the Imagining of Masculinities*. London: Routledge, 1994.

Demeritt, David. 'Visions of Agriculture in British Columbia.' *BC Studies* 108 (1995–6) 29–60.

Devens, Carol. '"If We Get the Girls, We Get the Race": Missionary Education of Native American Girls.' *Journal of World History* 3:4 (1992) 219–37.

- 'Separate Confrontations: Gender as a Factor in Indian Adaptation to European Colonization in New France.' *American Quarterly* 38:3 (1986) 460–80.

Dubinsky, Karen. *Improper Advances: Rape and Heterosexual Conflict in Ontario, 1880–1929.* Chicago: University of Chicago Press, 1993.

Dubinsky, Karen, and Lynne Marks, 'Beyond Purity: A Response to Joan Sangster.' *Left History* 3:2 and 4:1 (1996) 205–20.

Duff, Wilson. *The Indian History of British Columbia*, vol. 1, *The Impact of the White Man.* Victoria: Province of British Columbia, 1969.

Dunk, Thomas W. *It's a Working Man's Town: Male Working-Class Culture.* Montreal and Kingston: McGill-Queen's University Press, 1991.

Fabian, Ann. *Card Sharps, Dream Books, and Bucket-Shops: Gambling in Nineteenth-Century America.* Ithaca, NY: Cornell University Press, 1990.

Faragher, John Mark. 'The Custom of the Country: Cross Cultural Marriages in the Far Western Fur Trade.' In Lillian Schlissel, Vicki L. Ruiz, and Janice Monk, eds., *Western Women: Their Land, Their Lives.* Albuquerque: University of New Mexico Press, 1988.

Fingard, Judith. *The Dark Side of Life in Victoria Halifax.* Halifax: Pottersfield Press, 1988.

- *Jack in Port: Sailortowns of Eastern Canada.* Toronto: University of Toronto Press, 1982.

Fisher, Robin. *Contact and Conflict: Indian–European Relations in British Columbia*, 2nd ed. Vancouver: UBC Press, 1992.

- 'Contact and Trade, 1774–1849.' In Hugh J.M Johnson, ed., *The Pacific Province.* Vancouver: Douglas and McIntyre, 1996.

Fiske, Jo-Anne. 'Colonization and the Decline of Women's Status: The Tsimshian Case.' *Feminist Studies* 17:3 (1991) 509–36.

Forbes, Elizabeth. *Wild Roses at Their Feet: Pioneer Women of Vancouver Island.* Vancouver: British Columbia Centennial '71 Committee, 1971.

Foucault, Michel. *Discipline and Punish: The Birth of the Prison.* Trans. Alan Sheridan. New York: Vintage, 1977.

- *The History of Sexuality*, vol. 1, *An Introduction.* Trans. Robert Hurley. New York: Vintage, 1979.

Frankenberg, Ruth. *White Women, Race Matters: The Social Construction of Whiteness.* Minneapolis: University of Minnesota Press, 1993.

Gagan, Rosemary R. *A Sensitive Independence: Canadian Methodist Women Missionaries in Canada and the Orient, 1881–1925.* Montreal and Kingston: McGill-Queen's University Press, 1992.

Galois, Robert, and Cole Harris. 'Recalibrating Society: The Population Geography of British Columbia in 1881.' *Canadian Geographer* 38:1 (1994) 37–53.

Gartrell, Beverly. 'Colonial Wives: Villains or Victims?' In Hilary Callan and Shirley Ardner, eds., *The Incorporated Wife*. London: Croom Helm, 1984.

Gilbert, Arthur N. 'Buggery and the British Navy, 1700–1861.' *Journal of Social History* 10:1 (1976) 45–71.

Gillis, John R. *For Better, for Worse: British Marriages, 1600 to the Present*. New York: Oxford University Press, 1985.

Goldberg, David Theo. 'The Social Formation of Racist Discourse.' In David Theo Goldberg, ed., *The Anatomy of Racism*. Minneapolis: University of Minnesota Press, 1990.

Goldie, Terry. *Fear and Temptation: The Image of the Indigene in Canadian, Australian, and New Zealand Literatures*. Montreal and Kingston: McGill-Queen's University Press, 1989.

Gorn, Elliott J. '"Gouge and Bite, Pull Hair and Scratch": The Social Significance of Fighting in the Southern Backcountry.' *American Historical Review* 90:1 (1985) 18–43.

Gothard, Janice. '"Radically Unsound and Mischievous": Female Migration to Tasmania, 1856–1863.' *Australian Historical Studies* 23:93 (1989) 386–404.

Gough, Barry M. 'The Character of the British Columbia Frontier.' In W. Peter Ward and Robert A.J. McDonald, eds., *British Columbia: Historical Readings*. Vancouver: Douglas and McIntyre, 1981.

– *Gunboat Frontier: British Maritime Authority and Northwest Coast Indians, 1846–90*. Vancouver: University of British Columbia Press, 1984.

Green, Ranya. 'The Pocahontas Perplex: The Image of Indian Women in American Culture.' In Ellen Carol DuBois and Vicki L. Ruiz, eds., *Unequal Sisters: A Multi-Cultural Reader in U.S. Women's History*. New York: Routledge, 1990.

Gresko, Jacqueline. '"Roughing It in the Bush" in British Columbia: Mary Moody's Pioneer Life in New Westminster 1859–1863.' In Barbara Latham and Roberta Pazdro, eds., *Not Just Pin Money: Selected Essays on the History of Women's Work in British Columbia*. Victoria: Camosun College, 1984.

Griswold, Robert L. 'Anglo Women and Domestic Ideology in the American West in the Nineteenth and Early Twentieth Centuries.' In Lillian Schlissel, Vicki L. Ruiz, and Janice Monk, eds., *Western Women: Their Land, Their Lives*. Albuquerque: University of New Mexico Press, 1988.

Guitiérrez, Ramón A. *When Jesus Came, the Corn Mothers Went Away: Marriage, Sexuality, and Power in New Mexico, 1500–1849*. Stanford: Stanford University Press, 1991.

Haggis, Jane. 'Gendering Colonialism or Colonising Gender? Recent Women's Studies Approaches to White Women and the History of British Colonialism.' *Women's Studies International Forum* 13:1/2 (1990) 105–15.

Hall, Catherine. '"From Greenland's Icy Mountains ... to Africa's Golden

Sand": Ethnicity, Race, and Nation in Mid-Nineteenth-Century England.'
Gender and History 5:2 (1993) 212–30.

– 'Gender Politics and Imperial Politics: Rethinking the Histories of Empire.'
In Verene Shepherd et al., eds., *Engendering History: Caribbean Women in
Historical Perspective*. New York: St Martin's Press, 1995.

– *White, Male, and Middle Class: Explorations in Feminism and History*. London:
Routledge, 1991.

Hall, Henry S. *The Colonial Office: A History*. London: Longmans, Green, 1937.

Hammerton, James A. *Emigrant Gentlewomen: Genteel Poverty and Female
Emigration, 1830–1914*. London: Croom Helm, 1979.

Harkin, Michael. 'Contested Bodies: Affliction and Power in Heiltsuk Culture
and History.' *American Ethnologist* 21:3 (1994) 586–604.

– 'Engendering Discipline: Discourse and Counterdiscourse in the Methodist–
Heiltsuk Dialogue.' *Ethnohistory* 43:4 (1996) 642–61.

Harris, Cole. *The Resettlement of British Columbia: Essays on Colonialism and
Geographical Change*. Vancouver: UBC Press, 1997.

Hendrickson, James E. 'The Constitutional Development of Colonial Vancouver Island and British Columbia.' In W. Peter Ward and Robert A.J.
McDonald, eds., *British Columbia: Historical Readings*. Vancouver: Douglas
and McIntyre, 1981.

Heron, Craig. 'Towards Synthesis in Canadian Working-Class History: Reflections on Bryan Palmer's Rethinking.' *Left History* 1:1 (1993) 109–21.

Hitchins, Fred H. *The Colonial Land and Emigration Commission*. Philadelphia:
University of Pennsylvania Press, 1931.

Hoe, Susanna. *The Private Life of Old Hong Kong: Western Women in the British
Colony*. Hong Kong: Oxford University Press, 1991.

Hyam, Ronald. *Empire and Sexuality: The British Experience*. Manchester:
Manchester University Press, 1990.

Iacovetta, Franca, and Linda Kealey. 'Women's History Gender History and
Debating Dichotomies.' *Left History* 3:2 and 4:1 (1996) 221–37.

Inglis, Amirah. *The White Women's Protection Ordinance: Sexual Anxiety and
Politics in Papua*. London: Sussex University Press, 1975.

Jackel, Susan, ed., *A Flannel Shirt and Liberty: British Emigrant Gentlewomen in
the Canadian West, 1880–1914*. Vancouver: University of British Columbia
Press, 1982.

Jameson, Elizabeth. 'Women as Workers, Women as Civilizers: True Womanhood in the American West.' In Susan Armitage and Elizabeth Jameson,
eds., *The Women's West*. Norman: University of Oklahoma Press, 1987.

Johansson, Ella. 'Beautiful Men, Fine Women and Good Work People: Gender
and Skill in Northern Sweden, 1850–1950.' *Gender and History* 1:2 (1989)
200–12.

Johnson, Susan Lee. 'Bulls, Bears, and Dancing Boys: Race, Gender, and Leisure in the California Gold Rush.' *Radical History Review* 60 (Fall 1994) 4–37.
– 'Sharing Bed and Board: Cohabitation and Cultural Difference in Central Arizona Mining Towns, 1863–1873.' In Susan Armitage and Elizabeth Jameson, eds., *The Women's West*. Norman: University of Oklahoma Press, 1987.
Jolly, Margaret. 'Colonizing Women: The Maternal Body and Empire.' In Sneja Gunew and Anna Yeatman, eds., *Feminism and the Politics of Difference*. Halifax: Fernwood Press, 1993.
Kelm, Mary Ellen. 'Ross, Flora Amelia (Hubbs).' *Dictionary of Canadian Biography*, vol. 12. Toronto: University of Toronto Press, 1990.
Kidwell, Clara Sue. 'Indian Women as Cultural Mediators.' *Ethnohistory* 39:2 (1992) 97–107.
Killian, Crawford. *Go Do Some Great Thing: The Black Pioneers of British Columbia*. Vancouver: Douglas and McIntyre, 1978.
Kimmel, Michael S. 'The Contemporary "Crisis" of Masculinity in Historical Perspective.' In Harry Brod, ed., *The Making of Masculinities: The New Men's Studies*. Boston: Unwin Hyman, 1987.
Knapman, Claudia. *White Women in Fiji, 1835–1930: The Ruin of Empire?* Sydney: Allen and Unwin, 1986.
Knight, Rolf. *Indians at Work: An Informal History of Native Indian Labour in British Columbia, 1858–1930*. Vancouver: New Star, 1978.
Kranidis, Rita S. 'Introduction: New Subjects, Familiar Grounds.' In Rita S. Kranidis, ed., *Imperial Objects: Essays on Victorian Women's Emigration and the Unauthorized Imperial Experience*. New York: Twayne, 1998.
Lake, Marilyn. 'Between Old World "Barbarism" and Stone Age "Primitivism": The Double Difference of the White Australian Feminist.' In Norma Grive and Alisa Burns, eds., *Australian Women: Contemporary Feminist Thought*. Melbourne: Oxford University Press, 1994.
– 'The Politics of Respectability: Identifying the Masculinist Context.' *Historical Studies* 22: 86 (1986) 116–31.
LaViolette, Forrest E. *The Struggle for Survival: Indian Cultures and the Protestant Ethic in British Columbia*. Toronto: University of Toronto Press, 1973.
Lay, Jackie. 'To Columbia on the Tynemouth: The Emigration of Single Women and Girls in 1862.' In Barbara Latham and Cathy Kess, eds., *In Her Own Right: Selected Essays on Women's History in B.C.* Vancouver: Camosun College, 1980.
LeBourdais, Louis. 'Billy Barker of Barkerville.' *BCHQ* 1:1 (1937) 165–70.
Little, Jack. 'The Foundations of Government.' In Hugh J.M. Johnson, ed., *The Pacific Province*. Vancouver: Douglas and McIntyre, 1996.

Loo, Tina. *Making Law, Order and Authority in British Columbia, 1821–1871.* Toronto: University of Toronto Press, 1994.

Lutz, John. 'After the Fur Trade: Aboriginal Wage Labour in Nineteenth-Century British Columbia.' *Journal of the Canadian Historical Association* (1992) 69–94.

– 'Gender and Work in Lekwammen Families, 1843–1970.' In Kathryn McPherson, Cecilia Morgan, and Nancy Forestell, eds., *Gendered Pasts: Historical Essays in Femininity and Masculinity in Canada.* Toronto: Oxford University Press, 1999.

Lugrin, N. de Bertrand. *The Pioneer Women of Vancouver Island, 1843–1866.* Victoria: Women's Canadian Club, 1928.

Lytton, Earl. *The Life of Edward Bulwer, First Lord Lytton,* vol. 2. London: Macmillan, 1913.

McClintock, Anne. 'The Angel of Progress: Pitfalls of the Term "Post-Colonialism."' *Social Text* 31–2 (1990) 84–98.

– *Imperial Leather: Race, Gender, and Sexuality in the Colonial Conquest.* New York: Routledge, 1995.

Macdonald, Charlotte. *A Woman of Good Character: Single Women as Immigrant Settlers in Nineteenth-Century New Zealand.* Wellington: Bridget Williams, 1990.

McDonald, Robert A.J. 'Lumber Society on the Industrial Frontier: Burrard Inlet, 1863–1886.' *Labour / Le Travail* 33 (Spring 1994) 69–96.

McGrath, Ann. '"Black Velvet": Aboriginal Women and Their Relations with White Men in the Northern Territory, 1910–1940.' In Kay Daniels, ed., *So Much Hard Work: Women and Prostitution in Australian History.* Sydney: Fontana / Collins, 1984.

McPherson, Kathryn, Cecilia Morgan, and Nancy M. Forestell. 'Introduction: Conceptualizing Canada's Gendered Pasts.' In Kathryn McPherson, Cecilia Morgan, and Nancy M. Forestell, eds., *Gendered Pasts: Historical Essays in Femininity and Masculinity in Canada.* Toronto: Oxford University Press, 1999.

Mackie, Richard. 'The Colonization of Vancouver Island, 1849–1858.' *BC Studies* 96 (Winter 1992–3) 3–40.

– *Trading Beyond the Mountains: The British Fur Trade on the Pacific, 1793–1843.* Vancouver: UBC Press, 1997.

– *The Wilderness Profound: Victorian Life on the Gulf of Georgia.* Victoria: Sono Nis, 1995.

Marks, Lynne. *Revivals and Roller Rinks: Religion, Leisure, and Identity in Late-Nineteenth-Century Small-Town Ontario.* Toronto: University of Toronto Press, 1996.

Martinez-Alier, Verena. *Marriage, Class and Color in Nineteenth-Century Cuba: A Study of Racial Attitudes and Sexual Values in a Slave Society.* 2nd ed. Ann Arbor: University of Michigan Press, 1989.

Maynard, Steven. '"Horrible Temptations": Sex, Men, and Working-Class Male Youth in Urban Ontario, 1890–1935.' *Canadian Historical Review* 78 (June 1997) 191–235.

– 'Through a Hole in the Lavatory Wall: Homosexual Subcultures, Police Surveillance, and the Dialectics of Discovery, Toronto, 1890–1930.' In Joy Parr and Mark Rosenfeld, eds., *Gender and History in Canada.* Toronto: Copp Clark, 1996.

Meen, Sharon. 'Colonial Society and Economy.' In Hugh J.M. Johnson, ed., *The Pacific Province.* Vancouver: Douglas and McIntyre, 1996.

Mills, Sara. *Discourses of Difference: An Analysis of Women's Travel Writing and Colonialism.* New York: Routledge, 1991.

– 'Gender and Colonial Space.' *Gender, Place and Culture* 3:2 (1996) 125–47.

Mohantry, Chandra. 'Under Western Eyes: Feminist Scholarship and Colonial Discourse.' *Feminist Review* 30 (Autumn 1988) 61–88.

Monk, Una. *New Horizons: A Hundred Years of Women's Migration.* London: Her Majesty's Stationary Office, 1963.

Mouat, Jeremy. *Roaring Days: Rossland's Mines and the History of British Columbia.* Vancouver: UBC Press, 1995.

Muszynski, Alicja. *Cheap Wage Labour: Race and Gender in the Fisheries of British Columbia.* Montreal and Kingston: McGill-Queen's University Press, 1996.

Noel, Jan. *Canada Dry: Temperance Crusades before Confederation.* Toronto: University of Toronto Press, 1995.

Obeyesekere, Gananath. *The Apotheosis of Captain Cook: European Mythmaking in the Pacific.* Princeton, NJ: Princeton University Press, 1992.

Painter, Nell Irving. 'Three Southern Women and Freud: A Non-Exceptionalist Approach to Race, Class, and Gender in the Slave South.' In Ann-Louise Shapiro, ed., *Feminists Revision History.* New Brunswick, NJ: Rutgers University Press, 1994.

Parr, Joy. *The Gender of Breadwinners: Men, Women, and Change in Two Industrial Towns, 1880–1950.* Toronto: University of Toronto Press, 1990.

– 'Gender History and Historical Practice.' *Canadian Historical Review* 76:3 (1995) 354–76.

– *Labouring Children: British Immigrant Apprentices to Canada, 1869–1924.* London and Montreal: McGill-Queen's University Press and Croom Helm, 1980.

Pascoe, Peggy. 'Race, Gender, and Intercultural Relations: The Case of Intermarriage.' *Frontiers* 12:1 (1991) 5–18.

– *Relations of Rescue: The Search for Female Moral Authority in the American West, 1874–1939.* New York: Oxford University Press, 1990.

Peake, Frank A. *The Anglican Church in British Columbia.* Vancouver: Mitchell Press, 1959.

Peck, Gunther. 'Manly Gambles: The Politics of Risk on the Comstock Lode.' *Journal of Social History* 26: 4 (1993) 701–24.

Penfold, Steven. '"Have You No Manhood in You?" Gender and Class in the Cape Breton Coal Towns, 1920–1926.' *Acadiensis* 23:2 (1994) 21–44.

Peterson, Jacqueline. 'Women Dreaming: The Religiopsychology of Indian–White Marriages and the Rise of a Métis Culture.' In Lillian Schlissel, Vicki L. Ruiz, and Janice Monk, eds., *Western Women: Their Land, Their Lives.* Albuquerque: University of New Mexico Press, 1988.

Peterson-del Mar, David. 'Intermarriage and Agency: A Chinookean Case Study.' *Ethnohistory* 42:1 (1995) 1–30.

– *What Trouble I Have Seen: A History of Violence against Wives.* Cambridge: Harvard University Press, 1996.

Pierson, Ruth Roach. 'Colonization and Canadian Women's History.' *Journal of Women's History* 4:2 (1992) 134–56.

– 'Experience, Difference, Dominance and Voice in the Writing of Canadian Women's History.' In Karen Offen, Ruth Roach Pierson, and Jane Rendall, eds., *Writing Women's History: International Perspectives.* Bloomington: Indiana University Press, 1991.

– Introduction to *Nation, Empire, and Colony: Historicizing Gender and Race,* ed. Ruth Roach Pierson and Nupur Chaudhuri. Bloomington and Indianapolis: University of Indiana Press, 1998.

Phillips, Jock. *A Man's Country? The Image of the Pakeha Male: A History.* Auckland: Penguin, 1987.

Phillips, Paul A. 'Confederation and the Economy of British Columbia.' In W. George Shelton, ed., *British Columbia and Confederation.* Victoria: University of Victoria, 1967.

Pon, Madge. 'Like a Chinese Puzzle: The Construction of Chinese Masculinity in *Jack Canuck*.' In Joy Parr and Mark Rosenfeld, eds., *Gender and History in Canada.* Toronto: Copp Clark, 1996.

Poovey, Mary. *Uneven Developments: The Ideological Work of Gender in Mid-Victorian England.* Chicago: University of Chicago Press, 1988.

Pratt, Mary Louise. *Imperial Eyes: Travel Writing and Transculturation.* London: Routledge, 1992.

Rendall, Jane. 'Friendship and Politics: Barbara Leigh Smith Bodichon (1827–91) and Bessie Raynard Parkes (1829–1925). In Susan Mendus and Jane Rendall, eds., *Sexuality and Subordination: Interdisciplinary Studies of Gender in the Nineteenth Century.* London: Routledge, 1989.

Riley, Glenda. *Women and Indians on the Frontier, 1825–1915.* Albuquerque: University of New Mexico Press, 1984.

Roberts, Barbara. '"A Work of Empire": Canadian Reformers and British Female Immigration.' In Linda Kealey, ed., *A Not Unreasonable Claim: Women and Reform in Canada, 1880s-1920s*. Toronto: Women's Press, 1979.

Roediger, David R. *The Wages of Whiteness: Race and the Making of the American Working Class*. London: Verso, 1991.

Rosenfeld, Mark. 'Class and Gender in the Work and Family Rhythms of a Railway Town, 1920–1950.' *Historical Papers* (1988) 237–79.

Rotter, Andrew J. 'Matilda for Gods Sake Write': Women and Families on the Argonaut Mind.' *California History* 58:2 (1979) 128–41.

Rotundo, E. Anthony. 'Body and Soul: Changing Ideals of American Middle-Class Manhood.' *Journal of Social History* 16:4 (1983) 23–38.

– 'Romantic Friendship: Male Intimacy and Middle-Class Youth in the Northern United States, 1800–1900.' *Journal of Social History* 23:1 (1989) 1–26.

Roy, Patricia E. *A White Man's Province: British Columbia Politicians and Chinese and Japanese Immigrants, 1858–1914*. Vancouver: UBC Press, 1989.

Rutherdale, Myra. 'Revisiting Colonization through Gender: Anglican Missionary Women in the Pacific Northwest and the Arctic, 1860–1945.' *BC Studies* 104 (1994–5) 3–23.

Ryan, Mary P. *Cradle of the Middle Class: The Family in Oneida County, New York, 1790–1865*. Cambridge: Cambridge University Press, 1981.

Sahlins, Marshall. *How 'Natives' Think about Captain Cook, for Example*. Chicago: University of Chicago Press, 1995.

Said, Edward. *Orientalism*. New York: Vintage, 1975.

Sandwell, R.W. 'Peasants on the Coast? A Problematique of Rural British Columbia.' In Donald H. Akenson, ed., *Canadian Papers in Rural History 10*. Gananoque, ON: Langdale, 1996.

Sangari, Kumkum, and Sudesh Vaid. 'Recasting Women: An Introduction.' In Kumkum Sangari and Sudesh Vaid, eds., *Recasting Women: Essays in Colonial History*. New Delhi: Kali for Women, 1989.

Sangster, Joan. 'Beyond Dichotomies: Re-assessing Gender History and Women's History in Canada.' *Left History* 3:1 (1995) 109–21.

Scott, Joan Wallach. *Gender and the Politics of History*. New York: Columbia University Press, 1988.

Seccombe, Wally. 'Patriarchy Stabilized: The Construction of the Male Breadwinner Wage Norm in Nineteenth-Century Britain.' *Social History* 2:1 (1986) 53–76.

Sinha, Mrinalini. *Colonial Masculinity: The 'Manly Englishman' and the 'Effemi-*

nate Bengali' in the Late Nineteenth Century. Manchester: Manchester University Press, 1995.

– 'Gender and Imperialism: Colonial Policy and the Ideology of Moral Imperialism in Late Nineteenth-Century Bengal.' In Michael S. Kimmel, ed., *Changing Men: New Directions in Research on Men and Masculinity.* New York: Sage, 1987.

Sioui, Georges E. *For an Amerindian Auto-History: An Essay on the Foundations of a Social Ethic.* Trans., Sheila Fischman. Montreal: McGill-Queen's University Press, 1992.

Smith, Allan. 'The Writing of British Columbia History.' In W. Peter Ward and Robert A.J. McDonald, eds., *British Columbia: Historical Readings.* Vancouver: Douglas and McIntyre, 1981.

Smith, Erica. '"Gentlemen, This Is No Ordinary Trial": Sexual Narratives in the Trial of the Reverend Corbett, Red River, 1863.' In Jennifer S.H. Brown and Elizabeth Vibert, eds., *Reading beyond Words: Contexts for Native History.* Peterborough, ON: Broadview Press, 1996.

Smith, Sherry L. 'Beyond Princess and Squaw: Army Officers' Perceptions of Indian Women.' In Susan Armitage and Elizabeth Jameson, eds., *The Women's West.* Norman: University of Oklahoma Press, 1987.

Smith-Rosenberg, Carroll. 'Captured Subjects / Savage Others: Violently Engendering the New American.' *Gender and History* 5:2 (1993) 177–95.

– *Disorderly Conduct: Visions of Gender in Victorian America.* New York: Oxford University Press, 1985.

Smits, David D. 'The "Squaw Drudge": A Prime Index of Savagism.' *Ethnohistory* 29:4 (1982) 281–306.

Stanley, George F.G. *The Birth of Western Canada: A History of the Riel Rebellions.* Toronto: University of Toronto Press, 1960 [1936].

Stasiulis, Daiva, and Nira Yuval-Davis. 'Introduction: Beyond Dichotomies – Gender, Race, Ethnicity and Class in Settler Societies.' In Daiva Stasiulis and Nira Yuval-Davis, eds., *Unsettling Settler Societies: Articulations of Gender, Race, Ethnicity and Class.* London: Sage, 1995.

Stoler, Ann Laura. 'Carnal Knowledge and Imperial Power: Gender, Race, and Morality in Colonial Asia.' In Micaela di Leonardo, ed., *Gender at the Crossroads of Knowledge: Feminist Anthropology in the Postmodern Era.* Berkeley: University of California Press, 1991.

– 'Making Empire Respectable: The Politics of Race and Sexual Morality in 20th-Century Colonial Cultures.' *American Ethnologist* 16:3 (1989) 634–60.

– *Race and the Education of Desire: Foucault's History of Sexuality and the Colonial Order of Things.* Durham: Duke University Press, 1995.

- 'Rethinking Colonial Categories: European Communities and the Boundaries of Rule.' *Comparative Studies in Society and History* 31:1 (1989) 134–61.
- 'Sexual Affronts and Racial Frontiers: European Identities and Cultural Politics of Exclusion in Colonial Southeast Asia.' *Comparative Studies in Society and History* 34:3 (1992) 514–51.

Stoler, Ann Laura, and Frederick Cooper. 'Between Metropole and Colony: Rethinking a Research Agenda.' In Frederick Cooper and Ann Laura Stoler, eds., *Tensions of Empire: Colonial Cultures in a Bourgeois World*. Berkeley: University of California Press, 1997.

Strobel, Margaret. *European Women and the Second British Empire*. Bloomington: Indiana University Press, 1991.
- 'Sex and Work in the British Empire.' *Radical History Review* 54 (1992) 177–86.

Swagerty, William R. 'Marriage and Settlement Patterns of Rocky Mountain Trappers and Traders.' *Western Historical Quarterly* 11:2 (1980) 159–80.

Swaisland, Cecillie. *Servants and Gentlewomen to the Golden Land: The Emigration of Single Women from Britain to Southern Africa, 1820–1939*. Oxford and Providence: Berg and the University of Natal Press, 1993.

Tennant, Paul. *Aboriginal Peoples and Politics: The Indian Land Question in British Columbia, 1849–1989*. Vancouver: UBC Press, 1990.

Thomas, Edward Harper. *Chinook: A History and Dictionary of the Northwest Trade Jargon*. 2nd ed. Portland, OR: Binfolds and Mort, 1970.

Thomas, Nicholas. *Colonialism's Culture: Anthropology, Travel, and Government*. Princeton, NJ: Princeton University Press, 1994.

Usher, Jean. *William Duncan of Metlakatla: A Victorian Missionary in British Columbia*. Ottawa: National Museum of Man, 1974.

Valverde, Mariana. *The Age of Light, Soap and Water: Moral Reform in English Canada, 1885–1925*. Toronto: McClelland and Stewart, 1991.
- '"When the Mother of the Race is Free": Race, Reproduction, and Sexuality in First-Wave Feminism.' In Franca Iacovetta and Mariana Valverde, eds., *Gender Conflicts: New Essays in Women's History*. Toronto: University of Toronto Press, 1992.

Van Kirk, Sylvia. 'Bendixen, Fanny.' *Dictionary of Canadian Biography*, vol. 12. Toronto: University of Toronto Press, 1990.
- *'Many Tender Ties': Women in Fur Trade Society in Western Canada, 1670–1870*. Winnipeg: Watson and Dwyer, 1980.
- 'Tracing the Fortunes of Five Founding Families of Victoria.' *BC Studies* 115/116 (1997–8) 148–79.
- 'A Vital Presence: Women in the Cariboo Gold Rush, 1862–1875.' In Gillian

Creese and Veronica Strong-Boag, eds., *British Columbia Reconsidered: Essays on Women*. Vancouver: Press Gang, 1992.

Vibert, Elizabeth. *Traders' Tales: Narratives of Cultural Encounters in the Plateau, 1807–1846*. Norman: University of Oklaholma Press, 1997.

Walkowitz, Judith. *City of Dreadful Delight: Narratives of Sexual Danger in Late-Victorian London*. Chicago: University of Chicago Press, 1992.

Ware, Vron. *Beyond the Pale: White Women, Racism, and History*. London: Verso, 1992.

– 'Moments of Danger: Race, Gender, and Memories of Empire.' In Ann-Louise Shapiro, ed., *Feminists Revision History*. New Brunswick, NJ: Rutgers University Press, 1994.

West, Elliot. *The Saloon on the Rocky Mountain Mining Frontier*. Lincoln and London: University of Nebraska Press, 1979.

White, Luise. *The Comforts of Home: Prostitution in Colonial Nairobi*. Chicago: University of Chicago Press, 1990.

Whitehead, Margaret. '"A Useful Christian Woman": First Nations Women and Protestant Missionary Work in British Columbia.' *Atlantis* 18:1–2 (1994) 142–66.

Wickwire, Wendy. 'To See Ourselves as the Other's Other: Nlaka'pamux Contact Narratives.' *Canadian Historical Review* 75:1 (1994) 1–20.

Worsnop, Judith. 'A Reevaluation of "The Problem of Surplus Women" in 19th-Century England: The Case of the 1851 Census.' *Women's Studies International Forum* 13:1/2 (1990) 21–31.

Young, Robert J.C. *Colonial Desire: Hybridity in Theory, Culture and Race*. London: Routledge, 1995.

Theses and Dissertations

Belshaw, John Douglas. 'British Coalminers on Vancouver Island, 1848–1900: A Social History.' PhD dissertation, University of London, 1987.

Forestell, Nancy M. 'All that Glitters Is Not Gold: The Gendered Dimensions of Work, Family, and Community Life in the Northern Ontario Goldmining Town of Timmins, 1909–1950.' PhD dissertation, University of Toronto, 1993.

Johnson, Susan Lee. '"The Gold She Gathered": Difference, Domination, and California's Southern Mines, 1848–1853.' PhD dissertation, Yale University, 1993.

Kelcey, Barbara Eileen. 'Jingo Bells, Jingo Belles, Dashing through the Snow: White Women and Empire on Canada's Arctic Frontier.' PhD dissertation, University of Manitoba, 1994.

Mackie, Richard. 'Colonial Land, Indian Labour and Company Capital: The Economy of Vancouver Island, 1849–1858.' MA thesis, University of Victoria, 1984.

Morgan, Cecilia Louise. 'Languages of Gender in Upper Canadian Religion and Politics, 1791–1850.' PhD dissertation, University of Toronto, 1993.

Zaffaroni, Irene Genevieve Marie. 'The Great Chain of Being: Racism and Imperialism in Colonial Victoria, 1858–1871,' MA thesis, University of Victoria, 1987.

Illustration credits

British Columbia Archives: HBC's Fort Victoria in 1854 PDP02143 (James Madison Alden); male household in the backwoods, A-04468; Cariboo's Minnehaha Claim was a large gold-mining enterprise, A-03837 (Frederick Dally); archetypal gold-miner in 1864, PDP02612 (William George Hind); drinking in the backwoods, A-04437; Ah Bau and two companions, A-04279; Sir James Douglas, A-01229, and Amelia Connolly Douglas (R. Maynard) H-04909; Barkerville's library, A-03770 (L.A. Blanc); St Saviours Church, F-02310; John Good and flock, D-03971 (Frederick Dally); Lekwammen people settled outside the Governor's Garden, PDP02899 (Sarah Crease); Governor Arthur Kennedy, F-04608; Chinese male servants, D-09468 (Frederick Dally); sketch of female immigrants' quarters, 'Colonial Correspondence,' GR 1372, File 1638, Reel B-1366 (Gilbert Malcolm Sproat, Robert Burnaby and Jno. C. Davie to Anonymous, 29 September 1862); Hurdy-gurdy, G-00817 (Charles Gentile); Governor Frederick Seymour's wife presenting flags to volunteer militia, D-07233; St Ann's School, A-07737

Champness, W. 'To Cariboo and Back: An Emigrant's Journey to the Gold Fields of British Columbia' *Leisure Hour* 696 (29 April 1863): 249: 'To the Diggings and from the Diggings'

Cheadle, Walter B. *Cheadle's Journal of Trip across Canada, 1862-1863* (Edmonton: M.G. Hurtig, 1971): evening at a wayside house

City of Vancouver Archives: Lekwammen group, In.P.148, N.92 (J.C. Eastcott); Lekwammen people in Victorian dress, In.P.147, N.91 (J.C. Eastcott); Lekwammen housing in Victoria, In.P.145, N.89 (J.C. Eastcott); Crickmer's mission, Out. P825, N.381; A hybrid place: Lekwammen shed-houses, In.P.158,

N.105 #1 (Adm. Hastings); persistant object of regulatory efforts, In.P.144, N.88 (J.C. Eastcott); gendered and class disruption caused by the absence of white female servants, Out.P826, N.382 #1 &2 (Rev. W. Burton Crickmer)

Columbia Mission: Tenth Annual Report of the Columbia Mission, for the year 1869 (London: Rivingtons, 1870): missionaries and First Nations parishioners

Cornwallis, Kinahan. *The New El Dorado or British Columbia* (London: Thomas Cautley Newby, 1858): men cooking during the Fraser River gold rush

Mayne, Richard Charles. *Four Years in British Columbia and Vancouver Island* (Toronto: S.R. Publishers, 1969 [London: John Murray, 1862]): head-flattening among First Nations women; images of caring maternity alongside notions of depravity

University of British Columbia Archives: Frederick Dally's 'Types of British Columbia Indians,' BC-597

Index

STUDIES IN GENDER AND HISTORY

General editors: Franca Iacovetta and Karen Dubinsky

1 Suzanne Morton, *Ideal Surroundings: Domestic Life in a Working-Class Suburb in the 1920s*
2 Joan Sangster, *Earning Respect: The Lives of Working Women in Small-Town Ontario, 1920–1960*
3 Carolyn Strange, *Toronto's Girl Problem: The Perils and Pleasures of the City, 1880–1930*
4 Sara Z. Burke, *Seeking the Highest Good: Social Service and Gender at the University of Toronto, 1888–1937*
5 Lynne Marks, *Revivals and Roller Rinks: Religion, Leisure, and Identity in Late-Nineteenth-Century Small-Town Ontario*
6 Cecilia Morgan, *Public Men and Virtuous Women: The Gendered Languages of Religion and Politics in Upper Canada, 1791–1850*
7 Mary Louise Adams, *The Trouble with Normal: Postwar Youth and the Making of Heterosexuality*
8 Linda Kealey, *Enlisting Women for the Cause: Women, Labour, and the Left in Canada, 1890–1920*
9 Christina A. Burr, *Spreading the Light: Work and Labour Reform in Late-Nineteenth-Century Toronto*
10 Mona Gleason, *Normalizing the Ideal: Psychology, Schooling, and the Family in Postwar Canada*
11 Deborah Gorham, *Vera Brittain: A Feminist Life*
12 Marlene Epp, *Women without Men: Mennonite Refugees of the Second World War*
13 Shirley Tillotson, *The Public at Play: Gender and the Politics of Recreation in Post-War Ontario*
14 Veronica Strong-Boag and Carole Gerson, *Paddling Her Own Canoe: The Times and Texts of E. Pauline Johnson (Tekahionwake)*
15 Stephen Heathorn, *For Home, Country, and Race: Constructing Gender, Class, and Englishness in the Elementary School, 1880–1914*
16 Valerie J. Korinek, *Roughing It in the Suburbs: Reading Chatelaine Magazine in the Fifties and Sixties*
17 Robert A. Campbell, *Sit Down and Drink Your Beer: Regulating Vancouver's Beer Parlours, 1925–1954*
18 Adele Perry, *On the Edge of Empire: Gender, Race, and the Making of British Columbia, 1849–1871*